ALL ROADS LEAD TO WELLS

Caitlin Press Inc.
8100 Alderwood Road,
Halfmoon Bay, BC V0N 1Y1
www.caitlin-press.com

Text design by Vici Johnstone.
Cover art by Bob Masse.
Hand-illustrated titles and map by Kevin Easthope.
Printed in China by Prolong Press Ltd.

Caitlin Press Inc. acknowledges financial support from the Government of Canada through the Canada Book Fund and the Canada Council for the Arts, and from the Province of British Columbia through the British Columbia Arts Council and the Book Publisher's Tax Credit.

Canada Council   Conseil des Arts
for the Arts   du Canada

BRITISH COLUMBIA
ARTS COUNCIL
We acknowledge the support of the Province of British Columbia
through the British Columbia Arts Council.

Library and Archives Canada Cataloguing in Publication

Safyan, Susan
    All roads lead to Wells : stories of
the hippie days / Susan Safyan.

Includes bibliographical references and index.
ISBN 978-1-894759-76-2

    1. Wells (B.C.)—History.
2. Wells (B.C.)—Biography. I. Title.

FC3849.W43S34 2012   971.1'75   C2012-900547-9

ALL ROADS LEAD TO WELLS

STORIES of the HIPPIE DAYS
SUSAN SAFYAN

CAITLIN PRESS

Every book is, in an intimate sense, a circular letter to the friends of him who writes it. They alone take his meaning; they find private messages, assurances of love and expressions of gratitude, dropped for them in every corner...Of what shall a man be proud, if he is not proud of his friends?

—Robert Louis Stevenson

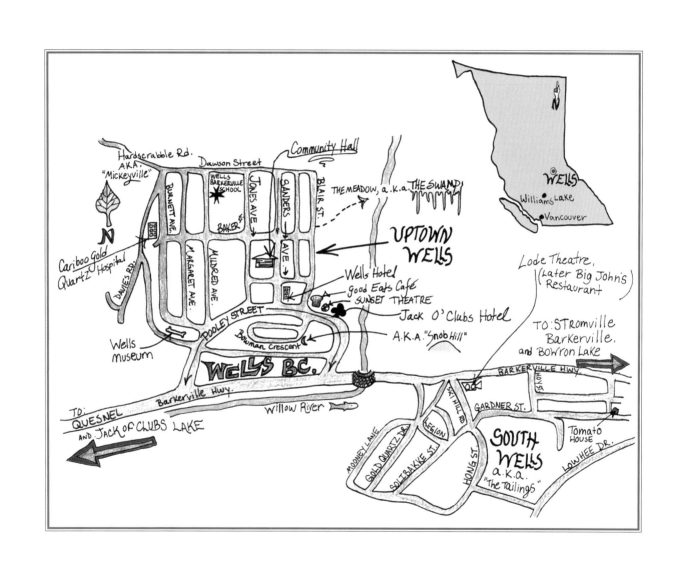

CONTENTS

Postcard of Pooley Street, 1980s. Photo: Dorse McTaggart.

PREFACE

IN OCTOBER 1978, I WAS WORKING AS A RECEPTIONIST/SECRETARY AT A PLASTIC letter manufacturer in Venice, California. I'd dropped out of university the previous year, and found myself doing odd and uninteresting jobs to make ends meet. My boss, however, was a charismatic teacher or guru of the Gurdjieff/Ouspensky school. One day, into the shop walked a former student of my boss, a handsome young "lumberjack" from Canada who took me out to lunch and swept me off my feet. A few days later, he returned to his home in Wells, BC (population 300), and we began to write letters (hand-written letters—not emails!) to each other. Within a year, I had gone to visit him, completed the Bowron Lakes canoe circuit with him, and decided to move to Wells and live with him in his rustic cabin.

We lived together in Wells for five years. I remember forty-below days in the winters and twenty-five feet of snow; frost on the pillow when the wood in the stove didn't last the night; dancing to the Zig Zag Mountain String Band at the Community Hall; playing Snowball (baseball in frigid and fierce February snows) on the frozen lake against the team from Cottonwood—the Cottonwood Peckers (or was that the Cotton Woodpeckers?); living in a place where there are many more trees than people; playing "O Canada" on stubby beer bottles with a contingent from the volunteer fire brigade at the annual town Talent Night; curling ("sweep! sweep!") in a Diana Ross and the Supremes costume against a team of jellybeans at the Ladies' Funspiel; appreciating old geezers like Lucky Swede ("Hey, Ducky!") and Ed "Ya dumb bugga!" Titley who sat drinking in the Jack O' Clubs pub every single day (we wanted to grow old just like them); cross-country skiing around

Moose Island—a stand of spruce in the middle of the swamp on the edge of town—at midnight while drinking homemade grog; walking home from a party on the other side of town at 2:00 a.m. and being absolutely, completely, unquestionably safe.

Jack O' Clubs Hotel, 1979. Photo: S. Safyan.

I made lifelong friends whom I still visit regularly in Wells and throughout BC. As most of them had lived in Wells in its hippie days, their memories were almost magically compelling and attractive to me; some were heroic, others romantic, and many were outrageous and funny. I loved hearing them; I asked my friends to tell them to me over and over, like a child does with a favourite bedtime story. So when, in 2003, I volunteered to edit a slim volume of memoirs for the Vancouver Folk Festival, I realized that I could do the same for Wells. While still in Wells, I had read Barry Broadfoot's remarkable book *Ten Lost Years 1929–1939: Memories of Canadians Who Survived the Depression*. Its format—highlighting the voices of the people who'd "been there" and diminishing the voice of the narrator—inspired and shaped the way I researched and wrote *All Roads Lead to Wells*. Another potent influence for me was the very 1970s concept of fractals, a word coined in 1975 to describe geometric or natural entities in which the shape of the whole is replicated in each of its parts.[1] What does this have to do with history? "As above, so below"; that is, the macrocosm, the zeitgeist (in the 1970s, the back-to-the-land movement) is reflected in the local and specific and small, that is, within one little town in the Interior of British Columbia.

The book you hold in your hands is my homage to my friends and to the town of Wells. I couldn't let the stories be forgotten. However, many stories and perspectives aren't included in this book; I wish I had persuaded more people to talk or write to me about Wells, and I wish I had been able to devote more time to this research/interview project in the almost ten years it's taken me to complete it. This is not a complete or definitive history of the town. I hope it's just the beginning and that former Wellsites will want to write their own stories and that academics and writers of fiction will turn their attentions to the gold that awaits them in Wells.

"Travellers that came into Wells in 1941 said that the Wells Townsite was the prettiest little town in the Interior. The houses were all nicely painted and the fences were all in good repair and all in all it was a very nice little town." A Brief History of the Town of Wells. *Photo: Fred Luckow. Courtesy of Julie Fowler.*

BACK TO THE GARDEN

Introduction

And we've got to get ourselves
Back to the garden.
—Joni Mitchell, "Woodstock" 1969

BACK TO THE GARDEN. THE SENTIMENT SOUNDS FEY NOW, BUT IN THE LATE 1960s, Joni Mitchell's "Woodstock" lyrics were a clarion call to action for millions of young people, a generation enamoured with the idea of going back to the land. They were trying to go "back" to an idealized, bucolic past, a simpler way of life they had imagined but not yet experienced.

Throughout the 1970s, the journey back to the land could mean finding and joining communes in the country, often under New Age gurus such as Stephen Gaskin at The Farm, founded in 1970 in Tennessee. For other hippie nomads, it meant settling into small towns. All over North America there were mining, logging, farming, or fishing towns, sometimes thinly populated or even abandoned, where hippie kids from big cities moved to drop out, evade the draft (if they were Americans who'd fled to Canada), start intentional communities, get in touch with nature, write their own rules, and escape "the system." In 1970 Charles Reich described the zeitgeist in *The Greening of America*, articulating the forces that drove many people in this generation out of the cities: "[O]ne of the gifts of the young," he wrote, "is to see through…the competitiveness and sterility of suburban living, the lone-

The town of Wells in fall/winter 1976. Photo: Sandy Phillips.

liness and anomie of cities, the ruin of nature by bulldozers and pollution, the stupid mindlessness of most high school education, the materialism of most values, the lovelessness of many marriages, and above all, the plastic, artificial quality of everything; plastic lives in plastic homes."

The brief prevalence and strong appeal of a rural, communal, natural, and free-love counterculture seems mostly forgotten now, or, if remembered, disdained as a failed and naïve experiment. But for more than a decade, "it appeared that the back-to-the-country movement might itself become a dominant social trend," wrote University of Calgary professor Jeffrey Jacob in *New Pioneers: The Back-to-the-Land Movement and the Search for a Sustainable Future.* "At a time when the *Mother Earth News* was becoming a mass-circulation magazine and the *Whole Earth Catalog*s were gaining in popularity, demographers discovered something they labelled the urban-to-rural migration turnaround." It has been estimated that there were over a million practising back-to-the-landers in North America by the end of the 1970s.[1] Many were inspired by reading the *Whole Earth Catalog,* first published in 1968, in which a new generation learned about tools for thoughtful rural living on the fringes of the current planet- and soul-destroying system. The *Catalog* "fed a deep hunger in America [and Canada]—a hunger to know new stuff not taught in schools...rural know-how (how to do stuff) collaged with adventurous intellect."[2]

Equipped with copies of Scott and Helen Nearing's *Living the Good Life* (Schocken

Books, 1970), *Living on the Earth* by Alicia Bay Laurel (Bookworks, 1970), *The Tassajara Bread Book* (Shambhala, 1970), iterations of the *Catalog,* and a wealth of other counterculture titles from that era, young people made their way from the cities and suburbs to rural refuges where they would make and grow their own homes, vegetables, hogs, quilts, candles, and recreational substances. You can hear the background music to this movement in the beginnings of the country-rock genre, on such albums as *Crosby, Stills & Nash* (their first, eponymous album), *Sweet Baby James, Bayou Country, Music from Big Pink,* or *Sweetheart of the Rodeo.* The back-to-the-land movement soon branched out into organics, handicrafts (think macramé and candles), the rediscovery of traditional and/or Eastern medicines, midwifery and home births, and other forms of self-reliance epitomized by a "grow your own" philosophy and a rediscovery of pre-industrial crafts.

Justine Brown, in *All Possible Worlds: Utopian Experiments in British Columbia*, observed that, by the early 1970s, "only two retreats" from an increasingly violent and oppressive urban scene "seemed possible. One was the cocaine-bright nights of discotheques like Studio 54. The other was the backwoods of North America…In the public imagination, BC was 'the end of the line,' the last frontier, the last place on earth."[3] One of the most well-known accounts of the back-to-the-land experiments in British Columbia was the *Eden Express*, written by Mark Vonnegut. In 1975, describing his experience on a commune near Powell Lake, BC, "twelve miles from the nearest road or electric light," he wrote:

The Mother Earth News *started publishing in 1970.*

> We hadn't taken to the woods just for a change of scenery and a different way of life. The physical and psychical aspects of our adventure were inextricably intertwined, but the head changes were what we were really after. We expected to get closer to nature, to each other and our feelings…We wanted to go

Forman's General Store, 1973.
Photo: Karin Ludditt.

beyond that and develop entirely new ways of being and experiencing the world. We had only vague ideas about the shape of these changes or when they would happen, but we looked forward to them eagerly. Since they would result from being free of the cities, of capitalism, of racism, industrialism, they had to be for the better.

It was a lot like taking some new drug and waiting for the changes.

The hippies who came to Wells between 1969 and 1979 shared much in common with these other sojourners who went back to the land. They were primarily under twenty-five, white, of middle-class backgrounds. Most had been in their teens during the Summer of Love in 1967. They came to Wells from as far away as Germany, moved up from the United States, or came west from Ontario. Most, however, had moved just one day's drive north from Vancouver or Victoria. They were leaving behind their parents' expectations and the increasingly consumer-capitalist oriented lifestyles of the late twentieth century. They were leaving behind attitudes such as that of Vancouver mayor Tom "Terrific" Campbell, who called the hippies "a scum community," "parasites" and "lazy louts...who contribute absolutely nothing to society" and instructed police to arrest them.[4] Wells' hippie settlers were students, entrepreneurs, travellers, and, for the most part, floaters in the economic system. They were still exploring which skills and inclinations they would develop as newly minted adults, still learning how to live in the world. Many, when they arrived in Wells, had no fixed careers—they had dreams. And Wells had always attracted dreamers; the town was built by gold seekers, those quintessential frontier adventurers.

In Wells, "you had the backwoods setting, which was the big thing back then," notes Judy Campbell, who's lived in Wells since 1974. "A lot of people who came to Wells in the '70s were part of the back-to-the-land movement."[5] Yet part of what set the Wells crowd apart from stereotypical "peace, love, and grass" hippies is that while they came to a rural setting, they did not find a climate in which food could be readily grown, and they did not come to live in a commune. Some came to Wells from communes, and a few came to dream and plan and organize a commune. But there were no gurus, no leaders, no pre-ordained shared principles (spiritual or dietary or political) that united these immigrants. There were no rules. The town itself was a community, and the hippies felt connected with each other, to some extent, because they often shared hippie values (sometimes stark against the values of the existing population), but they lived independently rather than communally. They were more permeable to the opinions and actions of the townsfolk than hippies who lived in communes nearby, for example, just outside of Quesnel. If there were shared enthusiasms (a love of Jerry Jeff Walker songs) or philosophical and practical differences (hippie vegetarians versus hippie hunters and trappers), they had to find these out for themselves. And these factors—the harsh weather and the circumstances of housing and neighbours—made the Wells hippies, on the whole, a fairly pragmatic and self-sufficient group of individuals, less dreamy and hapless than many. They may have arrived starry-eyed, but theory quickly had to give way to reality; it was a matter of survival.

By all accounts, the first hippies—the Ur-Hippies—to move to Wells arrived in the summer of 1969, the year the Apollo astronauts walked on the moon. In 1969 the movie *Alice's Restaurant* was released, and Trudeau's government had decriminalized homosexuality. It was the year of both Woodstock and of Altamont—the zenith and nadir of optimism that the peaceful, creative, freedom-loving Age of Aquarius had begun. The Beatles hadn't yet broken up, but Richard Nixon had been sworn into office in the US in January of that year. On campuses and in streets across Canada, students protested, activists rioted and, in February, members of the Marxist Front de libération du Québec bombed the Montreal

Courtesy of Bob Masse
www.bmasse.com

Courtesy of Bob Masse

Stock Exchange. A few months later, John Lennon and Yoko Ono held a Bed-In for Peace in Montreal's Queen Elizabeth Hotel.

In Vancouver in 1969, the Don't Make a Wave Committee (later known as Greenpeace) organized protests against nuclear testing in Alaska. The psychedelic counterculture was thriving in Vancouver's Kitsilano district near the University of British Columbia (UBC). Kits was described, in those days, as a Canadian Haight-Ashbury. In his 2004 history of Greenpeace, Rex Wyler recalls: "Fourth Avenue, Kitsilano's hippie row, lined with psychedelic shops and record stores, hosted scores of young people from across Canada who had found their way west in pursuit of rock music, marijuana, and sexual liberation. American draft resisters slipped north in Vancouver…[where] between 1966 and 1973, a fresh youth culture simply overwhelmed establishment resistance."[6] On "Love Street," as UBC history professor Tina Loo has dubbed Kitsilano's Fourth Avenue during the 1960s, there were "alternative clothing, book, and record stores; head shops; and coffee houses where you read the alternative press, *The Georgia Straight*."[7] At the Retinal Circus nightclub on Davie and Burrard or The Afterthought on Fourth Avenue, you could hear bands such as Papa Bear's Medicine Show, the Seeds of

Time, or My Indole Ring (lightshow by Ectoplasmicassault or Addled Chromish).

Since 1967 there had been free outdoor rock music concerts at the Easter Be-Ins in Stanley Park, attracting thousands of pot-smoking, LSD-dropping kids enjoying a big communal experience.[8] In professor Loo's analysis of Vancouver's hippie counterculture, the "flower children [of Kitsilano] were of at least two distinct varieties: hippies and student protesters. Cross-pollination and hybridization certainly occurred, but even in the fertile climate of the coast rainforest, the two strains remained separate, and provoked rather different reactions."[9] Those who went up to Wells were uniformly of the former species—the political radicals didn't seem to be interested in taking their struggles out of the city and into the Interior of the province. Wells was an end-of-the-road place to escape to, not a staging grounds for the Revolution.

At the end of the sixties, Wells was a town that time and the outside world seemed to have forgotten. It appeared to the hippies to have been entirely untouched by the social, political, and cultural revolutions of the 1960s.

Courtesy of Bob Masse

Postcard of Pooley Street, early 1960s. Photo: K. Buchanan.

GOLD TOWN

THE HISTORY OF WELLS FALLS INTO TWO DISTINCT PERIODS OF TIME: before and after the mines shut down in 1967. It is a history that follows the classic boom-and-bust template: the boom town of the 1930s, fuelled by gold, was in economic and social decline thirty years later. But this fading former gold rush town still contained numerous tangible reminders, both physical and personal, of its heyday.

History of Wells to 1967

In 1861, when Fred Wells was born in Whitefield, New Hampshire, pioneering prospectors were beginning to find gold in the Cariboo. Wells grew up not far from the Canadian border, and it is tempting to speculate that news of the gold rush might have fired his imagination in childhood. He left his hometown and family as a young man, and at the age of twenty-one came all the way west to BC. "Conflicting stories," reported Sandra Mather in her unpublished history of Wells' founding, "say he crossed over the Rockies from Calgary on an Indian pony, 'just to see what lay on the other side of the mountains.' Another story is that he came into the Windermere area to look after a ranch owned by a fellow he met in Calgary, leaving his employer shortly after to go prospecting."[1] In either case, it sounds as though he was, when young, on the kind of foot-loose and adventurous trajectory that the hippies followed to Wells almost ninety years later. Fred Wells was involved in various prospecting schemes over the years, but by the early 1920s he was working claims just a few miles from Barkerville, the gold rush town that had flourished as Wells himself was growing up.

L to R: O.H. Solibakke, J.R.V. Dunlop, Fred M. Wells, W. B. Burnett. First gold bricks produced at the Cariboo Gold Quartz Mining Company's property near Barkerville, BC. VPL Accession Number: 648.

Prospector Fred Luddhitt came to Barkerville in the 1920s and raised his family there and in Wells. In *Campfire Sketches of the Cariboo*, he remembered meeting with Fred Wells on "a summer evening of 1930":

> [Wells] was feeling rather dejected that evening. He told us that he had been prospecting for some years in the Barkerville area and felt sure that he had a potential mine a few miles from the town…
>
> Ever since the early 1860s miners and prospectors had been certain that a rich lode mine existed somewhere in the area…Over the years thousands of dollars had been spent but to date no one had been able to develop sufficient ore to make a producing mine.
>
> "It is most difficult to get anyone to take a further gamble," he said.
>
> Fred Wells was a tall, raw-boned, well-built man who would have been in his mid-forties at that time [he was clearly a well-preserved sixty-nine-year-old in 1930, if Luddhitt underestimated his age by twenty-some years!]. He had spent much of his life outdoors, and had been snowshoe champion at the winter games at Rossland in 1908. Slow spoken and deliberate in his remarks he nonetheless inspired in his listeners a deep confidence in the man himself and in all he said.
>
> Little did any of us realize that within the next three years Fred Wells' prospect would lift the Cariboo out of its slumbers into another mining boom, and would produce up to twenty million dollars in gold in the next two decades.[2]

With backing from Vancouver investors W.B. Burnett and O.H. Solibakke (the three partners were known as the "Three Musketeers"), Wells formed the Cariboo Gold Quartz Mining Company and drove the first adit into Cow Mountain, on the northeast end of Jack of Clubs Lake, in 1927. It was a lucky strike: the quartz veins under the mountain were rich with gold, so a mill was built to process the ore.

Pooley Street under construction, c. 1934. WP 01019 © Wells Historical Society.

Cariboo Gold Quartz Mine, January 1934: "Installing Engine No. 6." WP 00265 © Wells Historical Society.

The owners of the Cariboo Gold Quartz Mine weren't satisfied with simply reaping the profits and walking away from the workers when they'd made enough money; they saw the necessity of creating a more permanent habitation, of bringing in families and providing infrastructure and services. G.E. (Ted) Baynes, who worked at the Gold Quartz, recalled that Fred Wells was "always concerned that the employees of the Quartz be properly fed. Each fall he would journey to the Ashcroft district to buy truckloads of potatoes to be stored for the winter. It amused some of us 'city folk' that he would take a small pot and do a test boil of the potatoes offered before he would sign a purchase contract. [But] the food at the [mine's] cookhouse proved how wise he was."[3]

Across the valley from Cow Mountain, the Newmont Mining Company, with backing from New York financier J.P. Morgan (of General Electric and US Steel fame), opened a second mine, the Island Mountain Mine, in 1933.[4] The Wells Townsite Company Limited was also created in 1933 to "purchase, develop, and sell land" to prospective townsfolk. Fred Wells declared: "A town is essential in a neighbourhood where there are 200 men on payroll including Island Mountain Company and ourselves. At present, there are a great many shacks and cabins being built in the woods and along the roadside. It is much better to provide a proper place for people to live and this is what we plan to do."[5]

Throughout the 1930s, while the rest of the country (and continent) suffered during the Great Depression, the town named after Fred Wells became a thriving gold rush town. It's said that 4,500 people lived in Wells at its peak, drawn by the hundreds of jobs at the prospering gold mines, union jobs (the Rock and Tunnel Workers) that paid a living wage. It has been estimated that during the Depression one in five Canadians was on relief, and more than half a million people were out of work, but Wells was called a "pocket of prosperity in a land shackled by the Great Depression," and a "vibrant contrast to struggling towns in the rest of the country."[6] On April 15, 1933, a Vancouver newspaper headline trumpeted the Cariboo's second gold rush, declaring "The Depression Is Banished."[7] When the price of gold was first fixed at $35 US an ounce in 1934, "it was like a shot in the arm to all gold interests."[8]

In time the mines changed the geography of the area permanently and immensely, as massive amounts of "overburden" (trees, soil, gravel) was hydraulically removed from hills, creek beds were deepened by as much as two hundred feet, and "tailings"—great piles of gravel—were built up. Jack of Clubs Lake, now a quarter-mile from the southern end of town, once lapped up to the base of the hill known as the Crescent and, before it was filled in, the lake cut off land access to Island Mountain (hence its name). On the other side of the lake, a tailings pile from the Gold Quartz Mine formed a large hill.

Purpose-built for the mineworkers, Wells boasted a school and a hospital, a capacious community hall, general stores, hotels, bakeries, restaurants, and a movie theatre. Contracting the work out to two companies, Northey Construction and Gardner Construction, the gold mines built homes and apartments for the workers' families using standard patterns that varied according to the hierarchy of mineworkers—company managers in larger homes commanding views of Jack of Clubs Lake, and workers in smaller homes on "the flats." Because much of Wells was built to house and service its mine employees, its architecture, both residential and commercial, was relatively uniform (with some marvellous exceptions such as the Tudor Revival Wells Hotel,

Telephone directory for businesses in Wells, 1936. "All White Help" probably means no Chinese...

whose three fireplaces are faced with ore from the Cariboo Gold Quartz, Island Mountain, and Coronado mines, and the Art Deco-style Lode Theatre built by C.D. Hoy). Most of its buildings were locally designed by the contractor or owner and only "about six carpenters constructed almost all the buildings." The commercial structures on Pooley Street were built in the false-front style, appropriately "first developed in the gold rush towns of California" evoking earlier gold-town booms and busts.[9]

In its temporary affluence, the town of Wells offered its residents a ski hill and a horse racetrack, a pool hall, golf course and curling rink, and tennis, baseball, and badminton facilities and clubs. In *Barkerville Days*, Fred Ludditt recalled the vibrant community in its early days:

Uptown winter scene, 1930s. WP00605 © Wells Historical Society.

It is difficult to imagine a more beautiful setting for a town than that of Wells. It was built on a bench of the Willow River with the blue Jack of Clubs Lake lapping below and the river meadows stretching away to the north and east. From any spot in the town one enjoys a vista of meadow and mountain, lake or stream. The view of the lake from the Quartz Mine is breath-taking and on a sunny day can be compared to a blue gem in the wilderness. Farther to the east of the mine one looks down on meadows that stretch away off and around through Downey Pass, where the tip of Two-Mile Lake is just visible.

Wells was a vigorous little town from the start, and was to enjoy a lusty few years of high living. After the outbreak of the war it became more stable and settled. The population reached the two thousand mark when both mines were operating at their peak and hiring up to six hundred men. There were men from all parts of the country seeking a job. The saying was that there were three shifts of employees[:] those coming in looking for work, those working, and those leaving. Nonetheless many who found jobs remained for years and enjoyed a fullness of life which was being denied people from most of the rest of the province.

There was never a lack of something to do. In the summer almost everyone had a gold pan and could be found panning the gravels of the numerous creeks throughout the area. The cleanups of the larger hydraulic operations were ever a source of excitement, speculation and celebration. Nearer home there was always fishing. Dolly Varden, brook trout and salmon were caught within walking distance of the town. It's hard to believe that salmon used to come right up the Willow River. Pollution has long since put an end to this and the salmon runs are gone.

The two main holidays, July 1st and Labour Day, were days to remember. There were numerous sports events—softball tournaments, foot racing, mucking and panning

Dog sled races on Sanders Avenue were an annual winter event. Buildings lining the street are MacKenzies Store, Buckley's Pharmacy, and the Community Hall. WP00588 © Wells Historical Society.

contests and a boxing card. But the big attraction was the horse races. A circular track had been built on the meadows, and horses were entered from Quesnel, Prince George and Williams Lake…

In the winter months Wells resembled an alpine ski village. Wherever you went there was always someone on skis, or several pairs of skis standing on their heels in front of the cabins and homes. It soon gained prominence as a winter play-ground, and skiing events were established as an annual affair. For two years running it held the ski meet for the British Columbia semi-finals. These competitions ran for three days and included amateur entries in the cross-country, slalom, downhill and jumps. Throughout the ski meet the whole town had a carnival atmosphere; and each day culminated with a dance in the newly constructed community hall.[10]

But the first strike against the town's economy began not ten years after its initial optimistic beginnings, when, during World War II, gold mining was declared a non-essential industry; both supplies and skilled labourers became difficult to obtain. Because gold was kept at its fixed 1934 price until 1968, profits from hardrock mining declined over the decades.

By 1960 Wells' population had declined to about a thousand people. Harvey Bryant, who moved to Wells that year, recalled in his self-published memoirs, *Harvey's Story*, what the town was like when he moved there:

The town did show signs of neglect and indifference. There were two hotels with beer parlours, two cafés, two garages, a couple of coffee shops and three churches. There was a drug store, a gambling hall (the only licensed gambling hall in BC), a pool hall, a general store, a jewellery store, an electronics store, an accounting and real estate office, a telephone office, a meat market, a beautiful community hall and, of course, the theatre. One of the things that struck me was how friendly the people were.[11]

During the province's centennial celebrations in 1958, the dwindling gold rush town of Barkerville was made a historic provincial park. Despite several devastating fires, a few nineteenth-century buildings remained, such as the Barkerville Hotel, built just after the 1868 fire, and St. Saviour's Anglican Church of 1869. Park status involved the removal of all the town's residents, most of them to Wells, which, in turn, benefited as a "bedroom community" for those with jobs at the historic park.

The Luddiꞇt family was in the thick of these developments. Karin Luddiꞇt, the daughter of Fred and Esther Luddiꞇt, lived in Barkerville until she was seven years old and remembers the events vividly. Her father was the government agent there, as well as a prospector. But in 1958, as Karin told me, "The government said, 'We're not going to have this job in Barkerville any longer. We're sending you to Wells.' And my dad said, 'You know this is a crime, because if I were here one more year it would be one hundred years that the government agent had been in Barkerville.'" The irony of this was that the idea of preserving Barkerville's artefacts and buildings for posterity had long been championed by Luddiꞇt. But the government, recalled Karin (still strongly opinionated on the topic fifty-plus years later), said, "'No, no, no—we're shutting this baby down. We're shoving all you guys out of town, right into Wells. We're skidding the old people into the new townsite [New Barkerville, just outside of the historic park boundaries]—and screw history.'" While the Luddiꞇt family may not have looked forward to the move, according to Robin Skelton in *They Call It the Cariboo*, Barkerville lawyer Hub King apparently enjoyed the ride in his own home as it was skidded on a snow road from Barkerville to Wells.[12]

Karin recalled her impressions of her new hometown, where she had already been attending school, in the late 1950s: "The government agent's office opened up underneath the police station, across from the confectionary where you could get milkshakes and stuff. This was on Sanders Avenue. Bryant's Confectionary and Drug Store was right there beside the Community Hall. My mother and I would faithfully go to the Community Hall, up the stairs, once a month, to what was called the Open Shelf Library. And you would receive and order your books from Victoria through the mail in brown bundles. You could get four books at a time. You'd read them and then you'd send them back and you'd get four more.

"I can remember my first phone number in Wells was 78R. That was on the black dial phones. When we moved into Wells, we walked to school, and we didn't have to get carpooled by my dad anymore. School with a boys' entrance and girls' entrance. Boys lined up on one side, girls lined up on the other. I went to that school until grade six, and then...my mom and dad moved to Comox."

Bonnie May's father, Clarence Wood, moved to Wells in 1964, a few years after the Ludditts left. "My dad bought shares in Colter Creek Placer Mine. That summer, he went to work for the mine and stayed. He says he made his investment back. I moved in with my mom in Richmond, and came up to visit during the holidays...Then Dad worked at the Gold Quartz Mine as a mill operator. He worked for the highways for a while, then John Dunbar asked him to come to Barkerville as a display technician/curator. Dad bought a printing press from Harvey Bryant and moved it into the garage of his house on the Crescent.

"When I first came up as a kid, there were a lot of buildings that are now gone. Hong's store had a clothing section and hardware. Forman's store was open, as was Nick Warawa's hardware store. There was a liquor store, jewellery store, theatre, and a ski hill with a huge ski jump. I loved Wells the first time I visited."

But the mine—and therefore the fortunes of the town's residents—continued to decline throughout the 1960s. In 1967, the Cariboo Gold Quartz Mine, which in 1954 had bought out Island Mountain Mine, shut down.

After the Gold Rush

It was the Summer of Love all over the world, but in Wells 1967 was the year the last gold mine closed, leaving the company town without a company, decimating its economy and population. Wells legend has it that at a town meeting held after the mine closure, one of the old-timers got up, pounded the table, and shouted, "Shut 'er down! Just shut 'er down!"

Wells did not dry up and blow away like so many other former mining towns in BC. There were several contributing factors. First, some of the former miners who stayed in Wells found work at Barkerville Historic Park. Much of it was seasonal work, but there were some year-round jobs with security, maintenance, and the park's curatorial department. Second, in 1961, the provincial government had established Bowron Lake Provincial Park, creating seasonal employment for trail building and maintenance crews, carpenters, rangers, and naturalists—and adding recreational tourism to the list of Wells' saving graces. A 1974 *Rural Preliminary List of Electors* shows 261 eligible voters living in Wells in May of that year. The four-column list shows which individuals and families were living in town and what occupations were held by the people of Wells. A full fifty people in town, almost a quarter of the population, were employed by the Parks Branch, either in Barkerville or at Bowron. Third, beginning in the 1960s, the east Cariboo began to be heavily logged (the Bowron clearcut is one of the largest in the world, and is documented in Brian Fawcett's *Virtual Clearcut or the Way Things Are in My Hometown*), and for more than two decades logging provided another major source of local employment. And lastly, small-scale placer mining continued to provide seasonal employment throughout the 1970s. The town, with its abandoned and dilapidated buildings and diminished population and services, kept itself (barely) alive.

In *Harvey's Story*, Harvey Bryant recalled how he and his family managed to keep going just after the Gold Quartz Mine closed:

> In January, 1967 a headline in the *Cariboo Observer* announced that "Rich new Gold Veins had been Discovered" at the Cariboo Gold Quartz. In March the headlines read "Cariboo Gold Quartz to Close in April." This announcement threw the whole town into an uproar. What would now become of Wells? As for us, what would we do?
>
> Manpower started having seminars and job evaluations, some of which I attended, but I couldn't decide what to do...
>
> I was one of the last people to work underground at the mine. There was a lot of cleanup work to do and equipment to bring out. The mine had a telephone on each level. These old battery operated phones were antiques and they

Jack O' Clubs Bar in 1966 or '67. Photo: Bonnie May.

were going to be left behind, so I managed to bring out six or eight which I later sold or gave away as souvenirs.

After I received my quit slip at the mine, I applied for a job at Barkerville with the Parks Branch and was accepted on a part-time basis. Peggy also got a job at the museum. We were able to operate the theatre two nights a week during the summer months. We sold the garbage business, the drive-in café and the printing business.

We were still involved in various organizations, some desperately trying to keep Wells on the map. I was secretary for five of them! Peggy and I also belonged to the Chamber of Commerce and I joined the Masons.[13]

Brad Davies moved to Wells as a young teenager when, in April 1970, his father, Trevor Davies, bought the Barkerville Stage Line, a shuttle van that carried passengers and supplies between Wells and Quesnel five days a week. "At the very end of the sixties," Davies told me, "my father wanted to buy the Barkerville Stage Line...He brought the whole family up while he was doing the negotiating.

"You could sit on the main street there [Pooley Street], and you wouldn't even see a dog walk down the street. There was nothing. There was that quiet spot that happened at the very end of the 1960s. I remember when we were living in Cottonwood [about fifty kilometres from Wells] we could herd our cattle down the highway. There was nothing, not a car on the road. Our cattle would always run down to Cottonwood House to graze, and we could herd them up the middle of the highway—in the middle of summer.

"Wells at the end of the '60s was very strange. Being young, we would break into buildings and find complete households just waiting for someone to bring groceries to set up housekeeping (which a few of our Quesnel buddies immediately did). The cupboards were full of dishes, the linen was still on the beds, and the fridges were still running. The gambling club (the Sunset Theatre, now) had cards on the tables, and cues and balls

Sunset Theatre and Good Eats Cafe, c. 1972. Photographer unknown.

on the green felt of the billiard tables, as though the men had been called away to a fire but would be returning soon."

By 1970, the mining era in Wells was effectively over; only seventeen people described themselves in the elector's list as miners, a startling measure of the town's decline since the 1930s. However, twenty-seven people living in Wells are quaintly identified on the voters list as "Gentlemen." Known to the town kids as the "geezers," this group of old-timers either lived in town and drank regularly and heavily at one of the two pubs, or lived in primitive shacks in the bush, remote from even such civilization as was to be found in Wells. These eccentric characters shaped the town as much as its geographical isolation or its harsh climate, and though few lived to the end of the 1970s, they left lasting impressions on both the existing residents of Wells and the hippie newcomers who began to arrive in 1969.

Lucky Swede and Smiling Albert in 1971. Photo: Michael Weiss.

THE GEEZERS

WELLS WAS AN AFFORDABLE AND APPEALING END-OF-THE-ROAD REFUGE FOR its independent "Gentlemen," a number of whom acted as living links to the Barkerville gold rush. When they arrived in Wells in the 1930s and '40s, they met some of the original nineteenth-century miners who were still alive. When they, in turn, became the town's old-timers they were often happy to share their stories of the past with interested young people. They got by on their pensions and what they might make with a little occasional placer mining or trapping. Some had come to Wells in its heyday, worked hard in the mines or as merchants, been upright citizens, and raised families now long gone. Other old-timers had more mysterious pasts—they didn't tell anyone where they'd come from or how they ended up alone and poor and often drunk before noon—but a number seem to have been hardy survivors of the mining era. "I think mining towns are party towns; they've always been party towns," said Judy Campbell. "And then you have this propensity to have very individualistic people here, which I think attracted the old hippies…You have this background of hunters/trappers/prospectors, which are these very unique, individualistic type of people."

Many of the old-timers were known only by their colourful nicknames. This diverse group of eccentrics seemed less threatened by the hippies' arrival than the Town Fathers did, while the hippies appreciated the old-timers' quirky individualism, capacity for alcohol, and bizarre nicknames—qualities they emulated. And, like the hippies, many of the old-timers were more inclined than most of the townsfolk to thumb their noses at conventional notions of propriety, conformity, and what passed for success. The geezers provided an extraordinarily rich social and historical background to life in Wells in the 1970s and their stories, some of which are briefly told here, offer a rich seam of material, much of it still overlooked. Fortunately, a few photographs and stories have survived, and bring this community to life.

Harvey Bryant, who worked underground at the mine just before it closed, ran the Lode Theatre in Wells and the printing press in the summertime at Barkerville in the 1960s and '70s. In *Harvey's Story*, he recalled the colourful old-timers he found in Wells:

> Wells had many characters, some of whom I got to know through Alice [Barwise] and others quite by chance. The list of people is almost endless—there was Diamond Lil, Cold Ass Marie [Marie Roth, who ran a "sporting house" in Barkerville in the 1930s], Forty Below, Pooley Mike, Little Albert, Deaf Mabel, Lucky Swede, Blanchette Armstrong and Whiskey Dot. I'm sure there were more, but these are all I can remember. Some of these people had been "Ladies of the Night" and, at one time, operated a house of ill repute across the swamp [in or near Stromville]. There are many stories of raids on this house, but this was before my time.
>
> These persons got their nicknames in various ways. For instance, Pooley Mike owned and operated the pool hall on Pooley Street. Forty Below was a Chinese bootlegger who said that a bottle of 40 proof rum was good for forty below. Swede is reported to have found a very large nugget on a street in Barkerville. He was also an artist and painted murals on the walls of the beer parlours.
>
> Diamond Lil was raped near the Community Hall. In court she testified that she wouldn't have minded, but he was so rough. The case was thrown out. Blanchette Armstrong always looked like she had just come out of a band box. Her hair was set with tight curls and she appeared to be a woman of some authority and experience.[1]

Two correspondents have been unusually helpful to me in collecting information about the geezers—Michael Weiss and Brad Davies. Mike, a student of folklore and apprentice hippie ethnographer when he visited Wells (see next chapter), and now an author and journalist in Washington, DC, provided me with CDs and the full transcripts of his July 1971 interviews with some of Wells' old-timers, excerpts of which are quoted below. I have also been very fortunate to have had the input of Brad Davies, who moved to Wells as a teenager when his father bought the Wells Stage in 1970 and who has lived there on and off for the last forty years. Brad is considered the local expert on Wells' old-timers. Many of the following excerpts are from a group of character sketches that he wrote for inclusion in this book. They contain rare glimpses of mining characters whose working lives spanned the earlier decades of the twentieth century.

Alice Ann Barwise

TRACEY TOWNSEND-CARSON: "[Alice Barwise] or 'Gran,' as she was known not just to me (her granddaughter) but to all the kids in town in my era, moved to Wells in December 1946. She left her husband and moved up there. She briefly worked at the Sing's store (K.H. Sing), and then she was employed as an operator at Wells' telephone office by North West Tel and Tel (telephone and telegraph). She continued to work there until it became BC Tel and it went to auto-dialling. She also worked at the Lode Theatre part-time the whole time she was in Wells until she moved to Barkerville and was the post master there, after it became a park. Gran always had an open door to her house for everyone. She was a fantastic cook and was one of the first to let 'hippies' rent a room in her house."

Bill Terryberry

BRAD DAVIES: "A simple man—but a sort of town philosopher while he sat his weekday vigil in front of the Wells Hotel—Terryberry's life revolved around the arrival of the mail. When the Barkerville Stage arrived, he would leap up from the bench in front of the Wells Hotel and thrust everyone out of his way so he could wrestle the mail sacks away from the stage driver, and take them to the postmistress. There was no time for talk while the mail was waiting."

Ernie Brook

ERIC ACKERLY: "My friend Ernie Brook had more stories than you could possibly imagine. When I met him he claimed to be 103 years old. He had worked in the Gold Quartz Mine for a while before it shut down. He had only one hand and a third of one lung left, and he smoked three packs of Sportsman's [cigarettes] a day. He had out-lived two of his wives and was married to his third when I knew him. His youngest daughter was sixteen. He had twenty-eight kids, I think. Ernie had spent five years in the Arctic in the 1920s travelling with an Inuit family from Point Barrow, Alaska, to James Bay by dog team. He lived in the big white house on the Crescent looking over the Jack of Clubs Lake next to Clarence Wood's place by the old church."

Bill Brown

FRED LUDDITT (as told to Michael Weiss, June 30, 1971): "If there was any man on the job who could do more work than he could in a day, then he quit. He had the biggest shovel, he had the best axe, he could do anything better than any other man…He was still living when I came to Barkerville [in the 1930s]. He was 105 or thereabouts when he died…He was stooped way over…[Bill] was a big jaw-boned man, although when I knew him, he was very frail. But he had a long beard, about down to here, and he lived in a cabin not far from the new church…He had come [to Barkerville] in the [18]60s…

"[The townsfolk] thought, that poor Bill, he's in that shack, sleeping on a hay mattress, you know, no springs in it. So they thought they'd get a collection going. Someone took old Bill into the pub down there in Wells. Boys got busy, got his cabin all cleaned out, and put in a nice spring mattress, and a radio on his dresser. Well, when we got Bill back to the old cabin, everybody was standing around wondering what Bill's gonna do when he gets inside. All of a sudden, there was a revolution in the cabin, and out come the radio, and he said, 'By God, I don't want any of your new fandangles around in my cabin! What did you do with my bunk? I been sleeping on it for nearly fifty years! I'm not going to change now.' All the good intentions were for naught."

John Brown (Smokey)

BRAD DAVIES: "I never learned that John Brown's father was a historic personage until after John himself had died. Apparently, Big (Bill) Brown was famous as the guy who hand-shovelled the road through Devil's Canyon after every snowfall, using a special big shovel that the blacksmiths had fashioned for him.

"John first appeared in Wells in a little sports car outside the Wells school, where he tried to engage the Manthey girls in conversation. His hair was skin-head short, but he wore a turtleneck with a big peace sign medallion. Of course, all of us high-school guys were enraged, since these were some of the only girls in our class. But he disappeared again, and we forgot about him.

"Then a year or so later, he reappeared with long, shaggy hair and a bushy beard. And his sports car had been converted into a plywood-framed bush buggy with a sign that said 'Astronauts Only.' Now he didn't want to talk to anyone except the old men around the pool hall, and he made this plain whenever I tried to engage him in conversation. He moved into a piano box of a cabin down Jack of Clubs Creek and kept to himself.

"His last days were spent living in a bus at my cousin's campground in Cottonwood. Apparently he was very prompt with the paying of rent, but never really socialized with anyone there (though he was quite a coffee hound with the miner types around Quesnel, I'm told). When he passed away in the bus (from goitre complications due to neglect), nobody ever came to claim his last effects."

Alice Burns

BRAD DAVIES: "There was an elderly lady named Alice who lived in one of the shacks along the alley where Pooley Mike lived. Her big thing was Howard Hughes. She liked for us young people to come and visit, and would tell us the latest news from this old lover of hers. I was once told by her that this particular news didn't require the usual modes of communication, since Howard was such a whiz at science.

"Donnie MacNair and I helped move her to the Fraser Village [the old folks' home in Quesnel], and I went to visit her soon after. She confided the usual things to me, and as I was leaving I confided to her that, though others thought she was crazy, I myself did not (I was using psychedelics by this time). It was the wrong thing to say, and I was never invited back for tea."

Johnny Cannon

BRAD DAVIES: "Johnny was a diminutive man who never wanted to talk to anyone. He lived in a shack along the long, cold back street in the shadow of Barkerville Mountain, and seemed to run almost everywhere he went, the better to avoid people along the way. I did see him talking to a few of the long-term residents, but he wasn't looking for new friends."

Harold Christiansen

BRAD DAVIES: "Harold was a regular at the pool hall, where he and Pooley Mike and all the rest of their cabal would mumble and cackle about mysterious things. Judging by the *New China* magazines that were read by all of them, they were plotting the next communist revolution."

Tony Driscoll

Some will question his inclusion here, as he may not be much older than the hippies. In any case, he was/is a local character of note.

BRAD DAVIES: "There is a passage by Thoreau, written during his trek through the Maine woods, that explains Tony Driscoll better than anything I could say, and I've no doubt that Tony's read it at some time in his life, for Tony is the best-read man in the world. As Thoreau said, when we are farthest from the lights of town, the fire of the human race burns fiercest. Then, as we move closer to town, the idiots are found. It is only as we approach the heart of civilization that any sort of intelligence reappears, but it is a dim bulb as compared to the brilliance to be found in men who choose to embrace the wild.

"I've heard that Tony's childhood was not the best, though you would never hear it from him…

"My very first falling job was spent working under Tony and another fellow named Earl, and it was one hell of an education for a young, aspiring intellectual. Tony could hold forth at great length about all the philosophers of the world, and every now and then Earl would put in his own two cents' worth, teaching me that philosophers of every stripe can be found in the most unlikely of places—places as unlikely as pickup trucks parked in the middle of a winter landscape, miles away from town. And needless to say, those two taught me about falling trees, too, since that was why we were there."

Mike Duchak (Pooley Mike)

BRAD DAVIES: "Pooley wasn't given to sharing any great confidences with the younger generation. About the only time we could get him to be sociable was when we were trying to play one of the ancient billiards games that the pool hall was equipped to offer. Then he would become almost cheerful and quite voluble as he taught us how the old game was played. After that, though, it was back to being gruff and inarticulate.

"I think he enjoyed chasing us out the door and down the street for a ways, so we always played along by attempting to steal cigarettes from behind the counter. There was a period of time where a sign saying, 'Brat the Rat Steals Chocolate Bars' hung behind the counter, though I never saw it since I was barred for that same period of time. I guess he never figured out what I was after when he caught me behind the counter.

"As I've mentioned, there was a small cabal of elderly gents who gathered nightly around his heater. They read *New China* (when they read at all) and spoke in low voices

Pooley Mike on the front porch of the Wells Pool Hall, 1972. Photo: Rob Danby.

of mysterious things. Of them, I specifically remember Harold Christiansen and Smokey John Brown. We never found out what they were talking about, though, since they always shut down whenever we got close."

BONNIE MAY: "There were so many characters in Wells, but my favourite was Pool Room Mike. As teenagers we hung out at the pool hall all the time. Mike was so gruff with everyone; he would yell at us for taking too long to play a game of pool or complain about Gaylord's dog, Flag, being in the pool hall. Then, when you weren't looking, he'd go and let him in!"

Steve Errati

BRAD DAVIES: "Steve was the eternal working man. He was a craftsman (but slower than Methuselah), and there weren't too many jobs I took on that he didn't have some advice about. He was friendly with everyone, and well loved by all. His hounds were a bit noisy, and I think one or two of their descendants are still lying at Trapper Dave's door."

ROSE DANBY: "Steve had all those strange dogs; they were spotted hounds of some kind. One year, we put on a Christmas banquet at the [Community] Hall for all of the old-timers. That night, I found out that that man could dance! Holy mackerel! He danced with every single one of us and danced us off our feet until we were ready to drop, and then went and got the next lady and did it again."

Bella Fraser

BRAD DAVIES: "Such a cute old gal, but I think she was a bit dotty by the time I came to know her. I remember coming out of the Jack lobby one time to find her staring up at the full moon. 'It's the same old moon,' she crooned, 'and it's the same old tune.' If she was anything like her daughters, granddaughters, and great-granddaughters are today [including Ruth and Judy Peever], she must have been a power to reckon with."

Glen Galbraith (Heckpoint)

BRAD DAVIES: "Glen and Jesse Galbraith had a kind of a crash pad, the first crash pad in this town, as a matter of fact, before the hippies really arrived, when guys like Brian Humber were just starting to arrive. As the proprietors of the 'Hobo Jungle' in

Seniors' Dinner 1973: L to R: Bill Terryberry, John Boutwell, Steve Errati, and Roddy MacDonald. Photo: Karin Ludditt.

those early hippie years, Heckpoint and Jessie were central figures, beloved of the 'underclass' of Wells. Remember, there was no knowledge of 'countercultures' or 'hippie communes' at the time, and therefore Heckpoint named his home the Hobo Jungle when it began to fill with people. It was something that he understood.

"He had a story for every occasion, and time tells me they were true. Most of his stories brought hilarity to his audience, but on quiet nights he told some serious ones, too. He brought the house down time and again by explaining that he was certain it was the *big* trees that brought the snow. But you know something? I believe he had it right. In the years since then, I've seen as a faller that the water table drops once we've knocked down all the biggest trees. And wherever the trees are smaller, whether on the prairies or in the boreal forest, the snowfall is always less.

"At one point, some people in town were writing 'Heckpoint' on every dollar bill. Heckpoint used to have a story: At that time, the Canadian government had just changed the dollar bill. The bills used to say, 'Will pay to the bearer on demand.' And then all of a sudden the government came out with dollar bills that just said, 'This note is legal tender.' Heckpoint said that this meant that your dollars are no longer worth a goddamn thing, because you can't take it to the bank and get your gold back. These Heckpoint dollars circulated around town for quite a while.

"He also told us of early days around Smithers, where he knew Simon Gunanoot[1] personally, and spent a winter living with an outlaw named Hank Valloo. Some of his stories of the gold around that area gave fuel to a new generation of prospectors in this area, so that for many years afterward, the gold exploration around Wells was being done by hippies.

"Then on the quiet nights, he would speak wistfully of the time when he was 'in the truth,' and went door to door to speak about the Bible. Though he'd left it all behind by the time he arrived in Wells, Glen was once a highly placed member of his church, and he returned to that church in the last years of his life. He passed away in Armstrong, and was buried with much ceremony by Jehovah's Witnesses."

Vic Gardecke

BRAD DAVIES: "Mr. Clean came by his nickname honestly. A happy-go-lucky soul, he was not given to cleanliness by any stretch of the word. He often appeared to have just finished tearing a motor down, though this was highly unlikely. He loved to have people visit him and would usher them down the winding trails inside his shack to a place where he had cleared some space for company. Asked if they required a glass, the visitor would usually choose to drink from the bottle.

"Sadly, Vic got gangrene in his foot. Recognizing a special accent to the aroma that always lingered around him, someone sent the health authorities to check it out. I remember that he lost some toes over this, and I think he may eventually have lost his life. All I'm sure of is that he disappeared from Wells about this time."

Harold Garden

MICHAEL WEISS: "Harold Garden was a former surveyor in the Barkerville area in the 1930s who still believed that a gold vein existed on his property—one of two privately held properties in the Barkerville Historical Park. Born in Woodstock, New Brunswick, in 1889, he was a feisty eighty-two-year-old when I interviewed him. He spent most of our session criticizing the government for not offering him enough money for his property. His home was cluttered with yellow papers and books and the sitting room had a giant moose rug in front of a wood stove, a dog sitting nearby for companionship. He also liked to tell a story, really a shaggy dog tale, that he was the inventor of a portable mine shaft that you could just roll out and it would take you to gold riches underground. But I suspect he still felt he might do the same on his property for that long-sought strike."

Harold Garden in his Barkerville home, 1971. Photo: Michael Weiss.

Stefan (Steve) Gomboc

BRAD DAVIES: "If you were unlucky enough to call Crazy Steve by his nickname (as I was, just once), you found out just how sane and stern he could be. But he loved to perform, and my mother always said that his face was the most expressive face she had ever watched. My favourite performance was the one he would go into whenever we loggers were partying at Amboy's shop. He would dance around and start counting the layers of clothing that he was wearing, starting with the T-shirt that was closest to his throat, and proceeding outward to the collar of his outer coat: 'August, September, October, November, Christmas and January, February, March.'

"I remember when the police took away his driver's licence for a season—those days were much kinder—and when he needed to come to the general store for liquor or beer, he would don his hard hat and take up the wheelbarrow. Then he would run uptown making all the appropriate motor noises, and signal for every turn. The best part of the performance was always the part where he would parallel park the wheelbarrow in front of the store, since it usually took him at least ten minutes of back and forth to get that 'tractor' parallel to the curb.

"In the end he broke a leg or a hip and was laid up in the basement of his unfinished log home, and was dependent on others for his care. I went and split a few cords of wood for him with a wood splitter, and when we were sharing some comfort from a bottle beside his bed, he told me his life story. This terrified me, since he had never done this before, and I sounded an alert to everyone in town. He thought he was about to die, and the fact is, he was right. And without a doubt, the life story of this great performer would sweep the Academy Awards."

BEV DANBY: "I can remember trying to kick Steve Gomboc out of the Jack one night when I was bartending there. He was usually pretty mellow but he got owly this one night. Had a couple of chainsaw blades with him, and he starts to swing them at me. I say, 'I'm going to bar you if you don't leave right now.' He was just madder than hell, but luckily I got him out of there. I was scared, but I thought, I'm not going to back down to him or he'll have me by the throat."

Bill Hong

BRAD DAVIES: "The first month we lived in Wells, Bill grabbed me to come and work with him for a day. We went down to Slough Creek, where I got to see what is known to history as the last day of hydraulicking in BC. Then we walked up the mountainside and along a ditchline and in a little forest glade he told me to start digging down through the moss. There was an old town there, and we dug up artefacts. I heard later that he had a basement full of such things.

"Now, when I first got into the truck with him he handed me a cigarette (my parents wouldn't have approved), and got me to light us both up. Then he told me there was nothing wrong with smoking, but that drinking was bad. During that same conversation he mentioned that in the '30s, it had been cheaper to use Chinamen (his words) than it was to use dynamite.

"Bill's book [*And So…That's How It Happened: Recollections of Stanley-Barkerville 1900–1975*] was not written by him. He spoke into a tape recorder, and my mother then transcribed his broken English onto paper. He was quite taken with her, and would bring Chinese herbs in pots for her to grow as houseplants."

BONNIE MAY: "On our first New Year's Eve together as a married couple, we stayed home and didn't go to the dance at the Community Hall because Fred had a broken ankle. At around 9:00 or 10:00 at night there was a knock on our front door—which was a surprise, because we hadn't shovelled the snow at the front of the house. There stood old Bill Hong, coming to wish us a Happy New Year!"

Ray Hong

JUDY CAMPBELL: "One day, I went into Hong's store. I asked, 'Do you have any kerosene?' Muriel yelled back to Ray, 'Do we have any kerosene, Ray?' And Ray says, "Well, who's it for?'"

Jens Hansen (Lucky Swede)

BRAD DAVIES: "Lucky gets a lot of favourable coverage from people, but it needs to be balanced against the knowledge of those who have spent time with him. It's a complicated subject. And it should always be uppermost in our minds that his own family is not happy with his behaviour. Lucky left Norway with real forces chasing him…He did duty in the Canadian military, though whether he did this as part of 'the Zombies,' he never said. [Zombies was the derogatory term used for conscripts during World War II who refused to serve overseas.] I think any history of Lucky would have to begin there, but of course, all that would be dependent on the memories of people far more knowledgeable than me."

Lucky Swede at home, 1971. Photo: Michael Weiss.

LISA MARIE DUNCAN (NEÉ WOOD): "If you ask a lot of the kids my age that were there [in the 1970s], they will probably tell you about this cool old miner that use to live there. His name was Lucky; he used to pull quarters out of all our ears so we could go into Hong's store and buy penny candy."

MICHAEL WEISS: "The best-storyteller-in-town crown goes to a man I met one night in late June 1971 at the Jack O' Clubs...a man locals called Lucky Swede.

"Now, I should probably digress for a moment. At nineteen, I had already decided on pursuing a career as a writer, and I'd already started contributing articles to the University of Maryland newspaper. After graduating, in fact, I did become a journalist, a career that's so far lasted thirty years while I've written for publications ranging from *The Atlantic* and *The New York Times Magazine* to *People* and *Reader's Digest*. I've travelled around North America and Europe, writing three books, countless articles and even a radio documentary on folk music for National Public Radio. And I figure that I've interviewed probably five thousand people—generals and politicians, dancers and boxers, cops and crooks. That said, I think I can say without qualification that the best storyteller I ever met was Lucky Swede.

"First of all, Lucky wasn't even Swedish. His real name was Jens Hansen and he was born in Norway in 1905 and came to Canada when he was nineteen. He got his nickname throughout the Cariboo after he discovered a goose egg-sized gold nugget worth $500 in 1937, and then shared his fortune by buying liquor for all the other miners in the area— allowing them to enjoy what he described as 'a two-week drunk.'[2] When I met him, he was sixty-seven years old, with a full head of straight white hair, slicked back over blue eyes, and a square jaw. He lived in a tin-covered shack and still occasionally worked a claim outside Stout's Gulch, but I suspect he spent more time in the pubs. He was slight of build, walked slowly and had a fondness for beer and hand-rolled cigarettes. But he was one helluva storyteller, a classical artist of a storyteller, a man who'd begin a tale with the setting, embellish it with jokes, throw in some sex, mimic several voices, and end with a flourish—no matter if he were the hero or the butt of a joke. He told me how he found his first gold nugget in British Columbia in 1929 this way: 'I didn't know the first thing about the ground up here. And I'm down there, panning. I got maybe ten cents in the pan. But I took my cigarette, it's all soaking wet, and I put it right on a ten-dollar nugget. I says, "Hi!" From then on, I looked for nuggets.'

"That night I met Lucky, I knew I had to record him, so I bought him some beer and talked about coming around to his shack to do some tapings. He was amenable, but on one condition—I had to bring a bottle of whisky along. I agreed, and several mornings later, I showed up at his cabin with a bottle of Southern Comfort, my tape recorder and a harmonica. It must have been about 11:00 a.m., and he was already into a gallon of cheap wine with one of his cronies, a man everyone called Smiling Albert…

"We sat out in the sunshine, sipping whisky on two stumps while I asked him for stories about his days as a gold miner. It was probably one of the happiest days of my life, as he told me about his big gold strike and living through the Depression—The Hungry Thirties, he called them—and some of the characters in the area, like the beautiful woman who ran a whorehouse named Cool-Ass Marie. One of his stories concerned how, in a period when he was broke, he was able to ply free drinks from Marie by coming up with various ways to flatter her. As I recall one exchange, he knew that she was a high-kicking dancer so he challenged her to see if she could hit the ceiling of one of her rooms with a high kick. Well, she walked in front of Lucky and proceeded to kick the ceiling, prompting Lucky to say, 'Oh, Marie, what beautiful legs you have!'—earning him another drink as well as a glimpse of her legs.

"I knew Lucky had a good singing voice from his boozy baritone renditions of songs at the Jack O' Clubs. So I asked him for some songs, and he provided several that he claimed he learned 'off an old music box.' To this day, I still sing one to my wife and kids when we're driving back home on a long car trip. As I recall the words, it went something like this:

I'm only a crazy old mucker, my life in the mines I have spent,
Free, a fool and a sucker, and my back she is tired and bent.
No peaday [sic—payday?] was my heyday, as beer and rum I did drink.
Wake up in the morning, drunk, feeling punk.
I scoffed a man in that office, I called him belittlin' names,
But I realized as I grew older, I just might come back to where he's in his grave.
I can see my last days, they're nearing; I can see them only so clear,
When I been working, sweating, swearing, with a pick and a shovel in hell."

DUNCAN BRAY: "I wrote a song, one of my favourites, actually, called 'Crazy Bill and Lucky Swede.' I loved those two old geezers. Not many people liked or knew Bill, but I used to go and drink with him at his shack, and listen (with many repeats) to his wacky stories about being a speed addict in the '40s.

Crazy Bill and Lucky Swede
Lucky liked the booze, and Bill liked Benzedrine
Drinking in the bar
Lyin' 'bout their lives

Bill once played in a country band
Lucky panned for gold when he's a younger man
Living fast and hard
No way to keep a wife

Shooting speed back in '49
Jackin' cars and doin' time
Bill had a thousand tales to tell
The little pleasures and the livin' hell
Tears in his eyes at the memories
Reaching for the remnants of a dream

Bill lived down in the tailing flats
Outhouse and dilapidated tin roof shack
Burned the damn thing down
One dark and drunken night.
Lucky'd laugh and play his game
Might have the shakes, but he could shark ya'
just the same
Unless he got too high
Always ended in a fight

Lucky had come here looking for gold
Out in the hills where the black bears roam
End of the highway frontier town
He rode it up and he rode it down
Tears in his eyes at the memories
Reaching for the remnants of a dream

And I was still young, just seventeen,
Me, my guitar, and my crazy schemes,
Little log cabin at the end of town
Twenty-foot snow piled all around
Keepin' the fire stoked, haulin' logs

This little burgh of three hundred
  and four hundred dogs

Crazy Bill and Lucky Swede
Lucky liked the booze, and Bill liked Benzedrine
Drinkin' in the bar
Lyin' about their lives
Drinkin' in the bar
Lyin' bout their lives
Yeah, they're just livin' in the bar
Livin' out their lives"

Albert Lavine

(Smiling Albert, possibly also known as Little Albert.)

BRAD DAVIES: "In any history of Wells, Albert Lavine holds a major candle. And he damned well earned some kind of empathy from us all. So much can be said about this man, who was probably the first counterculture arrival in Wells. I'm sure there are people who still want to scrub him from any history…au contraire, assholes, without him, you have no history. Wino Albert came to us from time in a prison, and was here when I arrived. And he was here for all of us, whether you were a mere spectator when he showed up at the bar in drag, or whether you were someone (like me) who went in search of a hypodermic syringe from him and had to listen to his lecture to the young about how he didn't want to see us 'bo-o-oys getting wi-i-i-red.' He'd been through everything that Burroughs and the rest of the Beat Generation had been though, and long before we were willing to admit it, Albert Lavine was telling us where we were going. I guess he earned the nights that he would show up in drag, though there were not many people who could understand it at the time, including the hippies who had begun to show up around here."

MICHAEL WEISS: "He was a bit stocky and always seemed to wear a black hat over bleary eyes, and a lot of the hippies tended to think of him as just another old rummy who hung out at the pub at night. But I'd gotten a chance to talk to him and learned that he was a former musician who played harmonica with a band in the early days of Canadian television... It wasn't long before I gave him my harmonica to play. Then he did something I'd never heard done on the harmonica—he played a Scottish jig, screwing up his mouth so he could simultaneously play the drone notes on the left side of the harmonica while using the right side of his lips to play the treble melody. It was a virtuoso performance if ever I'd heard one."

ZUBIN GILLESPIE: "I came into his house one day, and he was looking into a tobacco can, because he had done LSD and he was watching TV in the tobacco can. He was way gone! Albert just did his thing...always had a wig on, this curly wig."

Richard Leggitt

BRAD DAVIES: "Leggitt lived in a cabin up the Swift River from Cottonwood. He was always walking the Barkerville Highway and sometimes appeared in Wells.

"My aunt worked in the Quesnel post office during the mid-1960s, and mentioned that they often got letters from him addressed to the Queen, on the outside of which would be further notes that he had forgotten to write in the letter. Apparently, he felt that he was her representative here, and wanted to keep her informed as to the state of her forests.

"A lot of people called him The Roadrunner and would stop to offer him a lift as he was swinging down the highway. Usually he would respond by saying things like: 'No thanks, I'm in a hurry,' or else, 'I can't stop right now, the other guy is catching up,' at which point he would motion to the empty highway behind him and keep on truckin'. One very cold day he rode in the Barkerville Stage while I was a passenger, and I heard him talking to one of the other passengers. 'Nine-foot-tall jackrabbits,' he was saying. 'Somebody should open your eyes, by golly, 'cause I've seen nine-foot-tall jackrabbits in the woods.'"

Fred and Ester Luddit at the Cornish Wheel in Barkerville, 1971. Photo: Michael Weiss.

Fred and Ester Ludditt

MICHAEL WEISS: "One day, I drove up the steep hills to the remote home of Fred and Esther Ludditt, alongside the plywood shacks of Fred's old mining camp. Fred was born in England in 1907 and came to Canada when he was two years old, first panning for gold when he was twenty. He was an owner and director of the Grouse Creek Mining Company in addition to building mining shafts and working as a government agent in an assay office. I showed up at his door because of his role as a historian and author of *Barkerville Days* and a pamphlet called *Gold in the Cariboo*. On the day I interviewed him, June 30, [1971], Fred was great company, a slight professorial sort who recounted the history of the area and told me stories from the books he'd published about the gold miners in the area. Esther even read two poems she'd written, and they were very generous with their time and tea."

Roddy McDonald

BRAD DAVIES: "Roddy was a wisp of a guy who walked around Wells very slowly, hunched over by a spine that wouldn't straighten. As he walked the streets, it always appeared as if the first big wind would blow him over, but he was much too strong-willed for that. When the wind blew, he merely stopped and leaned into it, like a tree. He loved everyone—laughed with a high wheeze of glee—but went almost apoplectic when he was angry, which was often."

TOM ADAIR: "Roddy was so thin. The coats he wore just hung on him, but they were his coats from when he was younger. He used to be big, the tough guy in town. Roddy didn't drink because he was a Jehovah, but he would invite people over to his place in the winter and it would be ninety-five degrees in there, and he would pour you a glass that had four ounces of whiskey in it."

JUDY CAMPBELL: "One night in the bar , Lucky was so drunk he could barely stand up, and Roddy was so doddering, but I thought the two of the them were going to come to fisticuffs, they were just flailing at each other."

Sherman "Spud" Murphy

BRAD DAVIES: "From the stories that he would tell about himself—like the building of ferro-concrete boats in Malaysia—Spud Murphy was a just a nomad who finally came to rest in Wells. He and Barb Tone presided over a tribe of the most wonderful people, many of whom are still residing in the area.

"I've heard it said of Spud that he never had to work for a paycheque or for any other man in his life, yet always had plenty of money to finance the affairs of his tribe. Certainly that is how I experienced him; he was a very sharp operator, though gentle in the application. I think the free spirit of this man had a lot to do with the way things evolved."

Nick Mole

TOM ADAIR: "Nick was a trapper out past the Cariboo Falls. And the first year I was here, he was on the corduroy [trail] crew between Kibbee and Indian Point with Nathan Kew and me…He ate only boiled potatoes, and wore long underwear, summer and winter. His theory was that it kept you cool in the summer and warm in the winter. When the long underwear got dirty, he wouldn't wash it right away; first, he'd turn it inside out and wear it some more."

Charlie Petersen

BRAD DAVIES: "I think if my father (who owned the Barkerville Stage during those years) had a favourite passenger, it was Charlie Petersen. Returning from town, Dad would always leave the highway to drive Charlie right to the front door of his cabin on Timon Creek (perhaps because Charlie liked to imbibe on 'town' days, yet was very old). There he would help Charlie inside, and if there were no other passengers, would pause to have a glass of cheer. Charlie, who was quite industrious, would sit there at the table and open all of the tins of Copenhagen that he had brought from town and proceed to add salt and pepper. Then he would pour a little dark rum into each tin before sealing them back up with tape. 'They're makin' it too damn weak, these days,' he'd say.

"One day Dad returned from a second trip to Quesnel very late in the day (these special trips were unusual, but did happen). This special passenger had insisted that they stop to bring Charlie along for the trip. Then, since Dad and Charlie returned from Quesnel alone (and because there was no official business such as the mail to worry about), they wound up sharing an entire bottle of rum before Dad returned home. Dad told me that when the last drink was done, Charlie shook his head with regret, then jumped up from his chair and went outside to continue cutting wood with the old bucksaw that he liked to use. Charlie was always cutting wood in front of his cabin, and apparently—never mind the excursion—this day was like any other."

Steve Rodencich

BRAD DAVIES: "A real joker, Steve made some damn fine beer and wine. All of us young guys were delighted to be waved in for a tasting. I remember once he started to dig a ditch alongside his house—it was 1973, as you'll quickly figure out—and probably never finished it. When my dad asked him about that few feet of ditchline with a shovel lying beside it, he looked at him in amazement and said 'You no heard about energy shortage?'"

Mabel Schmid (Deaf Mabel)

BRAD DAVIES: "When she lived upstairs in the Jack, Mabel kept to herself, but mumbled a lot. And then late at night I would hear her browbeating the old men who lived in the Jack, who would all be gathered in her room. They thought the world of her, and she scolded them like they were her wayward children. Maybe they needed that, or maybe there's a whole lot more history there."

Ski-pole John

BRAD DAVIES: "John had a cabin on the tailings for many years, and could be seen walking up the hill to the Jack on a daily basis. The kids loved to talk with him while he was resting over his ski pole at some point along his daily traverse. He moved into the Jack in his last years, and my fondest memory is of him telling me that for sure they were putting something into the beer to make people drink more of it."

Slim Anderson

BRAD DAVIES: "I only knew Slim as a tall, almost silent ghost who, throughout the day and night, slipped down to the kitchen before returning to his room upstairs with a plate, a mug or a glass of sustenance. You always knew he was coming because he breathed a kind of tuneless whistle to announce his passage through the Jack."

Mabel Schmid and Slim Anderson in the Jack O' Clubs, c. 1960s (mural on wall painted by Lucky Swede). Photo: Sam Thatcher.

Ed Titley

Ed worked in the gold mines during Wells' boom years and served in the volunteer fire brigade. By the late '70s, however, he was to be found most days sitting in the Jack O' Clubs bar, drinking steadily and accosting anyone who came near him as "Ya dumb bugga!"

Andy McGuire, c. 1972. "I don't know much about Andy, but he was around Wells for a very long time." Photo: Sam Thatcher.

BRAD DAVIES: "Now, Ed is a subject that even people in Quesnel want to be expert about. And why shouldn't they be? He spent the last chapter of his life there. But I'm gonna add a bit…

"When Ed first returned to Wells from his long sojourn in the wilderness he was a bit 'bushed.' We would see him bouncing along the street with a mountain man's stride and he would be talking to himself. To make matters worse, he ended up staying in one of the three cabins across from the curling rink (Lucky Swede lived in another one), and everyone in my generation used to party at his cabin.

"One night when I was too high from the LSD that we were taking, I went outside to vibrate under the stars, and there was Ed, who was vibrating too. But he'd taken no drugs. I guess it was this first real conversation that we had (and I don't remember what was said) that got me friendly with Ed.

"Ed moved into the Jack and became more sociable with people. He even spent a long period of time being a chokerman behind one of Amboy Logging's Cats (at his age!). But there was always that spectre hovering around him, the soul of a crazy hermit. When I visited him in his room, I noticed something that underscored all of this. I wrote a poem about it, but can only remember these words: 'The only room with half a view has tooth marks on the sill.'"

The Tregillus Girls, Margaret and Mildred

BRAD DAVIES: "I never knew Fred Tregillus [who first came to the Wells area in the 1880s], but I believe I knew one of his daughters. When I was in my late teens, and under the influence of alcohol, some chivalrous notion goaded me into asking her for a dance during one of the Community Hall events.

"'No, I'm too ugly,' she said, but I persisted.

"'No, I'm too ugly,' she said again, but still I persisted.

"'Look, kid, *fuck off!*' she said, and that was the end of our relationship."

✻

Missing from this selection of character sketches are stories about, for example, Andy McGuire, of whom little is known except that he was "around for a very long time"; Ella Price, a female trapper; Shakey Katie, of whom it was said that at dances, they had to follow her with a mop; Marion Dennis, who once regaled me with the story of how she'd run away from her strict upbringing in England and made it all the way to Canada as a teenager; Enar B. Tortensen and Wilfrid Thomson, the last ancient occupants of Barkerville, or scores of others. A well-rounded history of Wells, which remains to be written, would have to include far more representatives from this eclectic group of old-timers (in addition to providing information about Wells clans such as the Randalls, MacNairs, Williamses, and Drinkwaters, among others.).

L to R: Lottie Bowron, Margaret Tregillus, Fred LuddItt, Mildred Tregillus. Photo: Karin Luddltt.

The eccentricities and wild stories of the old-timers did not fail to exert an influence on some of the hippies who began to show up at the start of the 1970s as well as on some of the local youth. Brad Davies, in retrospect, told me: "I think there is no explanation for the counterculture revolution in Wells without an understanding of the elders who lived here in the heart of it."

Big Valley cabin in winter, 1977. Photo: Larry Fourchalk.

ARE YOU READY FOR THE COUNTRY?

THE WELLS MUSEUM WEBSITE (*WELLS.ENTIRELY.CA*) STATES THAT "THE LATER 1960s and '70s were a very slow time for the community, when nothing much seemed to happen." Nothing much if you don't count the arrival, into this time-warped ghost town, peppered with eccentric geezers, of paisley-clad, pot-smoking hippies who squatted in abandoned miner's shacks and listened to rock music, changing the town—and themselves—forever.

The first-hand accounts that follow from hippie migrants to Wells throughout the 1970s tell us what motivated them to go there or what accidents of fate drew and kept them there. Some stayed for just a few days or a season, others settled in for decades, but all were attracted by the possibility of living as they had never done before.

Filthy Larry's

In the Once-Upon-a-Time of Wells' history, the story of how the hippies came to town always starts with the names Brian Humber and Dale Ruckle, two hippies from Vancouver who opened Filthy Larry's Leather Shoppe. Brian and Dale's Wells arrival stories are told here by old friends: Brian was living in Vancouver when he died in 2006 but, regrettably, I never got a chance to interview him, and have been unable to locate Dale. Both Dale and Brian left

Wells' first hippies: Brian Humber and Dale Ruckle. Photo: Ann Moxley Humber.

Wells in the early 1970s, never to return, but they also left an indelible mark on the place. The leather shop, situated amidst a small cluster of rustic buildings outside of Wells in an area known as Stromville, was located on the side of the dead-end gravel highway to Barkerville. Within a year of their arrival, Filthy Larry's became known as "hippie central" in Wells before it was burned down in the early 1970s.

When asked to describe Brian Humber, his old friend Zubin Gillespie told me that, when they first met, Brian was considered "incredibly good looking; he was a football player, very stocky. He had a moustache, ponytail, curly hair. He was very charismatic. All the girls loved Brian; he just had a great personality." Brian grew up in California, and another one of his old Wells friends described him to me as a kind of "macho surfer dude."

Filthy Larry's sign. Photo: Ann Moxley Humber.

Brian's old friends don't know who, if anyone, Filthy Larry was. On the store's sign, there was what looked like a Neanderthal from the Ozarks, hairy and pot-bellied, dressed in tattered and very filthy garb. Was he based on a real-life character or a story Brian or Dale heard about a character, or was he entirely a product of their imaginations? Not even a shred of a legend remains, and just one blurry black and white photo.

Why did Brian and Dale think that Wells was a good place to start an entrepreneurial venture? There were head shops and leather shops and other hippie businesses turning tidy profits in Kitsilano, just blocks from the university where the two were students. It's reasonable to surmise that Brian and Dale, like thousands of hippies across the continent, were seeking a way to make a living from their own creative labours, literally from their own

Filthy Larry's Leather Shoppe business licence, July 17, 1970. Photo: Ann Moxley Humber.

hands, beyond the cities and the suits and their rules. Dale Ruckle appears to have grown up in Quesnel and may have known Wells. So, the two University of British Columbia students left Vancouver behind and headed north, where they unknowingly and irrevocably changed history for one small town.

ANN MOXLEY HUMBER: (Brian's widow, who shared with me a few precious old photos of Brian and Filthy Larry's in 2008, but, still mourning his untimely death, wasn't able to provide a detailed response to my requests for information about Brian's experiences in Wells). "Brian loved his early days in Wells...He was a history major and arrived in Wells through Dale Ruckle, whom he met at UBC."

ZUBIN GILLESPIE was one of the first wave of hippies to move from Vancouver to Wells as part of the Lord Byng high-school group. Stuart, who later changed his name to his grandfather's—Zubin—lived in Wells from 1971 to 1975. "Brian originally grew up in California and then moved up to Abbotsford, out in the middle of the farmlands, after his father died. They were friends with Fred Heringa, and Fred Heringa was from a real hillbilly family. They were always talking about making gallons of wine—goofy grape and rootin' tootin' raspberry! That summer [1969] was the first year Brian was up in Wells; he was there with Dale Ruckle. They had a leather shop called Filthy Larry's Leather Shoppe...I don't know how they ended up in Wells or why it was Wells, but they opened up Filthy Larry's, which was a little log house right at Stromville. [There had once been a dairy farm in Stromville (also spelled Strommeville and Strömville), named for original Wells resident Harry Stromme. There is also some archival and anecdotal evidence that, in the 1930s, this suburb was where Wells' residents found their sporting (prostitution) and gambling houses.]

"Brian had bought that property originally from a woman called Jerry Heskett-Bunting, and she was an incredible character herself. She lived in the Cotton-wood area, and she raised Manx cats. She would teach them to pray for food, so they would get up on their hind legs and go like this [puts hands together in prayer position]. She was quite a character! Brian paid $1,200 [for the 3.2-acre piece of property with its collection of rustic houses and shacks, without electricity, oil heat, or running water]. It was a lot of money at that time. "The shop was a little one-floored log house. It must've been miserable to live in. I recall walking through the front door; to the left was the living room. They were making leather sandals. Dale was very much an entrepreneur from the word go. It was a hippie-type thing; the big thing with hippies back then was candles and sandals!"

KARIN LUDDITT, daughter of Barkerville historian Fred Ludditt, lived in Barkerville and Wells through her grammar-school years and returned in the early 1970s as summer worker in Barkerville for a few years. "I think that Brian and Dale were fighting something. They were fighting society in Vancouver, and I don't know if all of them [the hippies who came to Wells from the city] had rich parents, but some of them did, fairly wealthy parents, and they were rebelling. It was their way of rebelling and getting back at people and doing something weird and off-the-cuff…We all do our own thing. My parents were very conservative and I turned out to be kind of wild. So that's my intuitive hunch, because I never obviously interviewed them at the time and asked 'Why are you doing this?' but over the years, that's what I've come to decide—that's why they did it. And, of course, they both ended up [decades later] being entrepreneurs and very rich businessmen. [Filthy Larry's] was the start…"

Karin Ludditt in Wells, early 1970s. Photo: Tom Adair.

Leather purses from Filthy Larry's. Photo: Ann Moxley Humber.

NATHAN KEW was born and raised in Vancouver, but his paternal grandparents settled in the Wells/Bowron area, so Nathan spent childhood vacations in Wells in the 1960s and lived in Wells between 1973 and 1986, intermittently. "Filthy Larry's was a really neat shop. They did a tremendous amount of leather work. They were very productive…They had all of these big, heavy purses, really the fashion, made from saddle leather, tooled and dyed and braided. The shop was quite small. I remember there was lots of purple paint, and when you walked in the store, it just smelled wonderful, all the leather and the dyes, and they burned a very heavy incense. It was a comfortable place to be."

BRAD DAVIES: "That first summer Dale Ruckle was the famous one. It was the first time the locals got to realize what LSD can do. He was running naked through the streets of Wells! They were down on Sanders Avenue, in one of the end buildings there, the night of his naked run through the town, stoned on LSD, which really blew the town away. Within a year or two of that, even the elders of this town were kind of, well, that's all okay, but he was a little early, it was just a little bit raw for their taste."

ELLEN GODWIN moved to Wells from Quesnel in 1970 and lived there for a few years. "In the summer of '69 a guy from Quesnel, whose name eludes me for the moment, and a very nice chap from Ruskin, BC, started the Leather Shoppe. It had the very 'Ren and Stimpiest' sign [the Ren and Stimpy cartoons, on TV decades later, featured off-the-wall violence and indecent humour]; one felt antisocial structure just looking at it. About the same fix as reading Marx's *Manifesto*. They also did fabulous leather work. They were there in Wells first, in 1969."

The First Waves

The first wave of hippies to arrive in Wells followed Brian and Dale from Vancouver; this was the Lord Byng High School cohort, also known as the Point Grey Pranksters. They came for the summer of 1970, then returned to finish school before moving to Wells over the course of the next several years. But in the fall of 1970, a second group of hippies, assembled from Ontario, the US, and Vancouver, arrived in Wells; they were planning an intentional community. Were they glad to find fellow travellers when they arrived in Wells? In a town of less than three hundred people, you might think the arrival of other longhairs would be hard to miss, but during their first winter in Wells, the hippies from the second group (living on the Jack of Clubs Lake side of town) didn't encounter those living in Stromville (on the opposite, Barkerville side of town). "I don't remember Filthy Larry's Leather Shoppe," Louise Futcher, who moved to Wells in 1970 with the Ontario cohort, told me. "I didn't have a vehicle and walked everywhere. I don't remember ever visiting [the Leather Shoppe]." For nearly four decades, she has believed that her own group was the first group of hippies in Wells. "Funny that our paths would not cross!" she now says. But Futcher became good friends with a few of the hippies from the Stromville contingent within a year of her arrival, and the two groups melded as people left and continued to arrive.

ZUBIN GILLESPIE: "I met Brian [Humber in Vancouver] in 1968 or '69. I was going to Lord Byng High School, which was an amazing school at that time in Vancouver. In grade eleven, I was living on my own. I was living off [the money I made from] a paper route and selling *Georgia Straight*s. I was living on the corner of Eleventh Avenue and Alma, renting in the basement of this rat-infested house. It was $50 a month. I was surviving by having my friends supply me with food from their parents' houses in exchange for party rights. I met a girl at one of the parties, Sunny Humber. Sunny was Brian's sister. I sort of went out with Sunny for a short period of time. Brian started coming down to the house. He was about two years older than us; he was in first-year university. He was coming [to these parties] to pick up girls. And that's how we got to know each other. And then I got arrested, finally, for [a B&E] in April of 1969.

"That summer, although I was on probation, I talked my parents into letting me go to Wells–Barkerville, and I hitchhiked up. I'll never forget: I get to the Quesnel–Barkerville turnoff, and I'm hitchhiking late at night. It's my first time in the bush, in a sense; I'd grown up camping and stuff, but really, we're in the middle of the north, and I'm seventeen. And these two hippies from New York City, two New York Jews, picked me up. A guy named

Zubin (Stuart) Gillespie at what was to become known in later years as the Tomato House. Photo: Jude Goodwin.

Mike, and I believe the other guy was David. They were amazing. They were totally organic. Nobody'd heard of vegetarianism or anything like that so, for me, they were the first; they were just really cool. I got in the car and told them, 'I'm going to see my friend Brian!' And we went up to Filthy Larry's and hung out there for about a week, all of us together. Then they continued on their travels…

"So that's how I came into the scene. I was only up there for a few weeks and really dug it. Then I went back to Vancouver, and I was hanging out with people like Brian and Alan and Jane [at Lord Byng High School]. After graduating from high school in spring of 1970, we all moved up to Wells.

"We would've been eighteen. For the very first time, our girlfriends came up with us. There was Alan McMaster, Don Rutledge, there was Marla Thirsk. There was Dale Foubister, there was Ben, and John Jordon, my best friend, who died back in 1973 in a car accident. Nora Baker was up there…

"Alan and all of them in Vancouver were starting to get the whole thing together with Eric and Ellen to do with the commune. It was called Spring Wind, which was going to be, what do you want to call it? A Utopian society. They all ended up on a farm outside of Prince George on a big commune…Eric came from America. He was very mysterious, nobody ever knew anything about Eric and what his story was. He was probably a draft dodger, I would think. He ended up with Ellen. Ellen was from Quesnel. She'd dropped out and moved up…

"So here we are, we're only eighteen, we've been in middle-class-land for our whole lives, and now we're in the middle of the bush with these people, and some of them are pretty wow; they're on another planet. That summer played living hell on Brian. It was really hard for him because we were all freaks, I mean we were working off and on, but we kept coming into the shop, and it was really disrupting his business. We were totally naïve young kids.

"That first summer in Wells we were working for the Parks Branch. We went skinny-dipping in Williams Creek, and the guys in the Highways Department would come out and hide in the bush and look at us"

"[In the fall] we all left, we went back down to Vancouver. Alan went to university. I was going to art school at that time. Then we went back up at Christmas time, hitchhiked up, and it was minus sixty. We ended up not being able to hitch from Quesnel to Barkerville. There were five of us, so we hired a taxi to take us up! At that time it was a lot of money, it was fifty bucks! But we did it."

MIKE HEENAN was part of the Lord Byng cohort and lived in Wells between 1973 and 1984, intermittently. "I visited Zubin and Alan in the summer of 1970, when they were all living in the log house in Stromville. Al told [my friend from Lord Byng high school] Duncan, and Duncan told me, and thus our first visit to Wells. I had just finished working for two weeks at a friend's grandmother's dairy farm, where I became very, very sick with sun stroke after bringing in and stacking hay. I was literally just out of my sickbed when I went to Wells…Filthy Larry's was in full swing. John [Angrignon] was not on the scene yet. Al worked at Barkerville with Mike Hall and Zubin. That was the year Zubin built the split-level tree house…My first impression that summer was that Wells must be in a semi-tropical zone because, for the week or two I was there, there was sheet lightening every night, people swimming in Williams Creek every day, and lots of kids swimming in the Jack of Clubs Lake.

"The magnet at that point was a couple of major hippies named Eric and Ellen, who were like the den parents and who held semi-guru status. They were planning a commune in the Rocky Mountain trench (south of Golden), where the tidal wave that was going to be generated from the nuclear test on Amchitka Island wouldn't quite reach them. Most of the West Coast was thought to be going under. Al and Jane and Zubin were true believers.

"My next visit was that winter—over school Christmas break—via the Greyhound bus to Quesnel and then the Stage. I can still remember the ride out with Trev Davies like it was yesterday, because that was the first time I'd ever seen someone have to scrape the ice from the windshield from *the inside* so that they could see where they were going. While the memory does play tricks, I believe it was about minus thirty degrees [F]. This was the visit that really cemented my obsession with the place, for a number of reasons.

"As still pretty much a teenager, this was my first experience of 'real' winter. Not only the minus thirty degrees, but there must have been over fifteen feet of snow at that point. (I loved the weather in Wells. Because my father grew up in Saskatchewan, I was inundated with stories of hot, hot summers and cold, cold winters, and I just could not relate, growing up in Vancouver. After my first experience with summer and winter in Wells, I could.) I vividly remember running and doing summersaults in the air, off the road, down into the swamp, and landing in nothing but pure-as-the-wind fresh powder. We did this a lot one night on our way up town to the Jack.

"This would have been early on in my teenage 'booze train,' and any experiences that ended up with me drinking too much were still pretty memorable. Abe and Alice Reimer [owners of the Jack] were putting on a free-beer-and-food New Year's Eve party in the Jack. We were so poor that when we went up around 9:00 p.m. we had to nurse our twenty-cent draft for almost an hour before Abe opened the free-beer taps.

"[That night], I went back to the Stromville cabin with [my friend's girlfriend] and, and, and, well, that was my first time! So from there on in everything was fairly memorable, at least until we broke it to her boyfriend!"

ERIC ACKERLY lived in Wells from 1970–73: "I met my wife in the Jack O' Clubs Hotel, and we were hippies for sure.

"I am an army deserter from the US. I came to Canada on the sixth of January 1969, and didn't get landed [immigrant status] until the twenty-third of February of 1973. I had renounced my US citizenship shortly after I got here, so I had no legal status and was paranoid as all hell of getting caught, because I had a lot of political charges against me down there. They don't like it when people in uniform object to their illegal wars…

"Dumb as only a lost seventeen-year-old can be, I had enlisted in the US Marine Corps on my seventeenth birthday, or at least signed all the papers. My mother was only too willing to get me straightened out, as I caused her a lot of grief. I was medically discharged. I liked the Corps; I knew nothing about 'Nam—never even heard of it. I never watched much

TV. Anyway, when I got out, I went to Florida and bummed around there for awhile…I was stuck there and had nowhere else to go, so when I turned eighteen, I enlisted in the US Army, but I didn't tell them I was medically discharged from the USMC (crime number one).

"I found army basic training a cakewalk after the USMC basic, and having just spent six months slaving on a ranch working from sunup to sundown, I was in fairly good shape. I still knew nothing much about the war. But I figured if I told them the truth now, they'd just give me a job and a posting somewhere and be done with it. That maybe would have been the case, but while they were trying to figure out what to do with me, a riot broke out in Jacksonville, South Carolina.

"Now, having lived for several years in the South, I knew how the blacks were treated, and if I were black I would have rioted too. I'm from New York and knew a few blacks pretty damn well, and there was no way in hell I could have shot one of them…so I had to do some soul searching and decided to desert (crime number two).

"I hung out in the backwoods of Maine for a few months, then called my mother, who talked me into turning myself in. I wound up in the Fort Dix stockade. I had seen a prisoner's body being taken out after the guards beat him to death with the butts of their rifles…A riot broke out that night; sixteen dead, many more wounded, and three hundred or so escaped…I escaped (crime number three). When I got to New York City, I went to Veterans Against the War, the Student Mobilization Committee, the Sixth Avenue Peace Parade Committee, the Young Socialist Workers' Party, and the United Jewish Women's League Against the War; they all shared the same office. The FBI was set up across the street on the same floor. I went to work in the anti-war movement while AWOL (crime number four). We organized the March on Washington (crime number five). I was arrested by the FBI and escaped again (crime number six), and went to DC for the march (crime number seven). Got caught the third time and escaped again (yep, crime number eight). Anyway, after running from The Man across the States, I wound up in California. I spent three months in a mafia house. Doc was the pickup man for twenty-eight states and had just been released from prison. One day, a priest shows up at the door. I knew him from Denver…The priest tells me that three hours after I left, the FBI kicked down the door of the rectory, with guns drawn, flashing my picture. I didn't want to draw heat to Doc, and I was sick of running. I decided to turn myself in and kiss my life goodbye. I went down to the highway and stuck my thumb out. The first car stopped, and it was another army deserter going to Canada…

"The story of [the commune we called] Spring Wind, on my part, had a lot to do with my paranoia and trying to find or build a safe and welcoming place for dissidents of all kinds. That and trying to live a life by more spiritually guided principles. Though I have had my ups and downs in those regards, it is still the main focus of my life. So Spring Wind came about as an idea to create a place where everyone would be welcome. It grew from there. Louise [Futcher] wrote a ninety-page brief while a whole bunch of us went to Vancouver to acquire land and funding for the project. We even made a presentation to Howard Hughes, who was staying at the Bayshore Inn [in Vancouver] at the time. We designed and built a model of the massive octagonal log cabin that was to be the town centre and main work area. We went about getting recommendations from 128 groups and societies—even one from David Suzuki, who was a friend of Peter Best's father, who was a professor at UBC. We spent three months nonstop on the project. Then Jacquie and I took a month off and spent that time wandering around Stanley Park stoned on acid; we were hippies, after all.

"I had never heard of Wells until I got there. I was hitching south in Quesnel when one of the most beautiful women I had ever seen asked me if I wanted a ride to Wells. I said sure, and I wound up in Wells at Ellen's. She needed someone to talk to at a painful point in her life so we talked…and talked…and this beautiful woman went upstairs to bed alone…and Ellen and I talked. I won't mention the beautiful woman's name but I haven't forgotten it. Anyway, that is when and how I met Ellen and how I wound up in Wells.

"Danny Flanigan was there when I first got there in '71. Harvey and Helga Armstrong lived in a cabin going out the road northeast past the school. He was a blacksmith. When I first went to Wells, Forman's Store was still running. Bud Williams had the motel and gas station on the flats. King was the name of his 'dog,' a pure-bred wolf. He is the reason there were so many wolf-dogs in Wells.

"In late winter of '72 or early spring of '73 we wound up on the farm in Aleza Lake for the summer, and that winter we lost the farm. In late summer of '73 some of us went back to Wells, some moved to Bella Coola, some had stayed in Wells; we all went off in different directions. Jacquie and I went back to Wells for a bit.

"When I think about how bloody dumb we were or (at least how dumb I was), it makes me cringe."

ELLEN GODWIN: "I was working in Quesnel as a reporter/photographer, after being a house-wife for ten years. I had two beautiful sons and a husband who had no interest in me beyond my ability to work and earn. When he forbade me to pursue a spiritual path, that is, 'have any of that junk around here,' one could possibly have laughed that off, if one were cal-lous. But he also said, 'I will teach your sons to despise those who do,' and that scared me pretty bad.

"There was a day when it was all over, and that was Kent State Day [May 4, 1970]. We found ourselves on opposite sides of the turf; he thought Nixon was a clever boy and would have borne arms under his command in a military sense. I was appalled, and a sick sense of futility came into my heart and I knew my marriage was over…I asked Jerry to leave, and he did. I quit my job and asked a friend to move us to Wells when the school year was over. We rented a house on the flats.

"Louise Futcher's Land Rover full of peasant wanderers arrived in September 1970—the same fall I moved to Wells—then Harvey, Helga, and Don, Bernice and her children, and Terry and Randy who did not stay very long. Then Louise, Becky, Mary, and Charlie Pace. The following spring, the Shapiros rented the white house beside the goat barn across from Filthy Larry's. There seemed to be new arrivals every day, and Eric was one of them… There was a young woman named Mary; she was seventeen, I think. She came west with Louise in her Land Rover…Mary found Eric at the Billy Barker pub in Quesnel one day and saw him hitching on the highway south that evening. She picked him up and, by the time he had explained that he was on his way to Vancouver, she was on the road to Wells, to the north, and they were hungry, so they stopped at the A&W, after which they were friends enough for Mary to ask Eric if he wanted to come to Wells. I had been there for maybe four months; my kids were in school.

"The Point Grey Pranksters did not show up until July of 1971. Peter Best came up and met Eric and me and had these strange thoughts about us being something, who knew what? It is like seventeen-year-olds getting all their information from twenty-year-olds. I really was not very ready for a job as civic-level hostess, sort of a Welcome Wagon person, or Social Services housing rep; it was a bit much after a while. There are those I regret not having had the capacity to know. Was I kind of straight to begin with? Yes, in some ways I still am. I already had identity, values, and a path, but they are mutable things. None of us knew the meaning of the word guru yet, nor had any 'knowledge' in particular...Peter touted Wells to the Pranksters and they thought they ought to go have a look. Eric did not renovate the goat barn until October. We moved into it in November, just as the snow flew."

LOUISE FUTCHER moved from Ontario and lived in Wells from 1970 to '75. "We had that idealistic belief that the world could change, and that we could be part of that...In the fall of 1970, a group of about twenty of us converged on Wells. We came from southwestern Ontario, Vancouver, and the US. The destination of Wells had been chosen by several of our members who had been scouting for possible locations. There were connections among the three different subgroups, but I do not remember what these were; perhaps some were brothers and others friends.

"I was part of a group of eleven living at a communal farm in southwest Ontario, near Kitchener–Waterloo. We were David Moore and Becky Campbell, me and Peter, Charlie and Mary,

The "Ark" in southwest Ontario; some of the people who moved to Wells in 1970. Photo: Louise Futcher.

Louise Futcher on her way to Wells, BC, in 1970. Photo: Louise Futcher.

and Roger, Tim, Linda, Annie, and Debbie. We were from a variety of backgrounds. I was working as a social worker and brought my salary into the communal coffers. The main heart of our community was David Moore, who also had a 'real job' and who did most of the work on the farm. Perhaps some of the group members decided to go to BC because that is where David was leading them. I went because these plans matched my romantic ideas of 'back-to-the-land' and 'living in the mountains.' None of us had much of an idea of what the reality would look like. We knew that Wells was an old, mostly deserted mining town in the mountains of BC and that we would be able to find cabins to live in. We combined money and assets and packed up all our worldly gear and convoyed across the country in a caravan of assorted vehicles. I owned an old Land Rover, whose ambience really added to the 'back-to-the-country' feeling of things. Most of us were idealistic—wanting to create a new community and live in the mountains. I can't remember how many of the eleven of us made the trek. Also on our cross-country journey, we met a married couple with children at a campsite who followed us to Wells. I don't remember their names.

"In Wells we connected, as planned, with the other two sub-groups. They were Terry Erikson and Bernice Fehr and Bernice's two children, Jeffrey and Karen, from Vancouver. There were Harvey and Helga Armstrong, from the US, and I think a fellow named Joel, and another man whose name I forget.

"We were the first hippies to arrive in Wells. The local Wells inhabitants were shocked by our arrival. They had no idea that we were coming! We represented a different culture and lifestyle, and they were not very welcoming to us. We did not become integrated within the Wells community, but remained our own separate group. I don't think [other hippies] were there in 1970. If so, we did not know them..."

JUDE GOODWIN (BRAY), one of the Lord Byng contingent, lived in Wells with her partner, Duncan Bray, in the early 1970s. "I visited Wells at Christmas during my grade twelve year. We were a bunch of kids who came up [from Vancouver] on the Greyhound following a dream, a communal lifestyle. There was a man, a guru really, named Eric who had built a model of this wonderful octagonal house and had a plan for purchasing land and building a community somewhere in northern BC. I wasn't part of the inner circle, so I don't remember much of it, but I do remember loving the idea of living away from the city, growing and making our own stuff, getting out from under the yoke of modern consumerism.

"All of us who ventured up to Wells that Christmas had the same feelings. I think most of us were from upper-middle-class families, and consumption was just starting to snowball. It was 1970. We stayed in cabins on the outskirts [of Wells, in Stromville], towards Barkerville. I don't know who owned them; there were so many people around, I never really learned all their names. The group I travelled with included Mike Heenan, Duncan Bray, Al McMaster, Jane Drummond-Hay, Don Rutledge, Peter Best, Marla, and Stuart Gillespie (now known as Zubin)."

PETER VAN DEURSEN lived in Wells from summer of 1971 to winter of 1973: "In 1971, I had been hired as a stagehand in the Barkerville show. I was eighteen years old. That show was a great experience.

Jude Goodwin and Duncan Bray in Wells, c. 1973. Photo: Jude Goodwin.

"When I decided to stay on in Wells after that first summer working for the show, I asked Bud at the Good Eats Café about a place to rent. He pointed to a small house with a sheet-metal roof shining in the sun across the little valley, and asked me if I could see the man working on the roof. He was introduced to me as 'The Skipper' and the little house was 'The Press.'

"The Skipper turned out to be Clarence Wood, who had lived on boats for many years before moving to Wells. His house was known as The Press because that is what dominated the entire first floor...a huge antique mechanized printing press where Clarence published the periodical local sheet. I can't remember the name of it now.

"Clarence invited me to the attic, where his living quarters were, and treated me to curry fry-up. He told me of his son, Gaylord, who was away in Castlegar learning to be a commercial pilot (he did get his commercial licence). When he found out I played piano, he said we should meet, as Gaylord played guitar. Clarence pointed me in the direction of Brian Humber's empire in Stromville, and that is how I came to join the little band of hippies living along the bend in the road there. I lived in the little shack across from Filthy Larry's, just below the house that later became known as Rosie's (after she intentionally, and to me, inexplicably, burned down her place at the lower edge of Wells, located on a high wooden foundation at the edge of the marsh, affectionately known as 'the swamp,' that bordered the town)."

JOHN SCOTT ANGRIGNON lived in Wells from 1971–76 and became known as the King of Stromville: "Brian bought his land the year I arrived there, and he found out the house beside it was for sale from a guy whose last name was Saunders. So I bought it for $1,000 off Mr. Saunders, and that was the beginning of Stromville and the Stromville Pirates. I soon became the King of Stromville and loved being there. It had a hand pump for water and a wood furnace in the basement. Getting wood with the other folks in Wells was always a good chance to drink rum, do lots of hard work, and have a good dinner at night with everyone. The outhouse out the back had a lovely view of the swamp, but you had to bring the toilet seat into the house in the winter so you wouldn't freeze your ass off when you needed to use the outhouse. On the kitchen wall was a dollar bill that we used to throw knives at for fun. The clock in the living room was permanently at 5:10, so no matter where you went in the world you always knew what time it was in Stromville."

MICHAEL WEISS: "I first came to Wells in July of 1971 as a nineteen-year-old under-graduate student majoring in English at the University of Maryland. It was my first and last stop on a trip to towns in British Columbia and Alberta as part of a project to collect occupational folklore in Western Canada. At least that was the formal goal. Actually, I just wanted an excuse to spend a summer hitchhiking around the US and Canada, and tape-recording miners and ranchers was the best I could come up with. I'd recently taken a class in folklore and loved the stories of fieldworkers like Alan Lomax gathering songs and stories of authentic Americans—so distant from my conventional, middle-class upbring-ing in the suburbs of Washington, DC.

Peter van Deursen, c. 1973. Photo: Jude Goodwin.

And somewhere I'd picked up a book by one F.W. Lindsay, who mentioned the cave-in of a gold mine in Wells after World War II. My plan was to hitchhike up to the towns in the interior of British Columbia and Alberta, carrying a pup tent and a cassette tape recorder in my backpack, and gather as many stories and songs as possible over the course of a summer. I'd write up my experiences for one of the folklore journals in Washington, DC, and then receive six academic credits for my effort.

"Somehow, I convinced my folklore professor, an elderly and straight-laced woman named Esther Birdsall, to approve the project. And on June 6, 1971, I stuck out my thumb on a highway outside College Park, Maryland, carrying an overstuffed backpack with few clothes, lots of maps, the tent, sleeping bag, some boxes of macaroni, and a cassette tape recorder with a dozen sixty-minute tapes. I also carried a blank journal, a red bound book, to record my experiences and stories of the people I met. And being something of a packrat, I kept that journal among my favourite books and photos, so today, as I look through the yellowing pages of sloppy printing, I can recall what happened to me in Wells thirty-five years ago.

"It took me several weeks to hitchhike to the Cariboo—I convinced one driver to stop at a bluegrass festival in Kansas and joined another for a visit to a commune in Washington—but eventually I made it up the West Coast and into British Columbia. Although I had a letter of introduction from the University of Maryland saying I was conducting a folklore project, I was still hassled by the border police who noted that 'there are 200,000 American draft resisters living in Canada and taking away jobs from Canadians.' Because I only carried $125 in cash with me, I was given a ten-day visa and told to report to immigration officials then and show that I had enough money to support myself while in Canada— something I never did.

"What I did spend time doing was talking to the drivers who'd pick me up, asking about areas that were known for gold mining, coal mining, cattle ranching, and sheep herding. North of Cache Creek, BC, I received a ride from a modern-day prospector who was still trying to find gold flakes ($80 an ounce at the time) and I knew I was getting close to Wells. On the night of Thursday, June 24, 1971, I entered the town in the car of a young couple who, with their toddler daughter, were looking for land to homestead in the Wells area. They dropped me off at a shop on the road between Wells and Barkerville called Filthy Larry's Leather Shoppe, which I soon learned was sort of the unofficial centre of life for many of the hippies up there. The owner, Brian Humber, seemed to be the most entrepreneurial of the young people, some of whom were working as guards and actors in Barkerville, the recently restored gold rush town, and living in rustic cabins on a mountainside overlooking the gravel road between Wells and Barkerville. Brian had a thriving business, a kind of head shop that sold leather belts and wallets to the tourists on their way to Barkerville, and with his long hair and moustache, he naturally attracted other hippies to his door. There were always young hitchhikers stopping at his shop, and always a phonograph on, playing the Rolling Stones, Elton John, or Emerson, Lake and Palmer; I still think of Wells whenever I hear one of their songs. As for me, I wasn't the usual long-haired drifter passing through. For one thing, I had gotten a haircut and beard trim before leaving for Canada, thinking it would be easier to get rides and create fewer hassles with the police (though I still carried a leather pouch on my side which carried my wallet and a knife). And Brian and I hit it off; I think he respected the fact that I had a reason to come to Wells to record the old-timers.

"Here's my journal entry from my first full day in Wells, June 25, 1971:

Awoke in Filthy Larry's Leather Shoppe and rapped with Brian, who lives in a cabin-with-a-loft in a rustic setting. All the heating and cooking is done with a wood stove, light comes from a Coleman lantern and the water is pumped from an underground spring. The floorboards buckle, food is kept in big sacks and jars, and strings hanging between wall pegs serve as a clothes closet. After crashing on the floor in my sleeping bag, I played guitar with Brian for awhile and then went fishing on Nine Mile Lake with two guys, Andy and Scott, who are very generous dudes. I didn't catch anything but Scott caught one rainbow trout and Andy caught two more. Then he built a fire and we roasted and ate all of them right from the fire. The scene was incredible: a mountain lake surrounded by lush pastures and pine mountains capped with new snow. In the afternoon, they drove me to the Barkerville campground where I pitched my tent and met some of the neighbours—heads with whom I played guitar and harmonica and talked for a few hours. Then we drove into Wells and a pub at the Jack O' Clubs Hotel where the nine of us drank about seventy beers over the course of the evening. I also worked the room a bit for my project and met a man named Beaver Trapper John who, for fifty-five years, had trapped for beavers by snowmobile along a 125-mile route in the Wells area. Got a ride back only to the leather shop, had tea and slept there.

"That day was typical of my time in Wells which, all told, lasted about six weeks...I spent a lot of my time during the days transcribing tapes and hunting down leads through the Wells Historical Society. But at night, I hung out with the other young people in Wells, drinking at the pub or sharing a spaghetti dinner at Filthy Larry's...

"But the weather was a mixed bag and, by the middle of July, I was getting weary from a string of rainy days. On July 12, I helped cook a farewell dinner at Filthy Larry's Leather Shoppe of spaghetti and Cherry Jack, though most of it went to waste because everyone had gone to the pub to drink beer for most of the night. But I do remember that farewell party as being pretty wild, with a lot of people stripping down at midnight to swim in the creek. The next morning, I said goodbye to the gang and hitchhiked away towards Williams Lake. Over the next month, I went on to fill all twelve tapes on my folklore study, recording cattle ranchers in Kamloops, coal miners in Banff and sheep herders and ranchers in Calgary.

"I never could get Wells out of my system and, on August 20, I hopped an open freight car in Jasper, Alberta, and rode across the Rockies to Prince George, arriving at six in the morning and finding an open Chinese restaurant for breakfast (chop suey and rice). From there, I hitchhiked back to Wells and spent another two weeks with the hippies and old-timers, drinking beer in the Jack O' Clubs and recording Lucky Swede one last time. I left

Wells for good on August 29, 1971, the last time with tears of regret.

"I came back to the University of Maryland in September and kept my promise to my professor from the previous spring. I wrote and published several articles about the miners and ranchers of Western Canada and donated all my audio tapes to the Library of Congress in Washington, DC, where they're still housed in the Archive of Folk Culture. I even sent a copy of one of the articles to Lucky Swede."

FRANK DOHERTY lived in Wells between 1971 and1987. "Well, I could have sworn it was the fall of 1970, but Sam Thatcher says it was the fall of '71! Jesus, now I have to figure where I was in the fall of '70. 'If you remember the '60s, you weren't really there.' Abe and Alice apparently bought the Jack in December of 1970. That's what I am using as a timeline. Julius Karpinski and I moved Dennis and Hilda Dobbin up from Keremeos with our 1959 three-quarter-ton Chevy. We were 'Mothertruckers.' Dennis told us he owned a fishing lodge at Cornish Lake. He hit the bar when we got there and never really sobered up after that! He didn't pay us for the move, so we had to stay the winter. We rented a house for $20 a month off Curly Fisher. Curly tried to sell it to us at a later date for $250, but we told him it was too much. I believe that is the Tomato House Judy Campbell now owns.

"Wells was like stepping into a time warp! Absolutely wonderful old characters there. I knew the first night I drank in the Jack that I was going to be there a while. Little did I know it would be almost sixteen years! Don't regret a minute of it, either! Long John, Lucky Swede, Shakey Carl, Deaf Mabel, Ed Titley, and the rest of the boys up on 'Death Row' [a wall in the Jack bar where photos of old-timers were hung]."

RICHARD MACKIE stayed in Wells for a few days in 1972 as part of a summer hitchhiking trip throughout BC. "I was fourteen. I was hitchhiking near Falkland and got a ride with a guy in an old 1950s pickup truck, who lived in Wells. I think his name was Paul, and he said he came from Prince Rupert, and his family was Dutch. [Thirty-eight years later, Richard discovered that this was Peter van Deursen.] He might have been eighteen or twenty years old, but he seemed much older to me. I sensed he was a recent convert to hippiedom. I think he

Richard Mackie, 1972, age 14, hitch-hiked to Wells. Photo: Richard Mackie.

had worked in a mill at Prince Rupert. He invited me to stay at his place in Wells.

"I never for a moment hesitated, and I was right to trust my intuition. On the way to Wells, he took me to a hotel restaurant in Kamloops and bought me a deluxe burger and fries, insisted on paying, and had the same himself. I was starving because I was living on granola and peanut butter sandwiches that I got from youth hostels…

"I was a kid with long brown hair, centre-parted, and I was regularly mistaken for a girl. I can still remember the chilling words somewhere in the Kootenays: 'Oh, you're a guy! I thought you was a girl. I wouldn't have picked you up if I'd known you was a guy.' Even as a fourteen-year-old this seemed wrong for at least two big reasons. I had an army packsack (a surplus US Army packsack that my dad got at Capital Iron in Victoria, but I got my mother to sew a Canadian flag over the stencilled 'U.S.')…

"It started to rain between Quesnel and Wells, and Paul's windshield wipers didn't work, so he had to reach out of the truck cab as he drove and push the blades across manually. This was slightly alarming, and I wondered what I'd got myself into. In Wells he lived in a house beside the road. I remember a leather workshop next door; behind, an enchanting tree house inhabited by a charming Englishman (who reminded me of Tiny Tim) and his girlfriend, with herbs hanging to dry all around the interior of the tree house.

"Paul's favourite music was Kris Kristofferson's eight-track tape, *The Silver Tongued Devil and I*, which was hardly a hippie or alternative choice, but to my surprise I liked it and can still remember the title track. It had a kind of naïve authenticity about it. I painted the inside of the main room while Paul went to work in Barkerville. He had the eight-track attached to a car battery, and I listened to Kris K. repeatedly while I painted.

"Paul worked in the theatre at Barkerville and took me there for a visit one day. I can still see him with his blond hair tied in a ponytail, Victorian fashion, with moustache and bowtie. One minute he was a hippie, the next a sort of uptight Victorian bartender or usher. Paul's sister (at least I think she was his sister) also performed something on stage at Barkerville; was she a hurdy-gurdy girl? She was dressed like a Victorian lady, blonde like Paul, and I thought her long dress was pretty nice, and I remember white frills and lace. At any rate, I was fourteen and rather overwhelmed by her! Like Paul, she also had two personas.

"For years I had a small tobacco pouch that I found in the leather workshop, which was then deserted. I think Paul said that the woman who ran it was away. I think I also scoffed a large satchel-type thing, basically a large pouch with a flap, which I had for a while. I also remember a house across the street from Paul's where some slightly younger and possibly 'straight' people lived...Their house was open to the public, as it were, with a kitchen at the back and a living room at the front where they partied from time to time. I stayed for only two or three days. Wells was a welcoming place with a friendly vibe.

"When I left Wells and hitchhiked to Quesnel, there was a big debate: 'I need some fries, man!' 'Yeah, I could use a hamburger! I think that rice had maggots in it! I can't remember when I last had a cheeseburger!' 'I need some grease, man! Far out!' 'Yeah, and a milkshake!' The driver did not approve but he was press-ganged and swung angrily and scowling into the A&W when—*crunch!*—the A&W roof was made for cars only. The collision smashed all the top lights and dented in the roof…

"This seemed to summarize some of the tensions of hippie life: idealism versus pragmatism, alternative versus commercial choices, meat versus vegetarian, and the cosmic message was: these things do not mix! I remember the driver's silent rage after this incident. He felt totally let down by the closet suburban appetites on the bus but was too cool to show it; he didn't want to freak out about something as superficial as a smashed-up bus, man. I mean, it adds character! And Freddie'll bang out the dents."

Rose Danby arrives in Barkerville, 1972, from Kitsilano. Photo: Rose Danby.

Volunteer Peasants

Throughout the 1970s, Wells would continue to attract self-described "volunteer peasants," those endeavouring both to "do their own thing" and to find and create a sense of community. Hundreds of hitchhikers, summer-only student workers, and temporary lovers passed through and out of town. Others fell in love with the clean, sweet-smelling air and endless vistas of green, treed hills and sparkling lakes, the evocatively dilapidated false-fronted buildings, or the crazy old geezers telling stories in the bar. The town felt like home, so they stayed.

ROSE DANBY lived in Wells from 1972 to '83 and 2002 to '11. "Oh my lord, how the hell did I ever get here? Well, I was a starry-eyed young hippie living in Vancouver. I graduated from high school in the mid-'60s into a full-blown hippie culture in Vancouver, which I took to like a fish to water as a way to snub my military upbringing [her father was a brigadier-general in the Canadian Army]. Went to the Retinal Circus regularly; strobe lights, black lights, loud music, crowded, everyone stoned on something.

"I visited Mandala Books on Broadway regularly, looking for spiritual inspiration and ate up anything like Sufism or anything Eastern. Regularly visited head shops for roach clips or other smoking paraphernalia—with a certain pride that these shops represented that our alternative culture was becoming accepted…Lots of second-hand and antique shops on Fourth Avenue between Alma and Granville with great old stuff for modest prices. Decorated our homes with old stuff, candles, and flowers—no particular style, just a mishmash.

"Everyone had long hair—men and women—and wore beads. It was a time of no deodorant, bras, or shaving. We wore long skirts and bare feet, tie-dyed T-shirts and patchouli oil, and burned incense. It was a time of earthy smells and all the colours of the rainbow.

"For years everybody'd been talking about going back to the land. And one day I just got pissed off. Everyone's just gonna talk about this and never gonna do it. Everybody's just too out to lunch, right? So I looked at my grand savings in the bank, a total of $700, and thought, well, I've got enough money to go out and seek my fortune in the great wide world and get back to the land.

"Then I thought it might not be quite enough, so I better find somebody who has as much money as me. The only other person on the earth I knew at that point who had that much money was my sister Bev. And Bev and I had been mortal enemies for years, couldn't be in the same room for five minutes without just going for each other's throats. But, I said, hey, she's the one with money! I approached her and said, 'Do you want to go look for land together?' She, being equally practical, went, hmmm, seven hundred and seven hundreds—wow! We could buy a whole town! We were completely clueless; we had no idea of the price of real estate at all. We borrowed Mum's car, because neither of us owned a vehicle, and headed north. Got to Hope. We were looking at prices throughout the valley and we were devastated. We didn't even have a down payment! What the hell were we thinking?

"Not being ones to give up easily, we thought, well, let's just spend all our money and go on a road trip. We've got the car, we said we were going to be gone for a couple of weeks, let's do it. So we just turned the whole thing into a party and went camping and partying and heading north, going nowhere in particular. When we got to Quesnel and we saw the sign that said Barkerville, we thought, we've heard of that; it's some kind of ghost town. Let's go check it out. We headed up the highway, still just following our every whim. The road at that time went right through Wells, right through the main street and down, and it wasn't paved most of the way from Quesnel. Devil's Canyon was a delight—one lane wide, gravel, twisting, sheer drop-off.

"When we drove through Wells, it was love at first sight. All of those 1930s false-fronted Western-look buildings; we were just ga-ga. So we went on to Barkerville and fell in love with Barkerville.

"In Wells, every second house in town had a 'For Sale' sign on it. We thought we'd better go check this out right now! So we came back and checked it out and found out that the ski hill [in Wells] was for sale. And we found out from some reliable locals that it already sold half a dozen times that year. We went down to the restaurant that was called, at that time, the Lucky Swede Café, and we were just sitting there, chewin' the fat with the locals and saying that we were looking for something to buy. Then the dish washer comes out and says, 'I hear you're looking for a house.' He had two houses for sale. The one down behind the Jack was $700 and came with the lot, and then there was one over on the tailings that was $750 but didn't come with the property because it was one of those ones where the mine still owned the land.

"So we looked at both of them. The house over on the south Wells side of town was actually maybe a little nicer house, but the location, location, location of the one right behind the Jack bar, and the fact that it came with deeded land was a hands-down winner. For $700. But by this time, we'd spent half of our money, so we made a deal, and we gave him half the money and said we'll be back in a week. We gotta carry on. And this was the part you'll somehow have to edit out of the book, because we went all the way up to Fort St. John to visit a friend of mine that I knew from Vancouver who was working on a ranch up there… and made enough money to come back and pay off the rest of the house! But then we had no money left, and winter was looming, so we went back down to the coast and worked for the winter to save up all our money.

"Do you remember Large Marge? She had a son, and they had approached us before we left about renting the house over the winter. We thought, well, that's a good deal, because it's better to have somebody in there. Really, all they wanted was a place to keep their horses, because down below the main floor it was all chicken coops and stalls. They kept their horses there, but they didn't live in the house, and they tracked horse shit and hay—they kept hay in the house—upstairs and dragged it downstairs to feed the horses, and so the place was just a disaster when we came back, it was just a nightmare. But hey, it was ours, so we got down and kissed the ground and proceeded to clean up."

ROB DANBY, younger brother of Rose and Bev, lived in Wells from 1973 to '84. "My first connection with Wells was through my best friend in school, Paul Guiguet, in grade eight at Our Lady of Perpetual Help School in Vancouver. He told me he was from this little town called Wells—he was born and raised there; his dad, Marcel, was the mine manager. When the Cariboo Gold Quartz shut down, Marcel was out of a job in Wells and they moved to Vancouver. They lived just a few blocks away from us. My first introduction to Wells was as this little mythical far-away town that my best friend had lived in.

"Paul and I [did grades eight to ten together]…and then my dad got transferred to the Canadian Embassy in Washington, so we moved. I did my last years of high school at an American high school in suburban Washington, DC, actually Virginia. We were in what was called a typical middle-class suburb. I came from Vancouver, and I was like—what?! These people are stinking rich and they're calling themselves middle class? And then there was the other side of the tracks. Right while I was there, 1967 to '69, was when all the forced integration was happening and the busing. I was shocked. Here they're busing these dirt-poor black kids from across the tracks to this stuck-up, rich white kid's school. 'Okay, get along, everybody! Why isn't it working?' 'I wanna kill you, I want your stuff! How come you got all that stuff and I don't? And you make me go to your stinkin' school!'

"Then, shortly after [we moved back to Vancouver] Rose and Bev discovered Wells… They bought the house on their holiday and came back to Vancouver and were telling me all about this amazing little town they discovered, and I'm going, that's the town Paul's from! I'd never been there, but I'd heard all about it from Paul...

"We were sitting around one night, we were in the bar in the Cecil Hotel and had quite a bit to drink. I'm telling Paul that my sisters just went up to this town he's from and bought a house. We decided, let's go to Wells. We drove all night—we drank beer and drove all the way to Wells. Got into Quesnel at some god-awful hour, probably six o'clock in the morning, stopped someplace there and then drove up to Wells and arrived at the Good Eats Café just as it opened at seven in the morning. That was my introduction to Wells, with Bud Williams behind the counter: 'Oh Paul, you're back!' So I had a real in, right?—I was with a local boy. It was just a weekend trip.

"I was fascinated; I thought, what a cool town, it was so different from anything I'd seen, but I went back to Vancouver and I was working in the photo finishing lab on Fourth Avenue…I was getting pretty sick of breathing these fumes and the darkroom had pretty yucky chemicals in those days. I was not thrilled with being in Vancouver. So in the spring of '73, I went up for Rose's birthday, May 15, on my motorcycle. I was looking for something different to do. My plan was to travel around; I was going to quit my job and travel all over BC on my bike for the summer, but the bike broke down and there were some really expensive repairs, so I ended up selling it and going back to Wells for a visit and ended up staying there. I thought, well, I need some money, because I'd spent all my money on my motorcycle, that whole plan's kind of dead, and the summer's just beginning. So I asked Rose, who said to check out what's happening in Barkerville, they usually hire people. I headed out there one morning and talked to [the park supervisor] John Premischook. 'Okay, we'll hire ya,' so I had a job.

"Mike and Dave were the established guys in Barkerville then. I worked in Barkerville the summer of '73 and stayed with Rose and Bev in their swamp house for a few months. I thought, well, this is a fun town, I'm having a pretty good time, why don't I just keep on staying? So I got my own place and I moved into that little cabin on the back street behind the highways yard down on the tailings."

TOM ADAIR lived in Wells intermittently from 1972 to '85. "I came up as a result of going to work out at Bowron Lake. I'd been working there the year before, 1972, and I'd just finished high school. I was eighteen.

"I took the bus up to Quesnel and ended up taking the Stage [a passenger van] to Wells driven by Trev Davies. Unfortunately, we only made it part of the way to Wells—the road wasn't paved—and the bus just stopped because they were putting in a culvert. So we sat there half an hour while they finished digging the road up. And then we kept going. Got further—and the bus wasn't very well that day—so it ended up that we were actually coasting from Devil's Canyon into Wells...

"Finally we got uptown in Wells, and I didn't know anybody there; somebody was supposed to come and pick me up [and take me out to Bowron]. I helped Trev unload the bus; the freight was for the Good Eats, all the food. I walked into the Wells Hotel and people were yelling, 'Heyyyy there, wanna beer?' I was horrified. I just backed right out. These people were nuts! I headed back out into the street and finally some guys that were surveying out at Bowron Lake arrived, and they gave me a ride out. The next morning I reported to Victor Bopp [the new park supervisor]...and he didn't even know I was supposed to start work. It had been done at the higher level, and he was just, 'Well, you're not supposed to be here till—' But I pulled my letter out, and went out to work on the Kibbee Lake trail crew...

Tom Adair at Stromville (freshly painted, sign just hung up). Photo: Marguerite Hall.

Nathan Kew enjoying the New Year's party at the Pelletier house, c. 1977. Photo: Sandy Phillips.

"I was only in Wells maybe two, three nights the whole summer long. We stayed at the Kews' family cabin on Bowron Lake—and it was a pretty deluxe place to stay—or I would go in to Quesnel. But one of the nights I came in to Wells was the Gold Rush Dance. I ended up staying at Stu's [Zubin's] tree house. He was gracious enough to offer me a chunk of floor, so I stayed there. The only people I really got to know that first summer were Mike and Dave, because both worked out at Bowron Lake chain that year.

"Then I went back to university. I came back the following year to work on the Bowron Lake chain. That next year, I spent more time in town. I ended up staying with Mike and Dave, because they had moved into Wells and were working at Barkerville, so I could stay at their place in town. They lived in the Gilbert house, which had dynamite crates from the underground mine in the living room. That's how I came to Wells."

NATHAN KEW: "I was sixteen in 1973 when I moved to Wells…I was leaving behind a lot of pressure that my school teachers were putting on me. My dad was a university professor at UBC. They all had this plan for me. I was supposed to have a doctorate in mathematics by the time I was twenty-six. And I was not prepared for that kind of pressure and expectations. I was a troubled student. Then I went to a private school, one of the free schools, so we smoked dope in the hallways…and it was a wonderful environment. I just kind of blossomed there, and skipped grade eleven. Didn't like grade twelve, so then I just tutored the younger kids and did my own math. My girlfriend at the time, Stephanie, had gone up [to Barkerville] and got a job, so she said, 'Why don't you work here?'…

"It was very familiar, and I had worked at Bowron the summer before. I was running from this pressure to this perfect spot, a hiding spot. My dad grew up in the Quesnel area, out in the bush and out on the chain, so he thought it would be a great life to be out there and maybe buy a trapline or something like that. And there was a big countercultural revolution at the time. I had tons of family there, relatives all over the place, because my family had lived in Wells and the Barkerville area since the 1930s...So everything was coming together, with family and familiar territory.

"My aunt lived on the Crescent with her husband, George Gilbert (known as GG). And GG's parents lived across town. So when I would come up there in the summers as a little kid, everybody in town knew who I was—I was Bea's grandson. I had instant friends all over the place as a kid...Tim Cushman and his sisters, we were all kids together…and Gaylord Wood was there.

"Growing up there as a kid and being allowed to roam wild in the bush was amazing, so I was very comfortable, and there was this whole countercultural society blossoming there, so it was, 'Oh, I'm home!'"

SUZANNE BESSETTE lived in Wells from 1972 to '81. "People will ask me what brought me to Canada. And I get to say, Richard Nixon.

Suzanne Bessette in Wells, c. 1974. Photo: Rob Danby.

"We were living in Chattanooga, Tennessee. I was married, and we were sort of disillusioned with American politics. We decided that we wanted to go west, but that was all we had in mind. So we got out. We had a home-made trailer; it was like an old back of a truck with a wheel well, and it was made into a little trailer. We hooked that up to my husband Mike's brand new truck. He'd made two payments on it. We had a brand new truck with a kind of hokey trailer with our cat and two dogs and everything of any value to us—mainly records!

"And so we drove across the United States. Before we'd left, we had heard of this couple, Barbara and Paul Barrows, who were living in British Columbia. Kind of in the back of our minds we thought we might do that, and also it was when they were building the Alaska pipeline, and Mike was a carpenter, so we thought, okay, he could get work on the pipeline. We just kept on going, and we got to BC. I think we knew they were living outside of Quesnel. The directions that we had to get to Paul and Barbara's were 'turn right at the Northern Lights Esso.'

"We got to Beaver Pass; at that point we blew the clutch on our truck, and that was when we met our first Canadians. They were this really nice couple, Bernice and Warren Partridge. He was like a trapper. We arrived at the Partridges' cabin, and we asked about the Americans, and they said, 'Oh yeah, they live three miles up the hill.' At that time I was a hippie, and I was a vegetarian, and I was very idealistic and pure, right? Back to the land, and Canada was going to be a part of that, and getting away from the American politics. But as it was moose hunting season, Warren had had the good luck that morning of stepping out and having a moose in his backyard, which he immediately shot. So at that point, they were busy taking the moose's head off with a chainsaw. I turned to Mike, and I said, 'I guess we won't be vegetarians in Canada!'

"Then we proceeded with our new Canadian friends in their four-wheel drive, and they took us up to The Hill. The guy who owned the place was John. He was from Pasadena, in California, from a wealthy family, and he'd been given some money. He had bought a quarter section of land, and he had invited different people to build cabins on the land… It was hippies, it was back to the land. He was a wonderful generous guy, but he had no idea about farming, ranching, house building. But he just threw himself into it and was doing it. His partner, Suzie, and he lived in one of the cabins. The cabins were all built around this quarter section. We said we were looking for Paul and Barbara and they said, 'Oh yeah, they're here.' And they came down and welcomed us. Everybody was like, 'Cool, you know, Mike and Suzanne from Tennessee are here! That's cool!' Right away, probably within the first week, John said if we wanted to build a house we could…

"Barbara taught me everything about chopping wood and hauling water—we had to melt snow for water! It was late September, October. There was a trapper's log cabin that John said we could stay in if we wanted to. We went and checked it out and it was one room; it had an old cookstove and airtight and an indoor woodshed with a dirt floor. There was no outhouse. All there was for an outhouse was a platform that they had built, but they'd never got around to putting the sides up…We had to get ready for winter right away, and there was wood that had to come in.

"Once we got all our wood in, Mike started going around, and there was a lot of dope smoking, of course, and he would just visit everybody in their different cabins and see what was baking and get stoned. I was melting water and getting the kindling ready, and doing all that, right? I was nineteen when we got together. But once we got out in this environment and Barbara taught me how to deal with all the things that were really terrifying to me, being out in the bush, I had a lot more confidence in myself, and I started to realize that Mike was basically doing nothing!

"One day…he decided he was going to Quesnel—this is the middle of winter now—to find work because we needed some money. So he told me that he would contact me, send me a radio message. I would sit there and wait for the message, and there was never a message. While Mike was away, it had been forty below, and I had been keeping myself alive by getting up in the middle of the night and putting wood in, stoking the fire. It was serious stuff. By the fifth night I went—'I'm leaving.'

"It was just the most beautiful day, one of those forty-below days, blue sky. I was all ready to go, and Mike comes in the door. 'Oh'! he said, 'What are you doing?' I said, 'Oh, well, um, what am I doing? I'm going to Quesnel. I'm going to look for a job.' He says, 'I'll go with you.' I said, 'Actually, no, I'm leaving.' I said, 'Yeah, I gotta go. I've got a ride.' That was that. And I walked out, and I had an old army coat on with the hood pulled tight around my face, and I felt amazing! With every step I took, the snow would come up in crystals in front of me. I was all by myself; everybody else had already walked down to the Partridges'. I walked out three miles…

Sharon Brown (probably baking something fabulous!), 1975. Photo: Sharon Brown.

[Suzanne travelled with a friend to California, Mexico, across the States, and Ontario.] "I left BC and Mike in February, and I came back in May. I went back up to The Hill and hung out there a bit, and I needed to find a job. Barbara...[had gotten a job at] the Wake-Up Jake [restaurant in Barkerville]. Marion DeWeese and I decided we would go up there…

"Marion had this dog called Moon. What a furball she was, just huge, like a collie mixed with something. We went to the Barkerville turn-off on the highway and we put Moon in the ditch so nobody would see her, and then we put our thumbs out to hitchhike. And who should come along to pick us up but Chris and Paul Guiguet? I think it was a little Toyota, and I could see the look on their faces when Moon got out of the ditch! We were sitting in the back and Chris just drove like a madman; I thought, oh wow, this is just a total karma trip, if he doesn't kill us. That was when the road wasn't paved the last bit, and dust was flying.

"We got out to Wells and there was a double rainbow over the town. It was so gorgeous. I thought, this is just meant to be; that's so cool. That's how I came to Wells. I think Chris and Paul must've told us there was stuff happening out in Stromville. Scott [Angrignon] was out there, and we partied. I had borrowed a sleeping bag. I had to sleep on the floor, and it was this horrible shag carpet, absolutely disgusting—roaches, spills—nasty. But we found out everything that we needed to know from Scott."

SHARON BROWN has lived in Wells, intermittently, since 1973. "In July of 1973 (I was sixteen at the end of May), my mother decided to move me and my four younger brothers to Quesnel from Calgary, where I had spent my life up till then, so my brothers would not 'get into so much trouble.' Ha! Way more trouble to be found in a small town! Luckily, they were all good boys.

   "I lasted about three weeks or so and then took off hitchhiking with a hippie I met at my waitress job at Shakey's Pizza. I was on the lam for that year, taking the train to Ontario, living in Rossland and learning to ski, staying in North Van with Simon Kendall

John Boutwell, Judy Campbell, and Fargo arrive in Wells, 1974. Photo: Judy Campbell.

(Doug and the Slugs), Holly Arnzten, and a Frenchman who they were involved in a triangle with, and just about moving to Australia where my father had 'my bedroom ready for me.' That turned me off, so I stayed in Canada. My mom called me a few weeks later with the news that her second husband (Lorne Lucier) had obtained the lease on the Wake-Up Jake, and would I like to be the head waitress? That first summer I was in Wells seemed to be an endless round of parties. Suzanne and I would hitchhike home from Barkerville and end up in Stromville where the music would be playing and the beer flowing. We would drink, and then I would go up to the Good Eats for supper (I had a tab there), and then we'd go to the bar…"

JUDY CAMPBELL has lived in Wells since 1974, and is now a Wells town councillor, the CEO of Barkerville Historic Park, and a great bagpipe player. "When I was in university [in Ontario in the early 1970s] I had an idea that I was going to go to the Peace River country and home-stead, because I'd heard that you could do that. And then I was going to go there and start a free school…I had definitely formed this idea that I wanted to live on a ranch, on a farm, in a small town—definitely not in the city. I wanted to live in a cabin in the mountains, so I was headed in this direction…

"The first time I came here I was working on an archeology dig at Ketza Lake, which is out the other side of the Fraser. The whole crew came up to Barkerville for the weekend because they were archeologists that liked history. We camped at Lowhee Campground. On the way out to Barkerville we pulled into Wells, and I went 'this is really neat.' This was the summer of '73. So we went into the Wells Hotel to have a beer. While we were in there, Fargo [my dog] jumped out of the back of my truck and came waltzing into the hotel and lay down under the table and nobody said anything. So I thought, I think I'll move here. It seemed a logical thing at the time.

"At the end of the summer I started another dig and then I went back to Vancouver. John [Boutwell, my husband] and I were living in a basement apartment in Kitsilano. He was building this thing, this little house, on the back of his three-quarter-ton GMC. So he somehow also had been to Wells in the course of that summer or in the course of some travelling that he did. Come November, we got into the truck, and we drove to his parents' place in Blind Bay in the Shuswap. We flipped a coin between going to Wells and going back to Bragg Creek, Alberta, which was where we had met, and where he could get a job as a log builder. In Wells we didn't have any prospects necessarily, we just both had been there and both thought it was a very good spot. John's memory was that there were all kinds of cabins in the bush, so we go there, we get a cabin in the bush, and don't have to pay rent, which was John's thing. So we flipped a coin in bed that night and Wells won. The next day we got as far as 100 Mile House. And it was freezing fucking cold—it was November 5. I didn't have any winter boots, and I went into the Co-op at 100 Mile House and bought my first pair of felt-packs, and it was like my life was made over!

"We arrived in Wells later on the next day, and we camped at what is now that pull-off at the Bar-X Mine. We had a little wood stove [in the homemade camper on the back of the truck]. It was in the day, and though there was snow, we were kind of comfortable in there, cooking dinner on this little tiny airtight, when, lo and behold, there's this pounding on the door and the two dogs, Kiyo and Fargo, started barking. Here is Scotty Thomson at the door. Rolled up in his fist is a copy of the *Parks Act*, which he proceeded to read to us in proof of the fact that we couldn't camp there. We'd gone to Lowhee [Campground, on the highway between Wells and Barkerville], and it was barred up, it was closed for the season, so we'd come back.

Mike Wigle on the trapline, c. 1973. Photo: Jude Goodwin.

Now he informed us we had to camp right in the parking lot at Barkerville where 'I can keep an eye on you'—I think that was the secret message there. And he was actually quite friendly after he'd had his little rant.

"The next day we drove into town and started to meet locals and look for a place to live. We went to the Wells Hotel—it being, of course, the place where we'd meet locals—and we met Frank Doherty and Gail and Robin Jacobsen, and I don't know who else at that point. We moved the truck to the back street by Larry Polowicz's place."

MIKE WIGLE lived in Wells from 1973 to '84. "I met up with a guy while tree planting in either the Indian River or Pitt River area in the spring of 1973. It was through him that I met [Mike]

Larry Fourchalk's first winter at Downey Pass, 1974. Photo: L. Fourchalk.

Heenan for the first time. They had friends in Wells, and one night that summer we decided to drop some acid and drive up to Wells. A long night of acid-filled confusion, and the next day we were in Wells. I remember driving down the main street and seeing what I thought was somebody's laundry hanging out to dry strung from the post office and across to the Wells Hotel. I thought this was the place for me. I later realized it was a banner twisted from the wind to advertise an event (Fred Wells Day, maybe). Anyway, I loved the place and was glad to be away from Vancouver. That summer I met Jude and Duncan, Al McMaster, the lovely Jane, Zubin, Louise, etc, etc., and Wells became my home base for the next eleven years."

LARRY FOURCHALK moved to the Wells area in 1974 and lived there from 1978 to '83 and 1991 to the present: "I was a hippie in Vancouver amidst a sea of other hippies talking about getting back to the land and was involved with various groups of people who were talking about doing things jointly, but nothing was ever happening. I wanted out and was looking around, but it was just down to me and Rick [Brownhill] who were kind of wondering what to do. Opportunity came my way first.

"My mother had a radio talk show in Langley, and one of the guests was a prospector from the Cariboo area. My mother ended up dating this guy—his name was Rob Souther…I went out to dinner with him and heard about Wells. He filled me with stories of 'the land,' and how cheap it was up here and how you could get gold; gold had just hit $90 an ounce, which was huge, a huge jump. I came up on the bus to visit him in June of 1974. They were paving the road in front of the Jack when I rolled in. I went into the Wells Hotel and there was somebody standing on a table dancing. One of those little round tables. There's somebody else winging bread across the bar; somebody else threw a pitcher. I caught the pitcher and got splashed with beer. So I left and went into the café. There's a table of local girls—Cindy Evans, Sam Thatcher—and I saw them eyeing me up, and I was eyeing them up. And Annette Dorish wanted to know what this hippie wanted to eat. I ordered a hamburger; turned out to be the best burger I'd had in, maybe, forever. My ride arrived shortly thereafter.

L to R: Larry Fourchalk, Gabe Fourchalk, Moose, Corinne Fourchalk, and Rick Brownhill in front.

"I spent probably only a week or two. I didn't meet anybody, I just hung out in the bush and thought, yeah! This is back to the land. And I saw gold, and that was okay. I went back to the coast and quit my job and moved up on Labour Day weekend. I built a cabin. I had an opportunity to buy a house…for $500, but why buy a house when I can build one? I built it out of green logs and frozen moss, a little too late in the fall. I was cold, really cold, that winter."

RICK BROWNHILL lived in Wells from 1975 to '88. "How did I end up in Wells, BC, one of the many hippies who flocked to the little gold-mining town during the 1970s when only a few years before, I had been a serving member of the Royal Canadian Mounted Police—second generation, at that? My police career lasted just under three years [1965–67], and, in hindsight, I'm surprised I stuck it out that long. The fact is, I was much too young and naïve to be doing police work…[By 1970, Rick had left the RCMP, attended and then dropped out of university, and in July rode from Ottawa to Vancouver on the back of a friend's Harley-Davidson bike.]

"I was standing at the hub of Vancouver—Main and Broadway—with not a clue where I could stay. Hotels were out of the question—too expensive and not particularly inclined to welcome long-haired, patched-jeans ex-college students with duffel bags slung over their shoulders. But it wasn't a hopeless situation. I soon learned that there were hostels available, hastily arranged by government agencies, to accommodate the influx of hippies arriving in Vancouver from elsewhere in the country.[2] One of these was set up in an old military armoury building, located on Beatty Street on the fringes of the city's downtown core. I found my way across town to the address and walked into an environment that I'd never seen before: A large brick building, quite old by its appearance, with an open interior that was filled with military-style bunk beds, row upon row of them. It was a hippie hotel, and there were dozens of my fellow travellers in residence there. As I walked inside, there was a reception area near the doorway, with several people available to handle registration and provide information and assistance to anyone who needed it. I was greeted by a young, dark-haired fellow with a shaggy beard who was wearing a pair of farmer's overalls and a train engineer's hat. As it worked out, I had just met the person who would become a lifelong best friend, Larry Fourchalk…

"Larry and his older brother, Ed, were just two of the people I met at that hostel. I became friendly with some of the others who worked there but, with Larry and Ed it was like meeting family. Larry invited me to move into his house in Port Coquitlam, which he was sharing with several other people. At the same time, I was offered a job with the hostel staff, as part of the security team that would deal with unruly visitors to the hostel… As summer rolled into autumn, it became apparent that we had annoyed some people in the community, to the point that a group of RCMP officers came to the door with a search warrant, alleging that we were selling drugs. Nothing was found by the police, but the handwriting was on the wall…Combined with all the political unrest in Canada—this was the time of the FLQ terrorist activities in Quebec—I felt it was time for me to put some distance between me and Port Coquitlam. Reluctantly, I said goodbye to Larry and returned to Ottawa and the university campus life I had abandoned six months earlier. It would be nearly three years before I got the chance to go back to BC…

[For the three years Rick was in Ottawa, he corresponded with Larry.] "We both talked about how we wanted to get away from the mainstream, to own a piece of land and structure our lives around a self-sustaining alternative to the urban lifestyle…

"One evening, Larry's mother came to visit us, bringing along her new friend so we could meet him. We were introduced to Rob Souther, a retired gentleman who had adopted the hobby of prospecting and turned it into his way of life. He told stories of a mining claim where he lived, out in the woods near a little town called Wells. This was gold country, close to the famous Barkerville of nineteenth-century gold rush fame. Life was somewhat primitive on the claim, he said, but there was still gold to be found if one knew where to find it. We learned that there were other hippies [in Wells] who had moved into the area in the last few years, and some even owned houses there. The more we heard, the more we liked the idea of exploring this place for ourselves. Larry was the first to make the leap, spending a long, cold winter in Rob Souther's humble camp. I made a trip to visit him around Christmastime. We felt like we were finally doing what we had talked about for so many years—being mountain men in the twentieth century!

"With my worldly possessions distributed in trunks and boxes piled in the back of a battered old Mercury pickup truck, I left the city behind in the summer of 1975…From this point onwards, despite the challenges of learning how to live and survive in the bush, regardless of the setbacks and tragedies that came along in the next dozen or more years of life in and around Wells, Larry and I both found, there in the foothills of the Cariboo Mountains, what we had been seeking over the previous five years."

MARGUERITE HALL moved to Wells in 1976 and lived there until 1989. "After graduating from the Outdoor Recreation program at Capilano College in 1976, I got a job as IC [In Charge] at the Bowron Nature House. There were four of us girls working at the Nature House. We went into the Jack for a beer one Friday, and this very cute, quite belligerent ringletted and moustachioed man began to piss me off by talking about taking a vehicle up into the alpine, but it was hard to get really worked up because he was so darned cute. Don Pegues, who was on the chain crew, invited the Nature House girls to a party in Wells at this girl's house—Judy was her name—and it was a quiet affair, with a fire in the backyard. That same cute fellow, Mike, was there, but I noticed that Judy was paying him proprietary attention, so I got the message (if she was sending one, anyway).

"I had met Tom Adair, who was on the Bowron Lake chain crew. He arranged for me to have his room in Stromville for a couple of nights so I could visit Barkerville (he was living there with Mike). I heard much later that Mike went on a cleaning rampage because I was coming to stay at the cabin, which really impressed Tom, since he had never seen Mike go on a cleaning rampage before. And when I went in, yes, Mike slept on the couch and I had his bed. I used my sleeping bag because that was proper and besides, the cleaning rampage had not reached the laundry stage.

"Not long after that, maybe when Tom had finished his ten days on, or maybe the next time he reached his four days off, Mike and Tom arrived at the panabode cabin at the youth crew camp where we four girls bunked at about midnight. They brought a blender, peaches, schnapps, rum, beer, and other liqueurs, and Mike proceeded to mix up a new drink called the Pink Floyd. It was pretty good…and eventually Mike passed out. Tom and I went for a walk down to the dock at Bowron, and he told me that Mike had just driven Judy to the airport so she could fly back east to visit her family and that Mike was interested in me (what a match-maker that old Tom was!). I was thrilled, but very calm and collected, you know? Then I had to go to work, as that day I was working a split. My sister and her family had arrived that day from the coast, and that evening were in the Nature House, awaiting my presentation on bears. Mike came in with a bouquet of wildflowers. Wildflowers for a naturalist in a Provincial Park? (Vehicles in the alpine?) But all my sister said was, 'Where did you find him? He's cute!'

"By that time, I was well and truly enamoured of this wilderness man with the golden curls. At the end of the summer, a job opened up for me to work in the Bowron Lake office, so I took it. Mike and his friends Dave and Ron and Deb went off to England for a three-week holiday, and I moved into Stromville and gave it a good cleaning and painting and prettied it up. Stinky Rex came for a visit and marvelled at what I had done (basic cleaning really impressed those young men back then). When Mike came back, the rest was history. We met in the summer of 1976, bought the house in Wells at the end of '77, married in '78 and had our first son, Graham, in '79."

ANNE LAING lived in Wells from 1979 to '89 and returned in 2009. "It was 1977. My friend Francine was living in Quesnel, and I came up from Victoria to visit. She said, 'Let's go to Wells for New Year's!' She had a date, and her date had a friend…So we piled into this Volkswagen van in Quesnel that had no heat in it, and it was thirty below. I'm

Marguerite Hall in the Wells Hotel, c. 1976. Note the pickled eggs and wieners in gallon jars! Photo: Nathan Kew.

Anne Laing with Elizabeth Laing.

from Victoria and had never experienced this kind of cold before. We all rolled up in the back in our sleeping bags; the defrost didn't work in the van because we had no heat, so we had to keep stopping and cleaning off the inside of the windshield, and we were freezing.

"They'd booked a room in the Jack. We were all going to stay in a room; Francine and I were going to sleep in the bed and the two guys were going to just sleep in sleeping bags on the floor…We went into our little room, and dropped our stuff off and then proceeded to the dance at the hall. It was fabulous; I'd never been to anything like that before; there were lots of women with long skirts, hippie women, and lots of children, and I just loved it. My friend Francine wasn't really much of a partier, and none of the rest of them were real partiers, but I just stayed and stayed and stayed. I travelled back to the hotel and there was a party in the lobby, so I hung out there for a while too. Then I finally staggered up to our room, and didn't lock the door behind me. I crawled into bed and passed out. I had this dream that somebody was sleeping between Francine and I—which, in those days, didn't seem that weird or anything, I just went, oh, it's so-and-so, and went back to sleep.

"In the morning Francine said, 'You know, I had weirdest dream last night.' I said, 'Oh, what was your dream?' And she said, 'I dreamed that there was someone in bed with us last night! I dreamed that I woke up and saw someone crawling into the middle of the bed, and then just kind of went, oh well, it's just so-and-so, and went back to sleep!' I said, 'Oh my god, I had exactly the same dream!' But nobody knew if it really happened or who it was, because whoever it was, they were gone in the morning.

"I was extremely hungover that morning. We went down to Big John's [restaurant, formerly the Lode Theatre, in south Wells] for breakfast. By this time it's about thirty-five below and brilliantly clear and beautiful. I remember sitting in the restaurant looking up the hill at the houses on the Crescent—that was the moment for me, when I looked up the hill and saw all these little houses and thought, 'this is so beautiful'…

[After returning to Victoria and taking a drafting course, Anne got a job with an archi-tectural firm in Prince George and there met George Laing.] "George had a friend in Ques-nel who was a logger, and his friend said, 'Why don't you come with me, I'm logging out-side of Wells.' So he did. By this time I was pregnant. George thought that Wells was really nice and houses were really cheap and suggested maybe we should buy a house there. I said, 'Well, I want an old two-storey log house.' The next time he went to Wells, he found one! Nathan and Stephanie were living in it. The asking price was twelve or fourteen-thousand dollars, and we offered ten thousand, and we got it.

"So we moved there at the end of September in 1979…It was tough at first. I could see who all the groovy people were—I remember Sally and Marguerite and Sandy and Suzanne…But from the instant we moved there, even though it took a while to break into the in-crowd and make friends, I loved it there. I absolutely loved it, in a way that I can't even explain; I felt like I had come home."

Back to the garden they may have gone, but it wasn't always paradise on earth. The hip-pies who moved to Wells did not always feel warmly welcomed. "My first week in town, I walked into the cafeteria in the Wells Hotel and asked the lady there if there were any houses to rent," recalled Sharon Brown. "She looked me up and down and said no."

Canada Day on Pooley Street with the Pink Pontiac: On porch, two kids from the Peters family and Pooley Mike. On car, Tannis (the Irish Setter), Monica Doyle with Mr. Ivan the dog, Heather Danby, John Fitton, Rose Danby (back row), Prudence Ryan, Duncan MacNair (back row) Alice Reimer (standing), Brian Humber, Shirley Decker, Al Reimer petting Murdoch the dog, Bev Danby, Kathy Danby, Edie Decker (standing).

GENERATION GAPS

WHEN THE HIPPIES ARRIVED IN WELLS, THEY ENCOUNTERED A RANGE OF attitudes from the locals, spanning indifference to derision to outright violence. Part of the challenges they faced as newcomers to a small rural town were ascribable to what was known in the 1970s as the "generation gap," a gap not only of age and experience but an often unbridgeable gulf in core values, awareness, understanding, and musical taste. It was the gap that, in the US, separated the Doves from the Hawks and Meathead from Archie Bunker. In Wells, a generational clash between the newcomers and the established, middle-aged, middle-class, home-owning, tax-paying residents defined social, political, and economic boundaries in town. In short, the hippies drank at the Wells Hotel pub, and the loggers drank at the Jack O' Clubs bar. But, by the decade's end, hippies not only drank but worked at the Jack, and, overall, age differences proved to be irrelevant; there were young people in Wells—people the same age as and even younger than the hippies—who remained untouched by the cultural revolutions of the 1960s and '70s, unmoved by peace protests, free love, and psychedelics and, as we have seen, there were Wells elders who are remembered today as a kind of countercultural "avant-garde." It turned out that not everyone over thirty was untrustworthy, and not everyone under thirty could be trusted.

The tiny town's demographics in the 1970s may be roughly oversimplified into two categories: Old Wells or the people who lived in Wells before the 1970s or came from families who did (including the geezers) and/or who epitomized "straight" values, and New Wells or the hippies, who moved to Wells after 1970 and embraced what was later termed

Postcard of Pooley Street: Jack O' Clubs Hotel, Pool Hall, Good Eats, Deluxe General Store, Wells Hotel, 1970s. Photo: K. Buchanan.

"the counterculture." On the *Rural Preliminary List of Electors, May 1974*, residents who would be considered New Wells account for around twenty-five people, or roughly a tenth of the list, but it is worth noting that only the ones who bothered to register to vote are enumerated, and it's likely that, as part of the "fuck-the-system" cohort, not all would have registered.

In 1969, the official local government was the Wells Improvement District, the local body of the Cariboo Regional District, based in Quesnel; its members were known as the Town Fathers. These were Wells' merchants, semi-professionals, and blue-collar workers; they ran small businesses in town or worked as loggers or truck drivers. They volunteered for the fire brigade and joined the Masons. They and their wives ran the post office, garage, general store, Legion, hotels and pubs, cafés, and the associations that sponsored annual beauty pageants where their daughters were crowned Miss Curling Club, Miss Ski Club, Miss Fire Brigade, or Miss Wells. Photos from the Wells Archives—taken around the time Prime Minister Pierre Trudeau wed quintessential West Coast hippie girl Margaret Sinclair—show local beauty-contest winners with beehive hairdos, long white gloves, and satin dresses. The crew-cut, tie-wearing men of the Wells fire brigade pose in front of their trucks in a snapshot that could be from the 1950s but was taken several years after the Summer of Love brought paisley and sideburns into the mainstream. Into this conservative scene came long-haired, pot-smoking hippies from "the city"—the latter term often used by the locals as an accusation of both ignorance and arrogance, for the divide was not only generational but between what were seen as urban and rural values. For their part, the hippie city kids brought their own biases about straight people, country folk, and authority figures. "I showed up in Wells in 1970," recalled Zubin Gillespie, "and there were these people there who'd never left the town. It was like a warp in time."

The age and cultural divisions might have remained unremarkable were it not for the fires. In the first half of the 1970s, several fires destroyed homes and businesses associated with hippies, starting with the arson of Filthy Larry's in 1972 and culminating in the 1976 cabin fire at Jack of Clubs Lake that took a man's life. No charges were ever laid by the RCMP for any of the fires. But even the violence of the fires didn't entirely negate the positive, mutually respectful relationships formed between some of the straights and the longhairs, between whom there were genuine friendships and mentorships. Just as the hippies discovered that some of their elders could offer them worthwhile tidbits of wisdom based on experience, the Old Wells residents gave a grudging respect to the newcomers as they

Wells Hotel, early 1970s. Photo: Sandy Phillips.

settled in and started to raise families, fix up their homes, work at steady jobs, and join community organizations. Or even before. Brad Davies remembers that in the early 1970s, "my mother confided that she'd been watching this big tall hippie named Stu [Zubin Gillespie], and had noticed that the dogs and the children all loved him. 'Nobody could fool the dogs and the children,' she said, and so it was there, in the confines of our bourgeois family, that I got the first intimations of how it was going to be. The barriers were falling, and it wasn't too long after that, that 'Old Wells' began to take up wife-swapping and smoking pot. And the beer parlours began to rock, and the house parties began to roll…"

Contact and Community

A Sunday afternoon in the kitchen at the Jack O' Clubs, 1971 or '72. Clockwise from left: Abe Reimer, Frank Everton, George, Slim Anderson, unknown, Marilyn Reimer, Blake Killins, Owen King, Charlie Walker, Alice Reimer, Mabel Schmidt, Mert Everton, and Archie Smith. Photo: Sam Thatcher.

The first years of the decade saw Old Wells, a rooted and insular Establishment, come face-to-face with New Wells, the mainly urban and middle-class hippies of a widespread counterculture. Old Wells contained local tribes and clans, stranded "gentlemen" from the mining era, the Town Fathers, the RCMP, and most of the loggers. The newcomers brought with them not only pot and psychedelics, Beatles' records, and notions of free love, they also arrived with a longing for community—albeit one that, at first, seemed diametrically opposed to the existing one. Some of the hippies were almost as suspicious of the Town Fathers as the other way round. "There was also the Masonic connection in Wells...I would suspect that all of the Town Fathers were Masons," Tom Adair told me.

But even in the early 1970s, the hippies organized dinners and dances for the old-timers at the Community Hall and held hot-dog barbecues on the main street for the town's children. Within half a dozen years, the newcomers got involved in the fire brigade, the historical society, the school board, and even the Town Fathers. In time, thanks to mutual efforts, a common sense of community was forged between Old and New Wells in the isolation of the Cariboo Mountains.

BRAD DAVIES: "The orderly side of life in Wells in 1970 seemed to be ruled by the Williams clan. The disorderly side of life was ruled by the MacNair/Randall clan. The Hongs presided over all, and Heckpoint and company [the Galbraith family] brought up the rear. I don't think a history of Wells would be complete without going into the names of the tribes that flourished in those days, since everyone that was outside the nuclear families of the middle bourgeoisie tended to form into a clan. A good example of this would be Spud Murphy and Barb Tone, whose offspring can be traced to the present day around Wells. It was no mystery why, when the entire town surged en masse into the counterculture a few years later, group marriage and tribal living arrangements became the norm for all.

"But when I first arrived [in 1970], I most vividly remember that the males wore ducktail haircuts and the females wore beehives. Johnny Cash or else Tammy Wynette poured forth from the eight-tracks in every truck and car. And the first dance that brought longhairs in any number erupted into a riot. It took a couple of years for the local males to realize that free love included them, too, at which point the war was over. The young females, of course, had long since realized this, which was probably what started the riot in the first place. Many of the young ladies of Wells flocked [to the hippies out at Stromville] until they discovered that these guys weren't going to fall in love with them.

"Most predominant, though, were the elderly people, who lived in all the shacks that have since been torn down...These people had lived in a time when it really did require some fortitude to make the journey out to civilization (i.e., Quesnel), and I don't think the town of Wells would have moved into the counterculture if it hadn't been for the influence of this starry firmament in our midst.

"The fellow who was in charge of the apartments and other [Cariboo Gold Quartz] Company properties was Sid Dannhauer [his occupation on the Rural Electors list is Carpenter and he was married to Mrs. Mildred.]. He was the only one being paid, I think, while the Town Fathers just functioned as some sort of council. I do remember that some real honest-to-god hippies brought a film to show these gentlemen in council. It was supposed to be about people living in harmony (maybe it was the Woodstock film, ha-ha), and I got so excited that I tried to enter the meeting where it was being held in the ballet room upstairs

Back row, L to R: Paul Pavich, Ray Hong, Helga Premischook, Betty & Herb Hadfield, unknown, Sid Dannhauer, Scotty Thompson, Trev Davies, unknown, Brad Davies, Nancy Davies. Front row, L to R: Olive Pavich, Leanne Davies, Marg Thompson, Ian Davies, unknown, unknown, Wade Davies, Gary Davies, Ida Williams. Photo: Leanne Davies.

in the [Community] Hall. But Ray Hong threw me out. Another meeting that has entered our lore concerns Lars Fossberg, who came first to Wells to ask about building his ski hill here. I guess they threw him out, too. [Fossberg built the ski hill at Troll Mountain, instead, about forty kilometres (twenty-five miles) from Wells, where it is still a small but thriving business.]

"It seems like the Town Fathers lost their mandate about the time of the federal government's expanding largesse [in the early 1970s], so a few of these men moved into supervisory roles with the Winter Works projects, employing some of the local unemployed. My mother kept the books, so I know a bit about it. They did some useful work, and when a very vocal group of newcomers began to complain about their administration, these gentlemen quickly stepped aside, leaving the field open for that very vocal group..."

ERIC ACKERLY: "I don't know if you heard the story of the 'gun-totin,' knife-packin' hippies of Wells that came out of Filthy Larry's Leather Shoppe? Well, when the hippies moved into town, they didn't get along so well with the loggers and the rednecks—understatement—and a couple of them came down to the shop to cause trouble. Brian [Humber] pulled a pellet gun on them. Now it did look like a military Colt 45, and one of the other guys was in the kitchen chopping veggies and came through the beaded curtain that served to separate the shop from the kitchen right at that moment, and the loggers freaked out and left. We didn't have much trouble with them after that for quite awhile.

"Another time we were sitting in the Jack and one of the good old boys put on the song "Oakie from Muskogee." All us hippies—and there were a lot of us in the pub that night—took the song and belted it out. We owned it after that. It was great. Poor Abe and Alice [the owners of the Jack] thought there was going to be a rumble in there for sure, but by the end of the night we were buying each others' tables beers."

MIKE HEENAN: "The Old Wells people were not all unhappy to see us because we, at least, provided some economic activity when we first moved up there. There wasn't any overt hostility or shows of aggression towards the hippies—other than from the loggers—but not from the townspeople. They didn't automatically throw us out. The only overt conflict was through a total lack of acknowledgement, especially if they were with others. Individually, they would actually acknowledge your presence, sometimes with only a grunt but, oh, we were thankful for even that…

"Abe and Alice were not really happy to see us when we first arrived, probably because we were smelly, broke, and tended to drink ourselves unconscious whenever we did have money. We also fucked up [the Hotel's] washing machines regularly, from putting in loads that were way too big—and washing sleeping bags and felt-pack liners probably didn't help a lot either…But Abe and Alice would also buy you a beer pretty much every time you walked in (remember, beer was only twenty cents a glass then). The impression I had then was that the old-timers were just glad to see people moving to town. They had all been there during the 1950s when things were busier and had seen the town slowly dying. I think they also welcomed the company—we were all more than willing to talk (and drink) with them. Maybe they liked to see the established boys and the loggers get their knickers in a knot?

Dave's Not Here

Living in Wells in the mid-1970s, when the population was about three hundred people, were: Dave Lockyer, Dave Thatcher, Trapper Dave, Dave Austin, Dave Spinks, Davey Davidson, Dave Williams, his father, David Williams, and David Williams' brother, David J. Williams, who was known as Bud.

"Dennis Dobbin seemed to be one of the happiest people of all that a new crew had moved to town. Working with him that first year in Barkerville, he couldn't do enough for me. I think he may have even come over and helped dig my house foundation for a day or two. I was invited for dinner just about every night, and you couldn't ask for a better person to cover your ass when you came to work hungover (he was good buds with John Premischook and would conveniently whisk him away from our job site whenever he came by and the smell of day-old cheap green beer wafted about). Bud and Ida Williams (more Bud than Ida) were always willing to load up your plate with extras, due to the emaciated look most of us had then.

"Pete Pelletier and Annette Dorish were running the Wells then, and because nobody—least of all me—was cooking in those days, Annette was a vital link to the Wells Hotel's hamburger. She hated the hippies, but she was forced to serve them food all day, burger after burger. No sooner would she whip one off the grill, than someone else would walk in and order another one. You could see the smoke pouring out of her ears. Herb Hadfield [the postmaster] was someone you had to know if you ever wanted to receive any mail, and everybody, I mean everybody, was on UIC, so you pretty much had to give Herb the *Coles Notes* version of who you were and where you came from…

"Mostly, though, I remember the old guys in the pub. You could hardly buy your own drink. Someone would always make sure you had a beer in front of you. I didn't have to buy a beer for the first few times I went into the Jack (my introductory bar), and I think they came from Bill and Lucky. Sometimes you just didn't know. It certainly was different than any bars I'd been in, in Vancouver!

All of the old characters were very friendly, not frightening as they sometimes appear to people in the city—sure, most of them were completely off their rockers, but it seemed perfectly natural. The old-timers really liked us; they were glad we were there, yakking and buying beer.

"The loggers and…were a different story. I don't recall them being outright hostile, but they didn't move an inch if you happened to be passing them on the way to the can.

The loggers displayed their loathing of us mostly in the open mocking of our dress whilst playing pool in the Jack. When they would venture over to the Wells they would put the boots to all of the hippie dogs that would be faithfully waiting (usually all day) for their masters to finish their beer. I remember being verbally assailed as I sat, surrounded by dogs, on the porch of the Wells Hotel. I'm surprised that there wasn't open arm-to-arm combat, but there wasn't. It all seemed very much below the surface, so that when Zubin's place at the lake burned down, it was very scary. The fire department in those days was definitely a closed shop, and run by some of the boys who we thought might have had a hand in burning down Zubin's cabin.

"As long as we 'hippies' stayed in the Wells Hotel and the loggers stayed in the Jack, everything was fine. When curiosity got the better of us, or when we were barred for being drunk and obnoxious, we would wander over to the Jack. Then things would get interesting.

"Most of the younger generation of locals were (from my point anyways) 'kids' while we, of course, were 'adults'—hippies, but 'adult' hippies. Most of the local kids in those first few years weren't old enough to go to the bar (small town; all the bar owners knew their parents and how old everyone was), so because that was where we spent the majority of our time, we didn't get to know them right away. I do remember that most of the local kids hung around Forman's general store, across from the Lode Theatre."

BONNIE MAY: "I don't remember the 'hippies' being anything different than new young people living and working in town. [My brother] Gaylord was friends with most of the new people, so we would have met them probably because of him, but Fred and I were so busy with each other and then our family that it didn't really change our lives at all when the hippies arrived."

RICK BROWNHILL: "There was a battle line drawn. The hippies didn't go to the Jack, and the loggers didn't go to the Wells. What changed that was when Pete Pelletier hired me to run the bar in the Wells hotel [in the late 1970s], and then I went down the street later on and worked at the Jack, and that just changed everything. At some point or other there was a curiosity factor, and people started checking out the other bar. 'Hey, it's not all that bad down there! They've got pictures of Lucky Swede on the wall and all that stuff.' So there was a slow shift that went on there."

LOUISE FUTCHER: "As hippies we faced disrespect and dislike. Many people were very rude and hostile to hippies, treating us without common courtesies, and/or being very disparaging to us. When we arrived in the fall of 1970, many locals were shocked and upset to have their town invaded by an unexpected flood of immigrants. Some, of course, were welcoming—we brought more money into the town (I am sure the Jack O' Clubs appreciated our business). But we really did not have much income, and aspects of our lifestyle were distasteful to many. I recall when I was living in the Tomato House that a nearby neighbour would not even say hello to me; it was as though I was invisible or a dangerous bringer-of-plague…It was bizarre, really, the contrast between our view of ourselves as peace-loving, kind, and spiritual, and outsiders' view of us as dangerous, monsters, immoral, tainted. And there were the cabins that were burned down by anti-hippie locals."

JUDE GOODWIN: "One story I heard was about a baby that was born to a local family. She was some kind of genius baby who started talking within a few months. The doctors advised the parents to put this baby in a room with nothing but a red light and zero stimulation—back in the womb, so to speak— until she was at an age where she was supposed to be doing these kinds of things. And they did it! So the story goes…"

ZUBIN GILLESPIE: "Now here's a story about [two brothers from an old Wells family]. I think it's true. Did you know both of them were missing one finger? They were in their teens, and one put his finger on the chopping block and said, 'I dare you to chop it off!'…And then, so he wouldn't get in trouble, [the other brother] put his finger down, and let his brother chop his finger off! We had just been living in hippieland [in Kitsilano in the late 1960s] but they're still in the '50s, being total greaseballs! But then again, we all became great friends in short order. They knew we weren't bad people, we were just really friendly. It was like the hippies in San Francisco and the Hells Angels. 'Let's be pals...'

"But in the winter of 1972 Rose and I went around town and collected money to put a big party on for all the kids because it seemed half of them didn't have enough clothes or anything. We had hot dogs and pop and Tang, which was big in the '70s, for all the kids, for free."

KARIN LUDDITT: "I came back one summer as a university student for a visit [after leaving in 1964 as a twelve-year-old] when my father found work back in Barkerville, running the Cornish Water Wheel. He said to me, 'You could probably get a job there in the summer and make some money!' One of the first people my dad introduced me to was John Scott Angrignon. I met people like Peter van Deursen and Frank Fitton and John Fitton, and all these people, they loved it there! I couldn't understand how

Heckpoint (Glen Galbraith) and Karin Ludditt, Wells Bar, 1974 (mural on wall painted by Lucky Swede). Photo: Karin Ludditt.

these young people liked this place. I got to know all the hippies that wanted to come back to the land—and I wanted to get *out* of the land! I used to say to them, 'What the heck? I can't stand this joint! I left it when I was twelve. I don't know what's going on!'

"The thing about me was that I was from the town; my parents were very well respected. The old-timers—they were my father's friends—would go, 'What's with all these long-haired guys down there on the edge of town?' But I straddled both worlds. In 1973 we did this transitional thing, where we had the Community Hall dinners for the old

Above: Seniors' Christmas Dinner, December 19, 1973. L to R: Mrs. Ortega, Steve Rodenchuck, Tom Adair. Photo: Karin Ludditt.

Below: Seniors' Dinner, 1973. Rose Danby plays checkers with Jimmy Corew. Photo: Karin Ludditt.

folks and tried to make the hippies be welcomed by the old folks. We rented the Community Hall and we all dolled up like crazy and cooked these huge turkeys…Some of those old-timers didn't come into town very often, but they all knew me. The invitations had to go out in my name, because I'm Fred Ludditt's daughter; people know Fred Ludditt, but they won't come if the invitation says it's from Stinky, King of Stromville. So I sent out the invitations in my name, basically saying: 'The young people of Wells would like to invite you to a very nice Christmas sit-down dinner.' That was so fun. John Scott with his hair all hippie, and wild dancing, and we were all in our little gowns. We had Christmas music. Dancing with the old farts! There was one old woman, and all the rest men. So that was a neat community thing that we did just on our own…"

BEV DANBY: "I remember dancing with old Leonard Carson at the old-timers' dinner…Even Wilf Thompson was alive for the first one—the last living resident of Barkerville. Then I got to know more of the old-timers. Some of them were pretty neat, some of the old guys who hung out at the Jack, like Charlie Walker, Roddy MacDonald, Lucky Swede, and Beaver Pass John. They thought it was kind of neat that people were interested in moving into this old town. When did I know I was accepted by people in Wells? I think it was that first summer, and Alice Barwise says to me, 'Hey, you dumb broad!' I realized that's what she called you if she liked you."

TOM ADAIR: "Doreen Townsend would have these dinners with cheese and meat and dipping materials, enough food for fifty people, always a house full of people, a warm, open atmosphere for everybody, no strings attached. She was always inviting people to her home with open arms; she just accepted everyone, and the more uptight people in town would eventually think that if Doreen likes you, you mustn't be too bad."

The Hippies

Among the hippies themselves were some notable characters, flamboyant and rebellious personalities, who, like the geezers, sported peculiar nicknames, showed a flair for imbibing, shared economic marginality and transience, and preferred rustic living to working for a living. Here are a few character sketches of hippies by hippies; more follow in the chapters to come.

ZUBIN GILLESPIE: "There was a couple living in Stromville, David and Catherine, and they were amazing artists. They were communists from San Francisco...But Brian Humber asked them for rent, and so they became ultra-enemies of Brian's. Brian went down to university in Vancouver, and when he came back up, in all the houses in Stromville were dead pig's heads, and written on the wall was 'pig' in blood—and this was just after

Above: Seniors' Dinner, 1973. Karin Ludditt dances with Ener Torstensen. Photo: Karin Ludditt. Below, left: L to R, facing camera: John Sikora, Tony Driscoll, Ener Torstensen, Wilf Thompson. Brian Humber in the background. Photo: Karin Ludditt.

the whole Charlie Manson thing. Brian was totally freaked out; it was really heavy."

NATE KEW: "I remember Ellen's husband in Stromville. He was a very charismatic man, with those very crystal, dynamic kind of eyes that just engage you. I was reading

The Cariboo Cannonball at Winter Whoopie, March 1975. Photo: Judy Campbell.

[Ouspensky's] *In Search of the Miraculous* at the time. I'd walk over to his place and we'd sit down and talk philosophy for hours."

MIKE WIGLE: "Bill and Greta were partners who lived in the log house at the bottom of the main street hill on the south side of town. They spent one summer cleaning out the old machinery at the [abandoned ruins of the] Gold Quartz Mine, cleaning out all the leftover black-sand ore. They hauled it to their house and spent the winter panning for gold through this material in their basement. I thought this was kind of nutty, but by the following spring, they'd found enough gold to buy plane tickets for themselves and their two kids to fly to Australia. As far as I know, they're still down there somewhere."

TOM ADAIR: "[Randy] was known as Cariboo Cannonball. He got the name because he won something like four events in the Winter Whoopie games. Everyone was on their sleds or toboggans and they'd wipe out at the bottom of the hill, but Randy waxed up his toboggan with blue super wax— it was for cross-country skiing, super skiddy—and then he just jumped right onto it and flew into the air, and into the tunnel. We thought his real name was Randy Russell, but it turned out that wasn't his real name, either. We never knew his real name. For a while, he lived in the shack on the back of a truck that John [Boutwell] had built; it sat out in front of John's house. Randy had lived outside of town, about two miles past the old garbage dump, in a trapper's cabin on the dump side of town, and it was just an amazing place. It was built from rough-cut wood, built right over a raging creek. He lived on something like $30 a month, lived on bannock that he made on top of an airtight. That was basically his food one summer. Cariboo Cannonball was a refugee, running from the US law enforcement authorities. He'd been in some big demos, something like the Chicago Democratic Convention, maybe? And he'd been arrested without cause. There'd been a huge class action suit, and it finally went all the way through the courts and there were settlements for everyone who had been arrested. He was eventually contacted through intermediaries to get his settlement money, and he left town…"

At Bill and Greta's cabin on the back street. L to R: Corinne Fourchalk, possibly Gabe Fourchalk, Rita Ralston, Mike Wigle, Bill Brown.

BEV DANBY: "Fraser lived in [the ghost-town of] Stanley for a while, lived in an old shack out there, and him and his buddies would hitchhike in to Wells and sometimes walk home at night after the bar closed, all the way out to Stanley [about fifteen kilometres]. And they still had to walk in from the highway, even when they got a ride; they were a good kilometre or so in. Then one winter, he and Maureen lived in a little cave at Hardscrabble Creek; it was like an old mineshaft. It was like they'd just dug a hole in the side of the hill and put a door on it. He was into living right out in the bush."

JUDY CAMPBELL: "I don't know who he was, but Mad John was creepy over-the-top. He lived in this little hut down the road from me, and he used to take the dirty diapers off the kids and just hang them on the line and let the rain clean them. He always gave me the creeps. It's funny how in those days we tolerated people who now I would just look at and say, don't make eye contact. It was okay in those days, but he was not okay."

JUDE GOODWIN: "There was Mad John. Did you know the average age of onset of mental illness, such as bipolar disorder, is twenty-eight? This is significant. We band together and become family in our younger years, but then slowly some of us go crazy. At first, it seems to be a personality thing, but I think this guy had a real illness. Have you heard any stories about him and Nora? They are extreme.

Sam (Sandra) Thatcher, c. 1972.
Photo: S. Thatcher.

"They lived for a while out on a trapline and for some reason (spiritual) agreed to not talk. So there they were, out in the middle of nowhere in the middle of winter and not saying a word to each other, eating nothing but roots and beaver. And it turns out Nora was pregnant. The story goes that she came into town for a month or so and drank some milk and ate some good food and suddenly she had this huge belly! They had something like five children over time. Nora was from my high school; Duncan dated her before me. I believe she ended up leaving the kids with John and moved back to the city. Social services got involved, and that's where I lost track of the story.

"One time, Mad John took us all into Quesnel in his Volkswagen van. Now that was one harrowing drive! The man was crazy. I wouldn't get into the van on the way home; we had to find another ride. John just shrugged and said, 'Well, keep your eye out for seven grins in the ditch!' Sure enough, on our way back, we found the van overturned in the ditch and its seven passengers standing by the side of the road."

How the Kids Saw It

Old Wells contained a population of thirty or forty resident children (judging from surviving school photos), some of whom were initially curious or alarmed by the arrival of the hippies. When interviewed almost forty years later, they remembered the hippies through the lens of youth. Some of the town kids would later become friends with the hippies who had seemed to them, in childhood, so grown up and exotic.

SAM (SANDRA) THATCHER: (née Reimer) "I thought most of the folks that came to Wells were great. I would have gone and lived with them if I could have. There was a group that came, and they stayed in a cabin in Stromville. The only person I can remember was a lady named Ellen. I don't think I ever knew her last name. There were probably about five or six people living there. Ellen made a great coleslaw with apples and sunflower seeds; I still make it now and then, it was so good…I don't know what it was about her; maybe that she was so quiet and calm, probably the quietest person I had ever met, that she has stayed with me all these years. Her hair was so blonde it was almost white, almost albino-like. Funny how some people stay in the memory forever."

Cindy Tone and Sandy Pelletier, 1975. Photo: Sandy Phillips.

SANDY PHILLIPS (née Pelletier): "My family came to Wells in November 1971 because my mom and dad [Stella and Pete Pelletier] bought the Wells Hotel, so they moved the family here. We came after the mine shut down; I think that is why the hotel was a bargain to purchase. There were still lots of people here and lots of logging in the area, so it was a bustling place with lots of business for a hotel owner.

"The first 'hippie' I remember was a fellow named Harry who rode in on a Harley (does that make him a hippie or a biker?). He worked at the Wells Hotel—Dad was always hiring these young people and actually helped a lot of them out. I remember falling head over heels over Harry—it was just so exciting, these self-sufficient young men who came through our 'boring little town' (is that a typical teenaged girl talking, or what!). The second hippie who made an impression on me was a handsome ponytailed fellow called Tumbleweed who Dad hired to paint our house. I followed him around like a love-struck puppy…I'm sure I made the same impression on him, too.

"After these two fellows, I don't really remember any hippies that stood out. I guess, by this time, the hippies were coming out of the woodwork, so no one over another stood out. They all stood out. It is funny, because to me, this influx of hippies seemed so 'untouchable.' I am not too sure if that is the correct word to use here, but it was like they were so out

Sloughey, Steve Parsons, and Wayne Diggins, mid-1970s. Photo: Nathan Kew

of reach for a kid like me because they were so much older and worldly. But then years later, and I do mean many years later, I learned that most of them were only four or five years older than me, practically the same age, but at the time it felt like they were light years older. I'm not saying that they seemed old in age—by no means—they just seemed so much older than the thirteen- or fourteen-year-old kid that I was. More sure of themselves. I guess this could have seemed exaggerated for me, because I was such a shy, self-conscious kid, and being raised by a strict father who kept me very much under his wing didn't help promote any worldliness in me.

"The word 'untouchable' came to mind because there were so many of them that it seemed like they formed a community of their own and didn't really fraternize with the rest of us. They tolerated us when our worlds did chance to collide, and most were very nice and somewhat intriguing, but for the most part it was like us kids sat on the outside of the hippie crowd, looking in at all the hippie parties and fun, but not really being included in it ourselves.

"I did make friends with several hippies, again usually ones that worked for my dad, or a few that kind of took me under their wing. They treated me very much like a little sister, but for the most part, we were just kids still living at home, which in itself made us seem worlds apart. I do know that over the years some of my friends did assimilate themselves into the hippie crowd, but that was later, when we were all a bit older."

LEANNE DAVIES: "My dad talked about 'the hippies' when I was a kid, and my impression was that a long-haired, gum-booted, long-skirted gal was a hippy, and a ponytail on a guy was a sign of being a hippy. There was a strong reference to hippies being unemployed, too. Plus they smoked pot! Stromville was a happening place, and I always loved going to Barkerville with Dad as we had to drive by Stromville and got to see what hippies were chopping wood, hanging out or [whatever] at the infamous house, the last one that stood on the left, the swamp side, just before you get to One-Mile."

Wells Justice

One classic example of intergenerational clashes was that between the hippies and the cops. The local RCMP constables were posted to Wells for several years at a time. They were therefore always changing—always had to be "broken in" by the townsfolk. Some were remembered with distaste for their letter-of-the-law attitude, some, like Constable Gillespie (no relation to Zubin), for their benevolent authority, and most were forgotten within hours after leaving town.

ROB DANBY: "When I first came to town on my motorcycle, I was a bit of a show-off, and I came blasting up the main street, cracking the throttle, *crraggghh*. And there was Don Gillespie. He didn't have a uniform on or anything, but he just walked up to me—it was really heavy—and just laid it on me right then and there. He said, 'No more of that in this town, or I'll get after you, big time.' And I just went, 'Hokay!' He didn't waste any time, didn't say who he was, but I knew right away. And after he walked away I found out that, yep, he really was a cop."

ROSE DANBY: "One of my favourite police officers in Wells was Constable Don Gillespie. Without his guidance, help, understanding, and occasional firm boot in the ass, I may very well have run afoul of the law to the point of incurring a criminal record. That's not to say that I was a bad person or criminally inclined. I was young, foolish, misguided, and struggling to find my way, as most of us hippies were back then. Constable Gillespie recognized that and guided us in his own way by enforcing the Spirit of the Law rather than the Letter of the Law.

"When he put new tires on any of his vehicles, he always gave us his discards rather than throwing them out because they were usually in better shape than whatever we had on our vehicles. He was always looking out for us young folk in ways like this, helping to keep us safe, and in so doing garnered a lot of respect from the so-called rebellious hippies. He attended many of our parties and was always welcome, and many of us shed the image of the police as them against us. He came to bonfires, wiener roasts, toboggan parties, and drove us home when we were too drunk to drive…

"One evening, we were having a typical party at the swamp house when Brian arrived, bragging about how he'd stolen a pickup load of firewood from the Lowhee campsite. Not to be outdone, P. and I hopped in my pickup truck and headed out to get a load for ourselves. We had just about finished loading right up to the top of the side rails (a good-sized cord) when headlights appeared. It was Ernie on security that night, and he was so proud of himself that he'd seen Brian's tire tracks earlier and noted the missing firewood. He figured the culprit would come back for more and had lain in wait. We didn't say anything, not wanting to incriminate Brian. Anyway, he went to get Don Gillespie while P. and I weighed our options. We decided that if there was no firewood in the truck when the police arrived, we couldn't be charged with theft. So we set to unloading and frantically picked up the pace as we saw two sets of headlights coming down the highway. Huffing and puffing and sweating, we unloaded the last piece as they both turned into the campsite. We quickly hopped into the cab (covered in bark, sawdust, dirt, and sweat) and pretended to be making out when Don approached the driver's window. Ernie was incensed that we had outsmarted him by unloading the wood, but Don didn't seem much happier. He did the usual official, 'Let me see your driver's licence, registration, and insurance,' which of course, didn't match the truck. He took them, kept them, and sternly told us to meet him at the detachment office at nine a.m., sharp.

"The detachment office was in the old Royal Bank building then, and Don's house was on the Crescent with a bird's-eye view of the detachment entrance. P and I were scared shitless and showed up right on time, only to be left sweating and pacing until Don finally showed up at 9:30. I'm sure that the waiting was part of the punishment, since our own consciences could be counted upon to be still functional, even if our idiotic young minds weren't.

"He took us inside and was cold and formal as he informed us that the truck had to stay parked until we could produce the proper paperwork for it. Since there was no wood in the truck when he arrived (thank god for that brainwave), we wouldn't be charged with theft. He believed us that we didn't take the first load and didn't press us too hard to rat out who did. He let us know in no uncertain terms how angry he was and that it could go a lot worse for us in someone else's hands. He left us with some parting words of wisdom, 'If you're going to do something so stupid ever again, don't get caught. I don't appreciate getting dragged out of bed in the middle of the night for something so petty.'

"We bent over backwards for a long time after that trying to do things 'right,' like getting the proper registration, insurance, and licence plates for the truck. (Although we did drive it around town at night after his lights went out and we knew he was asleep!) But to this day, he remains one of my most cherished Wellsians."

As in any small frontier town, justice was often meted out unofficially, without recourse to the law; disputes were settled directly between the parties (whether within or between the Old Wells/New Wells groups) or carried on as long-standing feuds, which affected the social relations between the families and friends of those involved in the disputes.

TOM ADAIR: "One night, the tires were stolen off my car in the Stromville parking lot. I had an orange Toyota Corolla. It was the middle of the night, and I looked outside because there was a truck with one tail light out, and it had a noisy muffler. It went by and then it went by again, and I wondered why it went by twice. And then I didn't think about it, and I went to bed.

"When I got up the next morning, my car had been jacked up and its wheels had been taken off. All four wheels. I found out that morning that the same night, George, who had a car with American mag wheels on it, had his tires stolen. I came across George's car in town and so we walked down to the police station together. It's about 8:30 in the morning. The police came and looked at our two cars.

"Now, R. had bought Mike Hall's old Toyota Corolla, which was exactly the same year, same model as mine, and it needed new tires. So the cops figured out that R. had taken my tires. Straightforward! And they knew that K.'s son had a Chevy that was similar to George's, and so on his car they found all of George's mag wheels. Well, it wasn't hard to find the two cars with the stolen wheels. It ended up that, by noon, the case was wrapped up. We'd reported it and [the RCMP] had just nailed the thieves dead to rights, so they took it to a court case. Of course, R.'s father just hated me and hated George from then on! It wasn't Wells justice, you know, because it went to the cops."

The cabin at the Jack of Clubs Lake. Photo: Alan McMaster.

The Fires

Fire was (and still is) a part of life in the Cariboo—many homes were heated primarily or only with wood stoves. A good fire could keep you from freezing to death. Chimney fires occurred most winters in Wells, and most of them were extinguished before they could do great damage. But every few years, a fire would burn out of control, and homes and businesses were lost. Lives were lost.

All of the suspicious fires that destroyed the homes of hippies, including the burning of Zubin Gillespie's house on Jack of Clubs Lake that killed Walter Smaill, occurred at night.

On some nights, two fires in separate parts of town started almost simultaneously. "On the one hand, you had this society that was very transient and remained very open, which doesn't explain what happened in the 1970s with the fires. What happened was that anti-hippie thing," said Judy Campbell. "If we think about what was going on in the '70s, what we had was fuelled by what people heard and understood about the hippie movement, which translated itself into a fear of these young people who smoked pot. It got magnified in some way." In total, about six fires, in clustered occurrences over three years, are associated with this conflict. In the wake of the fires, rumours and accusations endangered the sense of refuge that Wells had provided to its hippie immigrants. The stories of the fire at the lake cabin, in particular, accrued the status of legend. Some suspect that the fire that killed Walter was set by an individual or small group of persons in the Old Wells group—although it was believed to have been an accidental homicide—and that there has been, over the decades, "a conspiracy of silence" to cover it up. Unproven suspicions continue to divide Wellsites and former Wellsites.

RICK BROWNHILL: "There's a set-up premise to this story, which explains how it came to be Walter who died in that fire, and that is when Walter and I would go to town together and go to the bar, it was usually me who would get disgusted with Walter because he wouldn't leave and go home [Walter and Rick were both living in the cabin on the Jack of Clubs lakeshore, owned by Zubin Gillespie]. We'd walk all that way [from the lake into town], and at the end of the night, I'd say 'Are you going?' and he'd say, 'No, I'm going to stay and have another beer,' kind of thing. And it was always Walter who did that.

"On this occasion, though, he and I had taken three or four days and gone out the Jack of Clubs Creek watershed. We had that old dog with us, Knute. We were trying to teach Knute how to backpack, and all he did was bitch and whine the whole time we were out there! But we snowshoed and hiked all the way up…When we did this trip, there was still enough snow that it was an ordeal to travel cross-country. After three or four days of it we decided we'd had enough and we came back. We had no clean clothes and nothing in the house to eat. We were both tired and dirty and hungry, so we went to town and were going to have a shower and basically do everything that you would do on a trip to town. I got into the bar and started feeling pretty good, enjoying myself being back in civilization.

"Walter was totally bagged—the strenuous activity was more than he was used to and he was just worn out, so he decided to go home early and left me in town. So I lasted maybe another forty-five minutes and decided to head back. By the time I got to where the new lookout at the end of the lake is, you could just see the whole sky was lit up, and I thought, 'that's the lake cabin on fire. There's nothing else out there to burn.' It was still pretty cold at night, and I'm half-drunk trying to run to get out there, and eventually I couldn't run anymore and probably walked the last half mile as fast as I could. By the time I got there the place was fully involved, the whole building was just massive flames. Walter was nowhere to be found, and I'm running from one side of the house to the other yelling for him. I figured the side that was the least involved was the side that faced out towards the highway, the west-facing wall. There was a door there, but unfortunately the bed blocked the door, the metal bed that was always there had been parked right in front of the door on that side of the house. Couldn't get in. And then it started to get too hot, and I couldn't stay near it anymore.

"So I headed back to town. I think I met the fire brigade right at the junction, but they had not been able to get out of town because Mad John's house, down at the end of Mildred Street, burned down that night too. Right at the same time as this other one. So the fire brigade had responded to that call. And when they saw me, and I said, 'Hey, the cabin at the lake's burning down!' they said, 'Well hey, Mad John's place is burning down!' So eventually somebody got out there with the truck, but there was no hope of putting it out or getting inside or anything. The police and the guys from the fire brigade stayed out there and waited for it to burn itself out; the rest of us went back into town. I think I stayed with Trapper Dave that night…

"[Both places that burned down] were pretty heavily known as hangouts for hippies, and Mad John was about as weird as they came, really, when you think about it…Before that place burned down, there had been another place on the 2400 Road that had burned down that same winter, earlier in the winter. So there was definitely a precedent. I personally had my own theory, and some of it was based on innuendo and eyebrow-raising from a couple of people, one of whom lived in the house on the Crescent at that time, and could see everything that came and went...It's pretty apparent that the speed with which the cabin got so fully involved meant there was something that got it going really well, and for lack of a better excuse, the cops figured that Walter knocked over a lamp. They assumed he was drunk…

"The next day, the RCMP had to prove that Walter was actually in there [in the ruins of the cabin]. There was nothing left to identify. A little piece of Walter about that long, which would have been the middle of his spine, that was all there was. So they were just hunting for any possible thing that was left there that would prove that Walter was the bones on the floor. And really the only thing that there was, was a metal zipper off a sleeping bag that was mine, which was on that bed. There was nothing else.

"One of the real tragedies, apart from the fact that Walter lost his life, was that Walter was estranged from his wife, but they hadn't totally cut the cord. She was totally devastated. She lived out of town. But she showed up very shortly after he died, and I spent quite a bit of time with her because I'd been the last one to talk to him, and she was really anxious to know what his frame of mind had been toward her and that kind of stuff…

"There's some weight to the conspiracy idea. I doubt it'll ever be proven…But those particular houses that went up the same night were both places where a lot of 'less desirables' ended up, from the Town point of view. All that immoral hippie activity!"

JUDY CAMPBELL: "The other fire, of course, was Filthy Larry's. That was the first one. There was a gap, and then all of a sudden there was this rash of fires. The same night that the cabin on the lake burned, another place in town went up. Before that, the cabin that was across from the dump and the one that was behind Big John's [restaurant] went up on the same night. These were all within a couple of months. And then Peter MacDonald's cabin, which was at Jawbone Creek, between the two Stanley roads on the north side of the highway, went up with all his contents in it. They all happened, as far as I know, at night. And if they were part of a [clean-up-the-town] program, why wouldn't it be common knowledge for the fire brigade? And if the fire brigade was involved, they wouldn't be doing two at once. Doesn't make sense.

"At some point, Rose moved in from the cabin at Stromville to my house, because she felt that Stromville was a target. That might have been after Walter was killed, or it might have been before, but we used to leave Fargo [a large German shepherd] tied up outside so nobody could sneak up while we were sleeping. There was definitely paranoia associated with the whole thing. Then two weeks went by and nothing happened, and we all sort of relaxed afterward. But there was definitely a firebug.

"You can't say Old Wells was the people who lit those fires; it wasn't quite that simple. I think what happened on that whole fire thing was there were just a couple of personalities there that drove that, that were violent."

SHARON BROWN: "Judy, Rose, and I lived together for a week one time, because some crazed Town Fathers burnt down four houses. Two in one night and a month later two more. They did not do their research very well and Walter died in the beautiful house that was on the first pullout of the Jack Lake. We were pariahs to most of the town, I think."

TOM ADAIR: "I was away in California when the fire at the lake cabin happened, and when I came back, I got into the fire brigade. V. wasn't a member of the fire brigade anymore. He used to be, and I couldn't quite understand why he wasn't any more. I talked to him one night about it, and he said, 'Well, we were going out to the fire on the lake. I was on the back of the truck, and it got mentioned that Walter was living in this cabin. And [one of the firemen turned to the other] and said, 'We didn't know there was anybody in there!' And so V. quit the fire brigade; that was his last call-out. But another story I heard was that Don Rutledge had owed Walter $150 when Walter died. To pay it back, Don put $150 onto the tab at the bar after Walter died and invited everyone for a drink."

ERIC ACKERLY: "There was a lot of speculation about the fire at the cabin on the Jack...The loggers were the ones most people seemed to suspect. Some thought it was outright murder; most everyone knew it was arson. Either way, it wasn't very good, and I never did feel the same about Wells after that, since whoever did it got away with it."

MIKE HEENAN: "Once the house burned down, Zubin never did come back [to live in Wells]. He went straight to Bella Coola and started negotiating on that land there. And because Zubin's place was no longer there, there was no great stopping place for that particular circle of friends [the Lord Byng gang] to at least come and stay. When that was gone, there was no reason for them to stay in Wells."

BLAZE KILLS ONE

One person was believed dead following a house fire late Monday in Wells. Name of the deceased and cause of the fire in the log structure located beside the Jack of Clubs Lake on the main highway near Wells were not available at press time.

However, Wells resident and fire brigade volunteer Len Thatcher told the *Observer* Tuesday morning "rumor had it" the victim was a male and one of two people living in the house.

Mr. Thatcher said the one man came home around 10 pm Monday and the other arrived later to find the building on fire.

A second fire in Wells, around 12:30 am Tuesday, destroyed an unoccupied house on Dawson Street in Wells, said Mr. Thatcher.

The building was a total loss, he said, but there were no injuries.

Cause of that fire was also undetermined at press time.

Wells RCMP were investigating both fires.

Reprint courtesy of: Cariboo Observer, *Wednesday, May 12, 1976, p. 1*

[All rights reserved]

POLICE IDENTIFY ONE FIRE VICTIM

Wells RCMP have released the name of a man killed in a house fire there May 11.

Dead is Walter Barry Smaill, 26, originally from Quebec.

Smaill was one of two people living in the small house destroyed by a fire, which Wells police are investigating as an arson, said a police spokesman.

The $5,000 structure was demolished.

Police were also investigating what was believed to be arson in connection with a second fire the same night in a frame house in downtown Wells.

Reprint courtesy of: Cariboo Observer, *Wednesday, May 19, 1976, p. 1*

We may never know if their distrust of "pot-smoking hippies" bothered the Establishment in Wells enough to set fire to the hippies' homes. But while some of the young newcomers didn't even smoke pot (hard to believe, but true), others fairly openly enjoyed imbibing in mind-expanding drugs in the company of friends and surrounded by beautiful natural surroundings that were the envy of any fabulous freak.

Sitting on rounds of firewood in the Stromville parking lot, sharing gallon-jugs of Calona Red Dry, fixing trucks, and making the best home-grown music, were musicians like Dave Rodgers (L), Bob Campbell, and Gaylord Wood (back to camera with fiddle, at right). Photo: Rob Danby.

NO TURN UNSTONED

There was a band playing in my head and I felt like getting high...
—Neil Young, "After the Goldrush"

"UNFORTUNATELY, ALL OF THOSE DRUGS HAVE RENDERED MOST OF THE other memories unreachable," wryly apologized one former resident I interviewed about life in Wells in the 1970s. Drugs and alcohol—psychedelics and cigarettes, pot and high-test—were the hippies' boon companions. But because wild youth gives way to respectable middle age, and because drug use is still illegal, readers will find that some of the stories below that mention drug use are anonymously authored and that names are replaced with initials or [someone].

This was a generation known for taking drugs both recreationally and spiritually, who experimented with a wide range of substances. Marijuana was something new, and there was less cynicism and danger around drug use than there is today and a greater belief in its ability to enhance (rather than dull) awareness. "Grass is a subtle and delicate experience," wrote *The Greening of America*'s Charles Reich, "an educated experience (one that has to be learned)…[it] causes a concentration on what is immediately present: color, smells, sensory experiences, 'nowness,'" and because of this, it was seen as a potentially revolutionary and transformative substance. LSD, mescaline, and mushrooms could open the "doors of perception" and grace one with visions of self-knowledge, beauty, freedom and, sometimes, existential terror. These alternative states of mind were taken seriously and contemplated and discussed, as well as simply enjoyed.

Under the tutelage of the Geezers, the hippies did indeed move beyond pot and LSD to a heavier drug—booze. They drank a lot of Calona Red Dry (one of the cheapest options in alcohol at the time) by the gallon, passed around from hand to hand and chug-a-lugged from the jug. They became "Cariboozers." And whether under the influence or not, they were young and enjoyed their own and each other's exuberant appetites for potluck suppers, pranks, athletic tournaments, and parties. Stromville, the collection of cabins alongside the highway to Barkerville, was for a time, "party central," and the Wells Hotel and, later, the Jack became gathering places for socializing and drinking—two activities that seemed tightly intertwined.

Stromville parking lot party. Photo: Rob Danby.

ERIC ACKERLY: "In 1971 or '72, in that little log cabin in Stromville, we cooked Thanksgiving dinner for seventy-three people. It was a rocking party, and we had the drumming going good. The loft of the cabin was held up with four-by-fours at thirty-six-inch centres—not very strong. So I went out and cut a post, waited for the upbeat of the bouncing floor, and stuck the post under it. Later, when the crowd thinned out, the post fell down. The next day, when I stood the post up, it was about nine inches short of the ceiling.

"I'm sure you have heard the stories about the drumming from a number of people, but I've got to tell you that it was pure magic! There were four or five cabins that had drums, and on clear, moon-lit nights, someone would start a beat going, and then some one else would pick it up, and the dogs would start singing...I don't think everybody enjoyed it as much as we did, but it is one of my favourite memories of Wells."

Peter van Deursen: "The dinner parties we held were many and memorable, as were the various celebrations. I remember the great Tiddlywinks Championship, held during the late summer of 1971 while I still lived in Barkerville with Mike Brown. I think the tournament was the brainchild of Ken Scopic. He and Harvey lived in the old garage across from the motel, where they worked on old cars on their days off. They both worked for the Park as carpenters. They had a wood stove in their garage and often slept on cots there so they could go right back to 'wrenching' when they woke up.

"The Tiddlywinks Tournament was held at our cabin in Barkerville, just after Labour Day. It was organized like a big sporting event. The playoffs went all afternoon and evening. Everybody dressed in their hippy finery. Feasting and music-making went on for hours, until the final game in the late hours, and the champion went home with a handsome trophy made of a tin can and an oil funnel, assembled on a wooden stand and all painted and varnished. The whole bunch showed up; there were dozens of people.

"Dredge pond skinny-dipping was also a big social event. The dredge ponds were depressions left in the gravel creek beds by the big steam-powered dredges of the 1930s. All that was left were huge chunks of oversized chain, big steel dredge buckets, and these roughly rectangular depressions full of water, thirty or forty feet across and plenty deep. We would gather around sunset and build a roaring fire. Everyone would get naked, go swimming, drink a lot, and sing songs by the fire. Many townsfolk's daughters took their clothes off for the first time at a dredge pond party. It was a lovely thing."

Rose Danby: "That costume party down at Mad John's was the ultimate. We had talked about it for months. Deb Kell, Judy, Sharon, Bev, and I worked on our costumes in that big building beside Judy's house, the two-storey one. We worked upstairs there for months on our costumes, just having the time of our lives. And we knew we were going to win first prize. We wouldn't give anybody a clue about what our costumes were—not the slightest hint crossed our lips. We decided to incorporate my horses into it, too. It was this huge medieval troupe. Judy was the Lady, and I was the Knight. I had a tunic and a big helmet

Judy Campbell and Rose Danby dressed for dancing in the curling rink. Photo: Judy Campbell.

with a visor that went up and down and a big plume and the whole shebang, and I had a big cloak.

"I had my colt, who wasn't rideable yet, he was really skittish, so I had to just lead him. I had to lead Judy who was sitting sidesaddle on the horse. She had a long gown and a cone hat with the veil hanging off it. Sharon was the jester. She made the whole thing—the three-cornered hat and the shoes and everything. We had a brass standard that was an old lamp with a crosspiece on it, so we hung banners on it that Bev had made. Deb Kell was the page, and she had a tape recorder tucked under her cloak; we had medieval music to pipe us in. Bev was the executioner, at the tail of the parade, dressed in black. We got the horse dressed up and trooped all the way down the road to where the party was with the music blaring, the banners fluttering, and the horse prancing and snorting. Oh, it was just spectacular! Everybody had incredible costumes that night. Like Gaylord's tacky tourist was a winner, it was so good. I think that's where his Hawaiian shirt fad started. I slept outside by the fire that night, like a knight would, wrapped in my quilt, with my head on a rock, going, 'I'm so cool!' That was a memorable party."

MIKE HEENAN: "At the costume party that summer, I remember Rose arriving on her horse. That night there was a gorgeous sunset in the background. Everyone got dressed up.

We took over the whole street in front of Judy's. The Barkerville show performers just stayed in their costumes and arrived about 11:00 p.m. The RCMP arrived about the same time. He was more impressed than anything and simply sat back grinning from ear to ear."

By the 1970s, Stanley, BC was a remnant of a nineteenth-century gold-rush town with a population that had briefly exceeded that ofBarkerville. The town was little more than a collection of empty and decrepit buildings located down a gravel road off Highway 26, about fifteen kilometres (nine miles) from Wells. The Lightning Inn is now the last standing building in Stanley and was being renovated in 2011.

Costume Party, July 1975; Mark, Edna, Jan. Photo: Judy Campbell.

Tom Adair: "There was a party at the Lightning Inn in Stanley in '78. It was very, very cold, and there was lots of snow. There was a guy, Jim Skinner, at the Lightning Inn who'd sort of bought it, and he started renovating it."

Larry Fourchalk: "Skinner's idea was to have a private club out there where you could come and gamble and hang out and drink and smoke and be entertained by bands. Some of us didn't have vehicles and some just vehicles that wouldn't start, because it was so cold—it was October and it was minus forty—so we started walking from Wells, a group of four or five of us. I was packing my guitar. We walked most of the way there and got picked up by somebody around the top of Devil's Canyon and taken [by car] the rest of the way…Skinner threw an opening night party, and he had two bands. One of them was Dave Spinks and Kelly Winders, and the other band was me and Wayne Diggins. That was our first gig, our first paid gig! And everybody came! There were probably a hundred people there. It was wall-to-wall people. Most of us stayed over. It was some party!"

ROSE DANBY: "A film crew came to town in 1973 and did some of the filming in Barkerville, but the majority of it was at the Lightning Inn, in Stanley. They were looking for extras to be in the movie, so of course I signed up. The Lightning Inn was still in beautiful shape, really good shape. It still had windows and doors and all the floors and walls and everything in it, and it had furniture. It had beds and dressers and that sort of thing. The movie was a B-rated Mexican/Western, and we had to wear old-fashioned style clothing, which was really funky, long wool skirts and whatnot.

"Because it was spring, the weather was pretty tumultuous. One day, the director had forgotten something important that we needed for this next scene and had to go back to Wells. We were waiting for him and waiting for him and waiting for him. It started to snow, and it started to blizzard, and it started to rage and storm. The snow was stacking up like a mid-winter snowstorm. So we knew that he wasn't going to be back until morning, now, right? So we thought, well, what are our options? We had a nice cozy place; we had a fire going. There were all kinds of musical instruments and musicians there, and we were all dressed in these old clothes. So me and Sandy Pelletier thought we were going to snag a bedroom [in the hotel] before other people twigged that they were going to want to sleep somewhere! We went upstairs and got the room with the window overlooking the main road in Stanley. The two of us curled up into bed together and looked out the window and watched the snow coming down. And I was completely transported to another era. It was like I was her big sister and the family was having a party downstairs and we could hear fiddles, and everyone was clappin' and dancin' and hootin' and hollerin'! It was the most magical experience.

"Everyone proceeded to get drunk. We always had tons of dope on the set and brandy because when we were getting our scenes done, we had to run out into the snow and get shot and fall down and lay in the snow, so they always fortified us ahead of time. I've never seen the movie, but most of us were just hammered for most of it!"

With a Little Help from My Friends

Upon their arrival in Wells in the early 1970s, not long after graduating from high school, three eager hippies from Vancouver decided to plant "two thousand pot plants. But we didn't know anything about gardening, so we planted the seeds in the swamp—didn't even put them in little pots with dirt first," said Zubin Gillespie. "Then it snowed six inches on July 1 that year. At the end of that summer, we got one joint. But it was a good joint."

ZUBIN GILLESPIE: "I went out to Moose Island [in the swamp behind Wells] with my girlfriend and [some friends] and did LSD and [we] took our clothes off, lying around in three-foot-deep moss and going, wow, I think we may be elves. I could be wrong, but I'm the big elf, and these are my friends...

"Another day, we decided to do LSD and then we did a hike up Twin Sisters mountain to the lookout. Went all the way up whacked out, and got up to the top, and had the Rock Rolling Championships of the World."

ROSE DANBY: "Marijuana was smoked everywhere and the general impression was that the 'establishment' was weird, straight, boring, the cause of all the wars and injustice in the world, and they didn't comprehend the value of getting stoned, which was equated with being 'in love' or 'in tune with the universe.' Most of the people I knew also did mushrooms, LSD, mescaline, speed, etc., with no fear of putting chemicals into our bodies/brains—it was considered almost spiritual experimentation. Most shied away from heroin as an obvious addictive drug associated with degenerate street people, whereas we saw ourselves as a viable alternative to the status quo."

MIKE HEENAN: "We walked to the cabin on the lake when J. and I had taken some acid right before closing time at the Jack. We were amazed that the forty-below temperature really didn't feel that cold. We stood in front of Zubin's brand new barrel heater just waiting for the fire to build enough that we could take off our coats. One night we played Frisbee on the main street in front of the Friday evening supper crowd at the Good Eats Café while stoned on LSD and drunk on ouzo. I don't recall it being a pretty sight, and I did a lot of falling over. I think I was barred from the Jack later on that same evening."

ROB DANBY: "[One of the RCMP constables] walked in on me and B. smoking a joint one day—that was in the swamp house. B. and I had just showed up and…some guy who was visiting Rose had a bag of pot. They were heading out somewhere and he said, 'Help yourself, roll a joint.' I rolled up a joint, and the bag's sitting right here, and we fired it up and passed it back and forth and we're about halfway through, and I'd just had a big toke, I was like [inhales deeply] and there was this [knocks loudly three times on the table] and I say [holding his breath] 'Come in!' and [exhales, blows smoke out] Gillespie's standing there in his uniform. I've got a whole bag of pot in front of me, so I kind of scrunched it up and said, 'Yes?'

"He was totally cool. He hadn't come for that; he'd come specifically to talk to Rose about something. He stated his business and then he said, 'And the next time I come here, you better not be smoking pot,' and he turned around and closed the door and left!"

ANONYMOUS: "I remember bringing the pot to Wells one winter. I had a kilo of marijuana and brought it to town and sold it super cheap; I sold it for my price per ounce or something like that, making no money off it.

"D. came by one day, and I had six or eight bags of pot sitting out. He picked this bag up and that bag up, and said, 'Hmmmm…Do you have anything else?' So I ended up bringing all the bags down so he could figure out which one he wanted. We went through this whole thing. Finally, there was one bag he wanted, so I reached into it, grabbed a handful of pot, put it in another bag, and said 'Make your choice now!' The point was, I wasn't drug dealing; I was moving largesse on. Yeah, it was like a community service."

TOM ADAIR: "One night, a few of us got together and just decided to use some mind-altering drugs and try to achieve a new sense of nirvana. There was yellow windowpane in town one spring. We all piled into an old Meteor that was kind of stinky from winter, full of candy wrappers and empty cigarette packages, and we headed out the Bowron Lake road, fifteen miles out and fifteen miles back. No lights. We had a rope tow attached to the back of the car. G. was driving.

"So we were sort of in an alternate universe, and we were looking out the back window at someone skiing on the end of a rope. W. skied all the way out to the bridge at Bowron Lake and all the way back. And then we had two or three people on a toboggan being towed on a rope behind the car, all the way out and all the way back. It was probably just as cold as it was last night [about minus twenty-five degrees F]. G. turned the headlights off and put on the flashers. So you'd look out—you'd be back in the car after freezing to death in the toboggan—and look out the back window at the people on the toboggan, and the flashers were going red! red! red! red!— this sort of stroboscopic effect of faces going "ah, oooh, ah, eee"—and we were doing like thirty-five, forty miles an hour. Then finally we got to

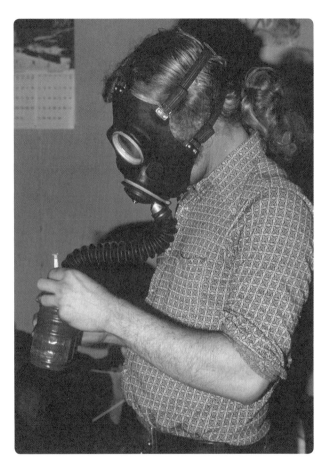

A new way to get high. Photo: Tom Adair.

Rose Danby and Judy Campbell in the log cabin at Stromville, mid-1970s. Photo: Judy Campbell.

the turn-off back to the Barkerville Highway towards Wells and only at that point we became paranoid that we might get caught by the police!"

ANONYMOUS: "One of the memorable nights was up at R's cabin. We were all doing a lot of mushrooms. I felt really tempted to go for a walk in the woods, but I got just a few feet in, and it was getting too intense for me. Went back down to the fire and R. was becoming this dwarf. He went into the cabin and was talking to his stove for about half an hour. He had stuff piled up all over the place. He finally came out, went around to the side of the house, and brought out this big square sheet of steel. He slammed it down beside the fire and jumped on it, just stomped on it, and then got his feet firmly settled—and we're all now quiet, looking at him—and he's got this big grin on his face. He says, 'I'm connected, man!'

"Another time, with mushrooms, it was Z. and G. and myself, skinning a moose. G. had shot it out the Bowron Lake Road. Then we got it back to town. Z. was totally tripping out on this; it was like his first real bush experience. He was sitting with the moose stomach in his lap, drumming on it, and just grooving."

A Night of Serious Drinking

ZUBIN GILLESPIE: "When I lived in the tree house [in Stromville], I spent my weekends there with Stan. He grew up in Quesnel. They were Pentecostal. Stan grew up speaking in tongues, being totally in the church. Fifteen years old, he went to university, because he was so brilliant, and of course he was opened up to all the great writers, it just opened up his mind. We became very best friends that summer because we were working in Barkerville together. He was living with Herb Hadfield, the postmaster. Stan and I would go to the liquor store every Friday or Saturday night after work, and buy three bottles of wine: the Gamza was the cheapest, it was a $1.60 a bottle; and then Yago, at $1.80; and finally the Dao was $2.25. We'd go over to my tree house and just talk literature and everything and drink all night. Then Stan would climb down from the tree house and ride his bicycle back to Herb's."

TOM ADAIR: "People would just come to these parties with drinks, and everything would get dumped into garbage pails. They were full. You'd drink out of that. One time, V. was wearing these scented beads he'd got in Thailand around his neck. When he got really drunk, he just bent over and drank right out of the garbage can, just dunked his head into it. Well, the beads fell off, but he didn't notice. Later, people started to notice it tasted weird, but we couldn't see anything. It was the next day they found the beads; they were sandalwood, I think, in the bottom of the sludge in the garbage pail.

"For a while there, we also used to have tequila bridge-playing parties. One weekend, we went through thirteen bottles of tequila.

"Think about when people came over. The question, when you came through the door, wasn't 'Would you like a cup of tea?' It was, 'What do you want to drink?' That's what you'd always ask, and it meant, drink alcohol. It wasn't meant to be coffee or tea, it was beer, whiskey—what do you want? And alcohol is a really friendly drink in its own way...I can remember getting up on a day off and then going, well, I'll go have breakfast at the Good Eats. Then the bar opens at eleven, and so I'd go into the bar and sit and drink beer and shoot pool and drink more beer. And it would be oh, five o'clock in the afternoon. Let's go to

Bud's, let's have supper. Then back to the bar. And then I'd drink till it closed. I'd be sober. I drank myself sober.

"The drinking that used to go on there—it was lucky we survived a lot of that. There were always these gallons of Calona Red Dry. I can remember partying in Stromville, and it would be three o' clock in the morning, and we thought, 'thank god we finished all of the Calona Red Dry!' And Scott would go, 'Ohhhh, no!' He'd bring out a gallon of Muscatel, which made Calona Red Dry seem like a really high-class drink! Muscatel was just sugar and water that they'd thrown in the jug two weeks before. Just gross stuff, like a few bucks for a gallon."

DEB KELL: "Yeah, Calona Red Dry will always remind me of Stinky, always, always! And everyone drank right out of the bottle; we used to pass it around."

RICK BROWNHILL: "How to Smoke a Chesterfield: I can't name the exact date, but the story that follows took place in late winter. There was still some snow on the ground, but it was old, rotten snow…not very deep. As it was, a few of us had closed the bar on a weeknight and, still in the mood for fun (and more beer), the decision was made to continue the party at Camera Dave's house. Dave lived in south Wells, in a small house that he shared with his girlfriend, Shelley. On that night, Shelley was out of town, visiting friends and family in the eastern US; she was due back in a few days.

"It's the middle of the night, someone had bought a dozen beers, and we had made the fifteen-minute walk from uptown, across the highway, and past the Highways yard to Dave's place. Brad, Frank, Dave, and I—all of us pretty drunk already. When we finally got to the house, Dave immediately got a fire going in the wood heater. Beers were opened and someone was lighting joints and passing them around. I can't remember what the conversation was about, but I recall that there was a lively discussion about something. Brad, who usually could be counted on for controversial opinions, was waxing philosophical from his corner near the door. Frank was sitting on a small couch across from Brad and opposite to the wood stove. Dave was in and out of the room; I was sitting on the floor, staying close to the heat. There was a point when Frank began poking around in the cushions of the couch where he was sitting. He had dropped his cigarette and couldn't find it. As he searched, the conversation continued to swirl around the room. We were all getting very drunk and stoned, so no one paid much attention to Frank's problem. It was soon forgotten.

"After several beers and joints, we were all at the point of passing out. Brad eventually gave up on trying to win the argument because no one was listening to him. He curled up on his bench and went to sleep. Frank stretched out on the couch and conked out. I was lying on the floor in front of the heater, by this time, watching the fire through the glass door. Dave said he was going to bed and left the room.

"The next thing I remember was opening my eyes and seeing a fire burning in front of me. I was pretty disoriented, at first, lying there on the floor. Looking at the flames, I suddenly realized that I was facing in the wrong direction to be seeing the fire in the heater. Rolling over to look behind me—there was the heater, flames still dancing behind the glass door. The room was smoky; even in the dim light, I could see a dense cloud of smoke above me. FIRE!! The couch where Frank was sleeping was in flames right beside his feet! I jumped up and started yelling at everyone, 'Wake up—the couch is on fire!' Frank rolled off the couch, and we started beating at the flames with a cushion, without much success. Things got pretty exciting, in a hurry. Dave had gotten out of bed by this time and came running to see what the yelling was about. He quickly filled a pot with water and doused the fire. The flames were gone, but there was still a lot of smoke in the air. Somebody opened the front door to let the smoke out. Through all the pandemonium, Brad was still asleep. We kept trying to wake him up, but he refused, told us to leave him be. The upper four feet of the room was full of thick smoke, and he didn't care.

"By now, the rest of us were wide awake and sober. Dave was moaning and groaning about the mess we'd made of his couch, which was still smoking at one end. We could see a hole where the lost cigarette had burned through the upholstery and gotten down inside the stuffing. Dave threw more water on it and we waited. Suddenly, the flames erupted again! More water! More smoke! We realized that we had to get the couch out of the house before the whole place burned to the ground. It took three of us to pick up the still-smoking piece of furniture and manhandle it through the front door. It was heavy and awkward and we had to tilt it at just the right angle to squeeze through the open doorway. And Brad was still asleep! Finally, the couch was outside, lying on top of the snow. The three of us stood there, watching it smoulder. We dragged it further away from the front of the house, just in case. Sure enough, it caught fire for a third time and there was no point in trying to stop it; it was ruined anyway.

"Dave was really upset, because he knew he was going to have a lot of explaining to do when Shelley returned from her trip. Dave was pacing around and lamenting the destroyed furniture; Frank and I had found a couple of unopened beers, which we drank while watching the bonfire on the lawn; and Brad, still lying on his bench, was sound asleep. In about twenty minutes, there was nothing left of that couch except a smoking pile of ash and the metal frame, all warped and twisted. Finally, after all the excitement had subsided, Brad decided to wake up and go home. He just got up and went outside, walked right past the mess in the snowbank, and kept going. Frank and I stayed for a while longer, trying to console Dave in his misery. Eventually, as the first light of morning appeared, we departed too.

"To this day, I don't know what it was that woke me from my drunken slumber. All I know is, if I hadn't woken up when I did, the fire in that couch would have jumped to the wall behind it. That little house was built entirely of wood; it was old and dry, and there would have been no stopping it from becoming a blazing inferno. If the smoke hadn't killed us, the fire surely would have. We were very lucky."

MARGUERITE HALL: "This is the wife's version of Mike's stag. Mike and I were married on April 30, 1978. On the previous weekend, Mike's good buddies in the fire department decided to throw him a stag. I think it was a Sunday night because the Jack O' Clubs was closed, so they had the stag in the restaurant part of the Jack. Ron and Dave made Mike a ball and chain in the [blacksmith] shop in Barkerville. It wasn't your dime-store variety; it was a real ball and chain, weighing about fifteen to twenty pounds. They spray-painted it black. It was very nicely done. That night they locked it around Mike's ankle and proceeded to have their 'stag.' When Mike came home, many hours later, he was covered in mud, because it was breakup time in Wells. He had escaped from his stag.

"I was mortified and disgusted with his overall condition. His only comment was, 'Marguerite, you don't understand.' I said, 'Did they sit on you and make you drink the beer and whiskey?' and he said, 'Yes!—you don't understand! Finally I told them I had to go to the bathroom. I went into the bathroom and broke through the door to the other side and ran away!'

"Mike had run down the dark streets of Wells through the mud and suddenly felt sick; he leaned against a car to puke, and when he looked up, he saw that it was—the cop car. He still had the ball and chain on him and was cradling the ball in his arms. Just as he got close to our house—I didn't know any of this was happening because I was at home, fretting— just outside, Dave and Ron and Herb caught up with him. To keep them away from him, he threw the ball and chain at them! Still attached to his foot! According to their stories, told to me much later, Mike threw the ball a few times, and each time the weight of the ball caused him to fall in the mud.

"Dave, Ron, and Herb gathered Mike up and brought him to our door, supported between them. When I opened the door, there was this very muddy and sheepish-looking drunk man with a ball and chain attached to his foot, and Ron and Herb and Dave sort of delivering him into the doorway. I was so upset, I was almost in tears that he had this thing on. I don't know if I was embarrassed for him or what. So I took him to the bedroom, covered in mud and the whole bit. I couldn't get his pants off because the ball and chain were around his ankle. And of course, there was no key in any of his pockets—I looked. After telling me that I 'just didn't understand!' he passed out on the bed, with one leg hanging out.

"I was in tears by this time, and I knew the only way to get the ball and chain off was to file it off. Downstairs I go, *bing, bing, bing,* the carpenter's almost-wife, and picked up a file. Apparently it was a chainsaw file. I managed to rub quite a bit of the black paint off, that's all, before I gave up! I hadn't made even a dent in the metal of the lock or the chain. I couldn't get it off.

Tom Adair mixes a Pink Floyd at the Bowron panabode, 1976. Photo: Marguerite Hall.

"The next day, Mike didn't even need the key because the swelling had gone down on his ankle and he was able to slip it all off his foot. Then that same ball and chain was used for Paul's stag. That was when someone put Everclear [190-proof liquor] in the punch and the party disintegrated within ten minutes. Tim broke the key in half and swallowed it; I don't know how they got the chain off Paul."

ANONYMOUS: "One time, R. was at a party in the old apartments...He drank too much and started to feel sick, so he went into the bathroom and threw up. But he missed the toilet. He grabbed a towel off the rack [and wiped up all the sick] and then thought—what should I do with the dirty towel? He was really embarrassed and tried to flush it down the toilet. Of course, the toilet plugged up, and everything ran out onto the floor. By now, someone's pounding on the door. So R. opened up the bathroom window and crawled out of it, jumped down, and walked home."

Mike Heenan: "I don't actually recall any occasions when alcohol wasn't consumed in excess."

Tom Adair: "First, we'd deal with a twenty-sixer of rum, and then—no more rum?!—kill a twenty-sixer of vodka, and *then* we'd go to the bar. First we had to get drunk before we went out to drink."

The Wells and the Jack

Mike Heenan: "The most memorable night in the Jack, for me (well, for the first few hours, anyway), was the free-beer New Year's Eve party at the Jack O' Clubs on December 31, 1971. I was such a young thing! I sat in the Jack with enough to buy one or two beer (at twenty cents per) and sipped those damn things for hours (it seemed like) until about 10 p.m. when Abe opened up the taps and brought out the goodie trays."

Rose: "We were in the pub one day, I think it was the Wells..."
Judy: "No, it was the Jack...oh, here we go."
Rose: "I'm sure it was the Jack!"
Judy: "No, 'cause the first two winters or so that I was here, we all drank at the Wells. All the hippies drank at the Wells. And all the rednecks drank at the Jack, and I was afraid to go in the Jack. I never went in the Jack O' Clubs Hotel for years."
Rose: "In my mind, that fateful night happened in the Jack."
Judy: "I'm sure it was the Wells. Anyway. There's these two out-of-town coots that had been holding the pool tables for some time and beating all the locals. And I think you and I were playing partners."
Rose: "Were we highball or lowball?"
Judy: "Was it headbands or earmuffs? I can't remember! But whatever it was, our name came up, and we started to play. I had hardly played pool, but Rose was a pretty good shot.

These guys were really good. But we held our own until we got to the eight ball, and Rose was hooked on the eight ball. So she swaggers up to the table in her Rose-like way, turns to me, and says, 'Well, I think I'll just have to do the Cariboo jump shot!'"

ROSE: "Total bullshit, right?"

JUDY: "And then she proceeds to give the ball lots of bottom; it just jumped over the other ball, hits the eight ball, and sinks it."

ROSE: "I was like, I do that all the time. And inside, I'm like, *Fuck! I can't believe I did it! It actually worked!* And they were just dumbfounded with us, because they finally lost the table."

Wells Hotel party, mid-1970s. Photo: Nathan Kew.

JUDY: "And then the next game we couldn't even hit the ball, but it didn't matter."

BEV DANBY: "Well, a whole bunch of us were drinking—that's always how these stories start! We were talking about the different streaking incidents in the news lately [c. 1974], and I said, 'I could do that here.' And whoever I was drinking with said, 'No, you wouldn't.' I said, 'For some beer I might.' So people started laying bets on whether we'd go streaking or not. I said, 'Okay, if my car starts, I'll do it, because I want to be able to take my clothes off in my car where it's warm. I'll go out and start my car, warm it up, and then run through the Jack and come back.' So I go to my car, and it's usually pretty iffy, but I stick the key in and *va-roooom*! it starts right up. Oh, darn. So Pat P. and I—he's now somehow got involved in this—are out in the car, stripping off our clothes, and it's minus twenty outside. We're parked up in front of the Wells Hotel, the lobby. We take our clothes off, leave our snow-packs on, put brown paper bags over our heads, and run towards the Jack. We were going to go in the lobby door into the bar and out the front door. People were hollering, and the old guys all of a sudden got real [makes grabbing gesture], so we get through the Jack, run down the street, go into the Wells Hotel, stumble over some chairs, almost get grabbed by somebody, run out, and jump back in my car. Pat's bag got twisted around in his face. That was a good one. I was running so fast, I didn't see Pat behind me. There was just dust behind me. It's twenty below, and I get to my car and grab for my clothes—and there's no bloody clothes! I went, 'You assholes!' Then I thought, 'Okay, don't panic, maybe they just threw them over the seat,' and luckily they did, they chickened

WELLS VOLUNTEER
FIRE BRIGADE
Wells, B.C.

Gold Rush Night

I STRUCK IT RICH

out. They were going to steal my clothes but they threw them in the back seat. So I grabbed them. Afterwards, I couldn't believe I did it."

ROB JOHNSON (via Mike Heenan)**:** "We would go up to the Jack for some hair of the dog and we ended up eating the whole dog."

The Community Hall

The Wells Community Hall was once, so it is claimed, the largest community hall in the province outside of Vancouver. The main floor, where dances are held, is a huge welcoming space, finished in warm, aged fir. The Wells fire department has held an annual fundraising event in the Community Hall called Gold Rush Night since long before the hippies came to town. In the early 1970s, they didn't attend, but as they became part of the town itself and joined the fire department, the event became a highlight of the year for longhairs and old-timers alike.

Fraser Critchfield (L) and Jack Tall at Gold Rush Night. Photo: Sandy Phillips.

MARGUERITE HALL: "The first Gold Rush I attended was in 1977. There was gambling downstairs, roulette and such like, with homemade old spinners and tables, etc. The firemen were dressed up in old-time gamblers' white shirts and black vests with white polka dots, string bow ties, and those armband elastics to hold the sleeves up. They had fake mutton-chop sideburns or moustaches, if I recall correctly and I do recall Ken Scopic in heavy rouge. I think all the firemen had rouge on, as part of the overall costume effect. Their women (wink-wink) were dressed in black and red cancan dresses.

"People bought fake Gold Rush money and used it to gamble, and I think they could cash in for real money at the end of the night. It was the fire brigade's big fundraiser for the year. Upstairs in the [Community] Hall that year was a local Cariboo band, dressed in white satin cowboy shirts. They had a female singer, and they played cowboy music and schottisches, rounds, polkas, etc. Mike was lubricated enough to dance, and we polka'd our way around the floor, 1-2-3, 1-2-3. Each time we twirled our way around the stage in front of the band, Mike would give them a raspberry. He denies it to this day, but I remember it well!

"I think the next year the set-up was similar, but then the brigade got more new members, younger, and Gold Rush Night got bigger, with a greater variety of activities, and different music to attract a larger crowd."

LARRY FOURCHALK: "What I remember most is all the great dances at the hall. We used to be able to bring the kids, and when they got tired, they'd just crash out up in the bleachers. The dances were always well-attended and great fundraisers for whoever ran the bar; it was common for the fire brigade, for example, to make a couple grand off of the bar, and that was thirty years ago! Volunteers for the door, security, and the bar got into the dance free, which made it affordable for some that couldn't have come otherwise, and it guaran-

Old Wells in drag for Gold Rush Night, 1974. Photo: Sandy Phillips.

teed adequate staffing. Some awesome dance bands played the hall over the years, which provided all of us with fabulous evenings then and great memories now."

CLOWNS IN WELLS

The Harlem Clowns Basketball team will travel to Wells, Thursday October 24 to play the equally famous Wells Allsorts. The Wells Allsorts is a local team comprised completely of residents of Wells. These include the school principal, the physical education teacher, the formidable R.C.M.P. constable and yes, even the local liquor vendor, not to mention many gifted high school

Snowball 1977, in front of old Snowmobile Shack at base of CGQ tailings pile: Back row: (L to R) Fred Boychuck, Brian MacNair ("Pogo"). Middle row: (L to R) Daylyn Laidlaw, Marilyn Reimer, Davie Williams, unknown, Ken Tingley, Dave Thatcher. Front row: (L to R) One of the Pelletier sisters, John Campbell, Marguerite Hall, Mike Hall, Dave Lockyer. Photo: Sandy Phillips.

athletes. The town of Wells is looking forward to this annual event. The game will take place in the Wells Community Hall, once famed as the largest hall outside of Vancouver. There will be admission at the door.

Reprint courtesy of: *Quesnel Cariboo Observer*, Wednesday, October 23, 1974

JUDY CAMPBELL: "We saw these posters up in town for the Harlem Clowns and went, 'What's this all about? We should probably check this out.' Now, these were good basketball players. I mean it wasn't the Harlem Globetrotters, but they were real basketball players. They had a donkey, and a clown rode the donkey into the middle of the basketball game and constantly disrupted everything. It was amazing."

Other memorable floor hockey tournaments played in the Community Hall, according to Tom Adair, included a game between "the loggers and the hippies" and "the town drunks and the RCMP."

SALLY HAMM: "I remember one New Year's Eve when we'd just come back from Mexico. It was—talk about culture shock—Mexico to the Vancouver airport to Quesnel to 'Eeehah!' in the Wells Community Hall. They had a big midnight spread of food, all potluck. Everyone was dancing, wearing felt packs. Gaylord and his band were playing and they had tuxes on—but they were wearing felt-lined boots too! I loved the dances in the [Community] Hall."

Snowball and Other Winter Whoopies

Wells was a bit of paradise for winter sports enthusiasts, as it had been from its founding, when its ski hill was the site of not only local downhill, slalom, cross-country, and ski-jumping races but also of the Western Canada Ski Championships in 1936. Snowshoeing, ice hockey,

The Stromville Giants win again! Holding trophy: unknown. Back row: L to R, Mike Wigle, Tom Adair, John Campbell, Mike Heenan. Middle row: L to R, Heather Cushman, Daylyn Laidlaw, Sharon Brown. Front row: L to R, Damien Laidlaw, Simon the dog, Roger Tierney, Marguerite Hall, Mike Hall.

and curling were also popular pastimes throughout the town's history.

The *Quesnel Cariboo Observer* of April 19, 1977, noted that Wells had "hosted its first Snowball Tournament, Saturday and Sunday, March 26–27." The following year, teams from around the Cariboo gathered in Wells to play softball in the snow, and tournaments were also held in 150 Mile House. In Wells, the game, which became an annual event, was played on the frozen Jack of Clubs Lake. (Q: How do you find a white softball in the snow? A: First, spray paint it red.) All the players wore felt-packs, which made running to base more of a challenge, but kept feet from freezing. Outfielders' hands, however, froze inside icy leather baseball gloves. Flasks and thermoses filled with warming cheer were a necessity.

Wells News: Stromville Takes Title

By John Campbell

The Stromville Giants, of Wells, are world champions.

Last weekend at 150 Mile House, the Giants won seven of eight games to beat out 16 teams of the world snowball championship. The 13-member team of five women and eight men defeated the home-town 150 Mile Hippies 13–3 and 12–10 in the finals to take the title. In the final game they overcame an eight-run deficit to defeat the Hippies, the 1977 champions.

Other victories were over teams from 140 Mile, Williams Lake and 150 Mile, including an exciting 1–0 victory over Williams Lake Unaccountables, the 1976 winners…Many of the same teams present at the 150 Mile tournament will be competing in the BC Snowball championship to be held here in Wells on February 25 and 26, where the Stromville Giants will defend

the provincial title they won last year. The Stromville Giants are: Heather Cushman, John Campbell, Margarite [*sic*] Conroy, Mike Hall, Dave Lockyer, Brian McNaughton, Peter McAulliff, Bruce Fraser, Paul Guiguet, Elodie Stauffer, Robin Jacobsen, Leslie Scarr and Michael Heenan; and they wish to thank all the Wells people who provided moral and vocal support for the cause.

Reprint courtesy of: *Quesnel Cariboo Observer*, Wednesday, February 15, 1978

Above: April in Stromville (1974). L to R, John Boutwell, Frank Fitton, Bob Hansen. Photo: Karin Ludditt. Left: John Campbell pitches to home. Photo: Tom Adair.

TOM ADAIR: "I played with the Stromville Giants one winter; it was a beautiful weekend, but with some challenging weather, as usual, and it was all over by three o'clock [on Sunday] afternoon. So we all decided to meet back at John Campbell and Daylyn's place. Everyone went home and cooked. We got there three hours later and there were about nine different desserts! And there was just this amazing variety of food that showed up so spontaneously. There were huge amounts of everything. It came out of nowhere, a kind of bounty that happened with the town spirit."

Gaylord kite-skies at the Winter Whoopie, April 1975. Photo: Judy Campbell.

Winter Whoopies—winter sports events, a parade, beauty contests, a dance—had been held in Wells for decades, even in the "slow" period of the late 1960s/early 1970s. The tradition carried on into the late 1970s.

TOM ADAIR: "Part of getting ready for the Wells Winter Whoopie was to go out and dig a trench for toboggans or sleds to come down. It was like a tube dug into the snow on the tailings pile [near the site of the Cariboo Gold Quartz Mine]. We all spent days digging this freaking tunnel in the snow. We dug and we dug, and finally we got right to where we were going to put the curve, and there was a mine car, right there, a big mine car. And it was frozen into the ground. Well, we thought briefly about tubing through that, but decided that would not be a good idea. We had limited time to get this done. We were going to put in a turn there, but instead we just had the trench come straight down the hill! No turns; it was just like a sheer drop to the bottom. Everyone coming down the hill made it to the bottom of this steep run and then went *poooff*!"

The following newspaper report shows a mix of Old Wells (e.g., Ida Williams, Mrs. Dorothy Seatter) and New Wells (e.g., Myron Kozak, John Campbell, and the author of the article, Val Harrison) working together at the Winter Whoopee to create a weekend of fun for the whole town and for participants and revellers who came to Wells from Quesnel and beyond. Divisions between the "hippies" and the townsfolk aren't apparent, but seem to have been replaced by a sense of "us" (Wellsites) and "them" (rowdy out-of-towners).

Cariboo Cannonball's big jump, Winter Whoopie, April 1975. Photo: Judy Campbell.

WELLS NEWS: MANY WINNERS AT WINTER WHOOPIES

By Val Harrison

This year's Wells Winter Whoopie was sponsored by the Wells Winter Whoopie Recreational Project and supported by the Wells Chamber of Commerce.

The Wells-Barkerville School Mini-Winter Sports Day program included snowshoe races, snowball throwing and other fun events. This was run in conjunction with school policy of house competition as opposed to individual events and the Yellow House won.

The Bingo Evening was a fun filled event for all ages. Chris Guiguet was the caller, aided by Cheryl Jefferies. A variety of different types of Bingo Games were played and the winners were: Robyn Esau, David Whylie, Kenny Robbie, Audrey Owens, John Campbell, Cindy Owens, Mike Goorew, Ida Williams, Dorothy White, Donna Chapplow, Myron Kozak, Valerie Harrison, Liza Lapine, Steve Kimmie, and Myron Kozak. During intermission a draw for the door prizes was made and Don Rampone won the Easter Rabbit cake made by Tracey Townsend and Dorothy Seater won the box of Turtles.

Winter Whoopie parade on Pooley Street, 1973.
Photo: Bonnie May.

The winners of the Saturday morning 'Suicide' Toboggan Run were 1st, Clay Wiley of Wells; 2nd, Marun Jackson of Prince George; and 3rd, Mike McGowan of Wells…

On the ski hill the local skiers and guests were participating in the giant Slalom races on a track prepared by Kathy Guiguet and John Boutwell. The men's event was won by Allan Williams with a fast time of 24.6 seconds, John Boutwell was second 25.1 and Murray Tossak was third with 25.6. The ladies event was won by Rose Danby with a fast time of 28.3; Kathy Guiguet was second at 28.5 and Leeane Davies was third, at 29.0. The junior event was won by John Foreman in 29.5 and his sister Jackie was second with a time of 29.6.

The Saturday Night Dance featured the Cow Mountain Boogie Band. Also highlighted was more great home-cooked goodies and the draw for the 1978 Skidoo-Elan won by Iqbal Bisal of Quesnel, the Cross-Country Skis and boots won by Don Williams of Quesnel and the 64-ounce stainless steel thermos won by Joe Lilienweiss of Quesnel.

Sunday's events began with a cross-country ski race on a prepared track at the Jack of Clubs Lake. The events winners were: Men, 1st, Ary Bouenherk of Quesnel; 2nd, John Boutwell of Wells; and 3rd, Myron Kozak of Wells. Ladies, 1st, Judy Campbell of Wells; 2nd Marguarite [sic] Conroy of Wells; and 3rd, Valerie Harrison of Wells. There were no juniors that turned out for this event so their prizes were presented to other participants, even the time-keeper received a prize.

The noon-hour tea boiling event was another fun-filled event for all ages. Participants were given a billy-can filled with kindling and with some soap in the bottom. They had to race for paper, and matches and then to the predetermined fire-lighting point. Then they had to light a fire on the snow, add snow to the billy-can and boil the melted snow until the soap suds spilled over the top and put the fire out. The children's event was won by Mark Lamb, ladies event by Daylyn Laidlaw and men's by Dick Hunter.

Miss Fire Brigade, 1973. Photo: Bonnie May

Snowball 1977, in front of old Snowmobile Shack.

The wrap-up event was an exhibition snowball game featuring the World Champion Stromville Giants and anyone else who wished to play.

The Wells Winter Whoopee Recreational Project wishes to thank all those people who helped to make the weekend an enjoyable success. This includes all those individuals who participated in the events and the many individuals of the town who pitched in and aided when an extra pair of hands was needed.

However, the success of the weekend was marred by some nasty incidents Saturday night after the dance. Drunken individuals tried to gatecrash at both the Hotels, windows were broken, doors were ripped off upstairs in the Jack O'Clubs Hotel and holes punched in the walls. Patrons of Big John's Restaurant were appalled at the behavior of some of the out-of-town visitors. As one local individual put it, "there seems to be a much larger percentage of (deleted) in town this weekend than usual..."

The people of Wells have no time for strange Yahoos from out of town who think because they are away from parental and police supervision that they can misbehave."

Reprint courtesy of: *Quesnel Cariboo Observer*, Wednesday, March 29, 1978

The Possibilities Are Meaningless...

What else can I say?

ZUBIN GILLESPIE: "In the summer of '71 we were all up here and Highways was doing road work [from Wells to Barkerville]. All the tourists were stopped in their cars while the construction was going on. Alan [who lived in one of the cabins in Stromville between Wells and Barkerville] had a rabbit-skin blanket, which looked very exotic to us when we were eighteen years old. It was about four feet wide by six feet high. Alan had very long black hair, down to his waist, and a big black moustache, and he tied the rabbit-skin blanket around his neck. He was wearing these cut-offs. Maybe we tied another piece of fur around his waist. He was running from tree to tree, just yelling and shrieking at all the tourists down in the cars who were looking up, like, Oh my god, our first Sasquatch sighting! And he's much shorter than we anticipated!"

TOM ADAIR: "I was living with Dave Lockyer, who had a two-bedroom apartment, at the top of the stairs. And Herb and Tim, some of the stuff they would do was legendary. One night, they ended up coming up to Dave's room and took all the clothes out of his dresser drawers and dumped them on the floor, upside down, just as if they were looking for something. And then I think Herb or Tim, one of the two, started a chainsaw inside the room.
DAVE LOCKYER: "They tried to chainsaw out my front window, but Herb got the saw tangled in the curtains, and it stalled out the saw. I think they broke the window out, because when I came home you could see the curtains, whisking out the window. Of course, Herb was drunk; he couldn't get it untangled, so there it sat."
MIKE HALL: "Herb liked his chainsaws when he was drunk…One time, he just put in a new window, from the inside of his cabin."
DAVE: "*Mrrrrrrrrrrrr* [chainsaw noise]."

MIKE HEENAN: "Tom and Don had been over at my place, and in the later part of the afternoon we headed to Stromville either to borrow a tool or something quite innocent. Mike [Hall] was putting a new roof on the chicken coop. We all decided to help him as it was getting dark and cold (it was late September or October). It soon became apparent, as it most always did, that the job would go a lot better with a couple of joints. It was within this haze that we hatched the plot to build a moose. Some bizarre interest in seeing how many wayward hunters would stop and fill Mr. Moosie with lead."

TOM ADAIR: "It was before hunting season and we, of course, hated hunters; we thought hunters were just scum! And when they shot near town that was even worse."

Walt the Moose with (back row, L to R) Tom Adair, Mike Hall and (front, L to R) Don Rutledge, Mike Heenan.

It was Mike Hall's idea to foil the moose-hunters with a plywood moose, installed in the meadows behind town near a clump of trees known as Moose Island.

TOM: "So we went and found some quarter-inch particleboard in the shed."

MARGUERITE HALL: "And I got out my *Mammals of Canada* book and drew an outline of a full-sized moose, as seen from the side. They cut it out with a chainsaw, and then they had to paint it. We had painted the house in Stromville that summer, that golden colour."

MIKE HALL: "With brown trim."

MARGUERITE: "And poured the house paint into the brown trim can, so we were thinking that's what colour the moose was going to be."

MIKE HALL: "You've got to realize it's pitch black

by the time we're painting the moose. And everybody was really drunk."

The mind-altered artists went to some length to make the moose look as realistic as possible, even putting grass into its mouth to make it look like it was eating out on the swamp. They dubbed the moose Walt, after Walt Disney.

Tom: "In the dead of night—it was dark, pitch dark—we carried it out to Moose Island. Cross-country, right across the swamp. We got incredibly wet."
Marguerite: "On the swamp it's all hummocks, it's not flat, and it's got that red, gross, oily water in between."

The moose, affixed to two-by-four posts pushed into the swampy ground, was set amongst the willow bushes.
Mike Heenan: "I can't recall if the night ended in the bar, but I somehow think that was inevitable in those days."
Mike Hall: "Well, we get up the next morning. Everybody goes up onto the highway to see how the moose looks."
Tom: "And you couldn't see it at all."

The golden colour they'd unintentionally painted their moose was nearly identical to the autumnal tawny colour of the swamp grass and yellowing willow bushes.

Their artwork remained camouflaged until winter, when Judy Campbell, who was cross-country skiing around Moose Island, found, riddled with bullet holes, a yellow moose.

Don't Fence Me In

When the hippies came to Wells in the early 1970s, the ideals of free love and feminism met small-town mores and small-town gossip. Over the course of the decade, almost everything about relationships between men and women—intimacy and jealousy, working and staying home, raising children in a nuclear family or singly, or choosing not to have children—was called into question in the name of sexual liberation. In Wells, the newcomers looked for love and lusted for sexual adventures, sustained and discarded relationships, and started families as the sexual revolution of the 1970s unfurled amidst conservative rural attitudes and opinions about gender roles.

The first hippies arrived with idealistic "tribal living arrangements" and an experimental approach to sex and love almost as new to them as to Old Wells. While many young hippies enjoyed the sexual freedoms made possible by the pill, feminism, and the mantra of "you don't own me," some of them found open, quickly shifting relationships—no commitments, no ties—emotionally difficult to navigate. It was a very small town, and no relationship could be kept secret for long, thanks to the ever-humming gossip grapevine. Romantic expectations were often stomped upon, but also given plenty of opportunity to recover afresh.

The boomers have always been ambivalent about monogamy, both desiring and dismissing it. In the Wells hippie cohort, it is possible to count on one hand the relationships begun in the 1970s that have lasted to the present day. However, a positive legacy of the open-hearted spirit of that era is that many former couples remained, or in time became, unembittered friends.

During his first summer in Wells, recalls Zubin Gillespie, he was one of a group living in one of the unheated, unplumbed, ramshackle log cabins in Stromville. The cabin, measuring roughly twelve by twenty-five feet, didn't have a bedroom; it had a loft accessible up a homemade stick ladder. Gillespie's girlfriend, he recalled, "wouldn't have sex with me" until they had more private accommodations. This motivated him to build a tree house for the two of them. "I was eighteen; I worked really hard for a month to build that!" The same log cabin loft vacated by Gillespie was where Mike Heenan recalled happily losing his virginity. Rose Danby remembers it as the place where, one summer in the mid-1970s, her daughter was conceived.

JOHN ANGRIGNON: "I fell in love my first summer in Wells, but we lived in Vancouver after that. Never fell in love again there, but did fall in lust a few times or more. As Kurt Vonnegut said,

'It was the seventies, and everybody was lining up for blocks to sleep with everyone else, so if you and I should slip away together, who's going to notice?' If I wronged a few along the way, I apologize. What can I say? PIRATE!"

BEV DANBY: "In that first year, oh, I had a good summer…I'd gone out with a few guys before, some real heart-throb stuff. Then I moved up to Wells. I met Alan, and he was way younger than me, but he was a lot of fun, so we just started hanging out. It was definitely a case of falling in lust. This was the start of a long tradition with Shirley; she used to say I was stealing her boyfriends. She'd been with Alan when I first moved up there, but they split up and I ended up going out with him. And then Mel was just breaking up with her and, in fact, the way we got together was one night he said to me, 'That Shirley's after me, save me,' and I'm like, 'Okay!' He just asked me the right question at the right time."

Barkerville, 1974: Mike Heenan (L), John Scott Angrignon, and Wanda Wilkinson.

MIKE HEENAN: "Are you sure you want to hear this? Paula and I got together right after [her boyfriend] left to work in a mine up north. I fell in love with her. She was the first woman I fell in love with, and I was completely innocent. I was so young. I never saw it coming. She was an older woman. I fell head over heels! I was working at Barkerville and Paula was living at the cabin on the Jack lake. Some weeks later, Paula went to work at a tree-planting camp out of town. The crew only came in every week or so, and the first week saw

Wells Winter Whoopee DANCE

Featuring
COW MOUNTAIN BOOGIE BAND

Saturday, March 18, 1978, 9:00 – 1:00

Available in Wells only, tickets in advance $4.00 each

me pining like a lost little puppy who kept checking the Wells Hotel for any sign that the crew had come in. After a week or so, they did come in but I only caught a brief glimpse of Paula who said very little but at least hinted that she missed me—enough to keep the hook set anyway, and I continued to pine for another couple of weeks until the next visit.

"When she returned, I recall walking into the bar with stars in my eyes and lust on my lips, and there she was with some hippie from camp who was obviously her new boy. I distinctly remember crying my eyes out in front of the big cottonwood trees just down the hill from my old place; it wasn't pretty. I went into a funk that lasted for weeks—until young A. took me aside and told me she knew exactly what I needed.

"I went to the Okanagan with Drew, looking for forest fires to fight (and make money). After that episode, I went back to Wells and continued on with A., eventually inviting her down to live with me in Vancouver. She moved in with me at the house on Maxwell Street in East Van with Drew, Duncan and Jude, and Louise. After a couple of days, she hooked up with my very good friend (right in the same house, in the very next room!). Well, as you can imagine, that was about all I could take. I took off to California to visit three young ladies I'd met—friends of friends—for a few months before returning to Wells."

DEB KELL: "I met Terry, who swept me off my feet when I was very young; I think I was eighteen when I met him...Terry was controlling and abusive; he just wasn't a nice guy, not a good guy to have a relationship with. He only liked me because I was really young. He was very much like the guy I'd left in Toledo, who was just a bad boy, and Terry came along and I guess it was familiar, at least! But one morning, I'll never forget it; it was my best coup ever in Wells. It was the night the tree planters came back to town. We're sitting in the Jack, and there's...one of the many girls he had the hots for, and as soon as she walked in, Terry was like [radar homing-device noise] *weeoooo*, and he actually said to me, 'You know, whenever you want to go, just go, and I'll come back later.' And then he said to me, 'You know what? Stinky's been saying lately that he's pretty horny; maybe you might want to consider...' So the next morning I was going to town, someone was picking me up quite early. I stood up, and I opened the door of the bus [we were living in], very dramatically with the handle, and I looked at him and said, 'I am so glad that I have your permission to fuck Scott—because I already have!' I walked out and slammed the door. I came back hours later from town, and he was still sitting on the bed with his mouth open!"

SHARON BROWN: "I was invited to a talk on Cariboo women. We went expecting something other than what we got. The speaker went on and on about women in Horsefly and Likely, with all their husbands and children. That was one huge difference between Wells women and those in the Horsefly area and in Quesnel who were all married and had kids—not very many of us did. Wells, for some reason, was very attractive to incredibly strong, independent women. I do not know why there was such a big difference. The altitude?"

R is For...

For the hippies, music was an essential part of life, both for those who could play an instrument and jam with other musicians or those who played only records; it was more than entertainment, it was even more than an emotional or creative outlet; the music of the 1960s and '70s was a social bond, a language used to connect with fellow travellers. "Music was our entertainment and voice of expression of that era," said Rose Danby. "The Beatles were equated with godlike qualities expressing 'All You Need Is Love' (and good dope)—and the world is transformed..."

In Wells, one song in particular became an anthem for the hippies.

SUZANNE BESSETTE: "When I was on a hitchhiking trip, I went through Texas and stayed with this guy who gave me a Jerry Jeff Walker album as I left, and I brought that album to

Wells. We played that album, *Viva Terlingua*, at all our parties…Oh it was just perfect [sings:] 'Up against the wall, you redneck mother /Mother who has raised her son so well/ He's thirty-four and drinking in a honky tonk/ Just kickin' hippies' asses and raisin' hell!'"

JOHN ANGRIGNON: "Suzanne introduced us to the music of Jerry Jeff Walker, the great country rock balladeer. The music seemed to be a force for cohesion amongst us in Wells; it just had the right sound and the right soul for all."

NATHAN KEW: "Everything was kind of a rockabilly in Wells. The theme song for the longest time was 'Redneck Mother.'"

TOM ADAIR: "The Cow Mountain Boogie Band would play 'Redneck Mother' at dances. Then other bands would come to town and we would demand it! 'You're in town; *this* is the song you have to play!'"

Wells boasted a substantial number of musicians who played individually and in variously rearranging groups, including Thin Red Line, Harry Hurst and the Shifters, Cow Mountain Boogie Band, and the Zig Zag Mountain String Band, as well as spontaneous groups who might come together to play at a dance or party but never got named.

JOHN ANGRIGNON: "[In the early 1970s], five or six people were invited to a party, destination unknown, in an effort to keep some undesirable people from showing up. Gaylord and Andy and I picked everyone up at ten in the morning and fed them all illegal substances and drove them out to Slough Creek, where we had set up a stage across a creek from where they were all to sit. The Slough Creek Rock Festival. We played it up like Woodstock: 'Wow, there's ten of you fuckers out there,' and 'Slough Creek Freeway is jammed, man,' and 'This is basically a free concert now.' Then we entertained them with classic hits like 'The Scottish Soldier,' 'Terryberry Waiting for the Stage,' and our finale was 'Goodnight, Irene.' The final verse, about jumping into the river and drowning, led us to leap off the stage into the creek and emerge with a gallon of Black Jack (from the fine family of Jack wines). Everybody was stunned by the professionalism and sheer brilliance of our performance, so they all jumped into the creek with us and shared the gallon all around."

BEV DANBY: "I remember my thirtieth birthday party was pretty good. Gaylord and Greg started playing; Gaylord had his fiddle and Greg had his guitar, and they were just going. This was at a little shack next to Steve Errati's place. There was a lot of spontaneous music like that around town, with the band being like Bob Campbell, Gaylord…We used to let them practise at our house. That was a lot of fun! Lots of people around to stoke the fire, make music. We had room just for the heater and the band, the house was so small."

On stage at the Sunset Theatre, Larry Fourchalk (L) and Wayne Diggins. Note the felt packs!

Cow Mountain Boogie Band (L to R): Peter van Deursen, Gaylord Wood, Duncan Bray, and Craig Armstrong in the back.

Cow Mountain Boogie Band

JOHN ANGRIGNON: "Peter Van Deursen, Gaylord
Wood, Duncan Bray, and Craig Armstrong.
These guys were good and got even better in
later life. Duncan was an eccentric musical
genius. Peter was a very talented piano player
who later became a pilot and still plays R&B
with some of the best in the Lower Mainland.
Craig Armstrong, whose talents for doing
anything just kept blossoming, was a musician who could have had the world if that's
what he wanted. And Gaylord, the loving
energy at the front, looking like General Cus-
ter, loving and laughing. I saw him stub his
bow at the beginning of a song and just burst
into laughter, delighting everyone."

The Jack of Hearts

Gaylord Wood came to Wells as a boy with his
father, Clarence Wood, in the mid-1960s. As a
young man, he started his lifelong career as a
working musician (guitar, banjo, and fiddle)
in a series of country-rock bands. He became
good friends with many of the Wells hippies
and was admired as a great ski-jumper. His
sparkling smile, charismatic warmth, and gen-
erosity made him well-liked by all. Gaylord

Gaylord on the fiddle. Photo: Rob Danby.

On stage at the Sunset Theatre, Gaylord Wood on fiddle. Photo: Rob Danby.

contracted lung cancer, although he never smoked, and died, still a young man, in 2001.

BONNIE MAY (Gaylord's sister): "He was a huge part of my life…One of the summers I went up to Wells to visit, Gaylord and I took Dad's truck out and drove around Wells, playing hide-and-seek with another group of kids in another car. It was really fun, and hard to believe how long you can lose a car in such a small area! When Dad left for work in the morning, after this, he made it as far as the bottom of the hill of the road that used to run down the front of the Crescent by Berlin's Garage. He wasn't happy with us.

"The first winter that [Fred and I] were married, Jay and Gaylord were living in my father's cabin on the lake. It got so cold one week—the usual forty below—and they'd go there from the bar and forget to light a fire, so I was sure they were going to freeze to death. I made Fred go out one night and get them. He lived with us till the spring.

"Musically, he was amazing; he could pick up any instrument and play it. He went to play with a band that needed a fiddle player, and so he learned how to play the fiddle. He used to go out to One Mile and practise.

Stromville parking lot party, 1976: Gaylord Wood on banjo (L) and Bob Campbell on guitar. Photo: Karin Ludditt.

"Gaylord used to borrow our trucks to go to gigs because he never had a reliable vehicle himself. He borrowed our Blazer one time, and Fred told him to be careful driving through Quesnel as it had really loud pipes. Well…he came back on Sunday with a little blue piece of paper, courtesy of the Quesnel Police Department, with a list of things that needed to be fixed on the truck. Lucky that Fred loved him, too.

"Since I met Fred [in 1970], we've had beads hanging on the mirror of our truck. I bought them at the store at Cottonwood. They were bright pink and green, but faded out to nice natural colours fast. Anyway, Gaylord hated those things and when he was in the truck, he would always take them off and throw them in the glove box. When we went up to Wells for his memorial, I had a vial that they said they put some of his ashes in. It kinda grossed me out, but then it felt like he was with us, so we hung the vial off the truck mirror for the weekend."

PETER VAN DEURSEN: "Gaylord and I, along with Craig Armstrong and a drummer, formed a band after Gaylord got back from college. First it was called Harry Hurst and the Shifters, then we changed the name to the Cow Mountain Boogie Band.

"Our first gig was at the Wells Community Hall. Gaylord played his red guitar with the 10-watt Fender Princeton amp, and I played the hall piano. We played a mix of songs by the Everly Brothers, Hank Williams, and the Band.

"Clarence [Gaylord's father] was an early supporter. We would all go down to the Press and use up his stock of paper and ink for posters. He would come to all the rehearsals and gigs, always wearing a corduroy jacket with the leather elbow patches and smoking his pipe, smiling away as we played. I can still see him as clear as day…

"I was playing in the band at Gaylord's wake [in 2001]. I will never forget Clarence at the memorial dance we held for Gaylord at the Community Hall. Clarence came up to the stage, wearing that jacket, smiling up at the band. I could have sworn that time had stood still. For one second, as we were bringing our gear into the hall that day, after all those years had gone by, I actually thought I saw Gaylord carrying some equipment through the door.

That day just evoked such strong memories, and I had always wanted to play a reunion dance with the band in that hall. Having Clarence coming up to the stage, watching us with a smile on his face as he always did in the old days while we played in memory of his son that afternoon, just like before. Well, that was about the peak of that experience for me. It was very moving."

JOHN ANGRIGNON: "Gaylord—what a force. The most positive guy ever. I can see him walking in his long underwear from his house to the post office next door, twenty-five below zero, big smile, and saying 'Ain't life grand?' I drove up to Whitehorse with him one time. We were delivering a van for a friend and decided we would eat some hash for the gravel part of the trip (twelve hundred miles worth), so it became fear and loathing on the Alaska Highway; you know, hallucinating Vancouver police at gas stations on the highway, getting lost 'cause we weren't sure if we were going north or south, the usual stuff. Gaylord loved his music. He started playing the fiddle at one time so he could get more girls, but he had enough already. When he tragically died way too young, me and a friend breathed a sigh of relief and said, 'Now maybe there'll be some girls left over for us.' Gaylord loved life and had a blast—all he ever wanted to do was play country music in bars in Western Canada, and so he lived his dream."

The drip torch brigade, (L to R): Sharon Brown, Judy Campbell, and Rose Danby.

WORKING TO LIVE

WORKING TO LIVE VERSUS LIVING TO WORK. THE SPIRITUAL VERSUS THE MATERIAL. Being versus doing. That's what it seemed to come down to, and few hippies in Wells were living to work, to pursue professional success and wealth. In the cities, it was said that the 1960s hippie movement—that is, the questioning of the materialist paradigm—was dead by the 1970s. But it lived on in rebel outposts such as Wells.

In *The Greening of America* Charles Reich described the new generation's values and the factors that made a place such as Wells attractive to those wanting to step off the education/career assembly line and focus instead on friendship, fun, and freedom. Reich wrote, "Unsympathetic observers of the new generation frequently say that one of its prime characteristics is an aversion to work…[The hippies'] attitude toward career is indeed based on the belief that most work available in our society is meaningless, degrading, and inconsistent with self-realization." In Wells the hippies took seasonal work to survive; the rest of the time, thanks to "pogey" (unemployment insurance), they could sleep in, read, think, talk, learn, and just be. Louise Futcher has wondered, in hindsight, "if some disrespect [the hippies faced from Old Wells] was because we did not hold down 'real jobs'; we were living outside the mainstream of society, not contributing, [and were] probably seen as having no work ethic, being willing to milk the system and live off others."

From their arrival, however, the hippies had self-divided into two camps—the hard-working "entrepreneurs," which included the two young men who opened Filthy Larry's, and those who took a far more casual attitude to making money. There was, inevitably,

Dave Lockyer, wheelwright at Barkerville, early 1970s. BP09011 © Barkerville Historic Town Archives.

resentment between the two groups. Some of the young people who moved to Wells in the 1970s, had long hair, smoked pot, and lived in funky shacks, insist to this day that they were never hippies *because they had steady jobs*. Government jobs with good wages were not impossible to come by in the 1970s, even in isolated Wells. The economics of the town were the opposite of what they are today; there was relatively well-paying work, both year-round and seasonal, guaranteed unemployment insurance, and ultra-low house prices.

The voters list (*Rural Preliminary List of Electors*) in 1974 didn't include "hippie" as an occupation, so newcomers to town can only be identified by their names and the jobs they held at the time of the enumeration, e.g., Parks Employee, Miner, Waitress. This list also shows that Old Wells had a Liquor Vendor, a Meat Cutter, a Stage Driver, and a Pool Room Operator, three Teachers, several Students (of voting age), a few Unemployed, a small group of Widows, a Maid, half a dozen Highways employees, a Hairdresser, a Dressmaker, and a Constable. Most of the married women in town, the Mrs., have no listed occupations at all, though some were given the occupation "Housewife."

Employment was available at Barkerville Historic Park or Bowron Lakes Park (about twenty-five percent of the population of Wells in the mid-1970s worked for Parks Branch), Highways, Forestry, or "in town," usually serving beer in the bar, or waiting tables in one of the cafés.

Barkerville, then firmly dedicated to faithfully recreating the 1870s, fostered employees who were keen to learn nearly forgotten pre-industrial skills such as wheelwrighting, log-house restoration and building, carpentry using hand tools, or blacksmithing—skills that were making a comeback in the early 1970s. Just as the hippies' interest in organics developed into what is now a multibillion-dollar, worldwide health-food industry, their discovery of woodworking, gardening, and handicrafts evolved, over the decades that followed, into today's hugely

Rob Danby (L) and Mike Hall in Barkerville. Photo: Tom Adair.

profitable DIY industry. The renovated gold rush town also offered a bonus for a generation infatuated with the fashions of the Old West (fringed leather vests and jeans, cowboy boots and long full skirts, granny glasses, handlebar moustaches, and long hair)—getting to dress in nineteenth-century period costumes while at work. The old ghost town offered the hippies opportunities for personal creativity.

Bowron Lake Park, about nineteen miles (thirty kilometres) from Wells, employed park rangers and naturalists who lived on-site, generally ten days on and four days off during the summer months. The rangers were then all male; they built shelters, trails, campsites, cut firewood, and helped canoeists and other campers in need. The naturalists gave talks, led walks, and taught visitors from the cities about bear, bush, and canoeing survival skills and etiquette.

Gold Rush Town

Barkerville, just five miles up the road from Wells, provided the greatest amount of work for locals in curatorial, security, and restoration and maintenance of the historic buildings: in the contracted-out retail gift shops, bakery, and root beer saloon, or as summer street actors doing "interpretation" of historical characters from the 1870s. Every summer, a troupe of young actors came to town to work in the vaudeville/music-hall shows for tourists at the Theatre Royal. Romances, rivalries, and friendships between the actors and the locals flourished.

PETER VAN DEURSEN: "I worked as a stage-hand at the Barkerville show with Fran Dowie in 1971. Fran was a difficult man, but one of the last true vaudevillians. I worked with him on set construction for a week before the show began. He could work magic with rough materials—sheets of plywood and house paint, stuff the works yard had in stock. In the evenings at the Nicol Hotel [in Barkerville] the cast would assemble the show from bits and pieces they had. The cast in those years had all worked together for years; Fran and his wife Louise; Norman Long on piano; Tink Robinson, the charming womanizer and his lovely wife, Judy; Sid Williams, 'the man with the rubber face'; Franklin Johnston and his portrayal of Judge Begbie, 'the hanging judge'; and always one or two beautiful young women to sing and dance and add sparkle. During that first summer I lived with the stage manager, Mike Brown, in a cabin on Barkerville's main street. That was a summer of wacky characters…"

JOHN ANGRIGNON: "I worked in security in 1971 when I first went to Wells. The head of security was a tough old Scotsman who took his job maybe a little too seriously. So some people decided to have a little fun. They tied up the night shift security guard so that when the security head showed up at eight o'clock in the morning, he found the poor guy in the back room tied up. He told Scotty that the bad guys had headed up into Barkerville. I had just arrived also, and we looked up the street and there were some cowboy-looking characters with bandanas over their mouths running out of the government office. Scotty yelled at me, 'They're after the safe!' then he called up the RCMP in Wells. He and I went running up the street, and as we got to the flagpole at the office, we saw a toilet seat hanging from it with a sign that said 'Government Seat. Through This Portal Great Deeds Are Done!' Scotty went running up the steps into the office where we found the office clerks had been tied up and fed whiskey.

"'Did they get the safe?' the security head screamed.

"'No,' the clerks said, 'all they got was the toilet seat.'

A quiet morning in Barkerville, spring 1974. Photo: Judy Campbell.

"Scotty then realized he had been totally had, so when the RCMP arrived the poor guy was totally humiliated.

"I worked in Barkerville another summer doing maintenance, hauling hay from Quesnel, chopping wood, making cement parking-lot barrier blocks, building dams. It was all interesting and often quite slow-paced in a government job sort of way. One day, I saw a whole crew of workers under a building in Barkerville, laughing their heads off for several hours in a row, and I wondered what they had ingested that day."

Barkerville crew, 1977, (L to R): Herb Carter, Mike Hall, Mike Heenan, Ken Scopic, and Hilda Dobbin. Photo: Judy Campbell.

MIKE HALL (via Marguerite Hall): "In 1972, Mike Hall and Dave Lockyer [both of whom had been working at Bowron Lake] were asked to work for Barkerville as Park Assistants. That first winter, they shovelled a lot of snow from the streets and roofs. One day, Mike and Herb Carter and Ron Candy were on the roof and they managed to cut Ron onto his own square of snow, which, with one shovel push, they sent over the side of the building, with Ron along for the ride.

"Mike worked out of the carpentry shop, where Bert Rosin and Harvey Bryant also worked. In addition to shovelling, he remembers building and fixing wooden picnic tables and building campgrounds for Barkerville.

"He worked at the park for ten

years. When he started, Mike worked under the umbrella of Recreation and Conservation. In Barkerville, Mike worked on just about every building in town, repairing or restoring. He helped build the Lung Duck Tong, broadaxing and dovetailing the logs together. Lloyd Saunders was the Park Carpenter then, and Mike learned many skills on the job. He made scores of Cariboo Tippers [an easily tipped-over chair designed to keep sentries awake].

Mike Hall (L) and Dave Lockyer in Barkerville, summer 1975. Photo: Judy Campbell.

"At that time, there was a lot of money available for parks in BC, not just Barkerville. Bowron got trails and a Youth Crew Camp, and had enough crews to cover the park every day of the week. BC Parks used to be the envy of the world, but slowly the money was removed, and it was disheartening.

"He quit when the government lost sight of the history and focused only on dollars and cents."

ZUBIN GILLESPIE: "People like Mike Hall and Alan McMaster were really responsible and got all the good jobs in Barkerville because they showed incentive, wanting to do something interesting like building log houses. The rest of us were put out on the street and we had to rake rocks. Which was hilarious, because you knew just below the surface of the street was about five miles straight down of rocks. But we were raking rocks off the street so the tourists wouldn't trip on them.

"We were so eff-ing useless, just didn't want to do anything. We didn't know; we were just out of high school. We also worked out at the new campgrounds at that time. They had us peeling logs for making outhouses and things for around the campfires. There was a crew of about ten guys. Now, if you've got a crew of ten guys peeling logs, you should be able to do, I don't know, at least fifty a day. Well, we'd get three done a day, if we were

Ron Candy (L) and Mike Hall in Barkerville. BP1609 © Barkerville Historic Town Archives.

lucky. We just sat around; we did everything we could not to work—smoking cigarettes, telling stories. We'd have a lookout up on the hill. The foreman was some wanky young guy just out of university, clean-shaven; we didn't like him, he was the epitome of everything anti-hippie that we didn't like. We always had somebody on lookout to see the highway, and as soon as we saw him drive up, the lookout on top of the hill would yell, 'Why not!' And we'd all start working really, really hard, and he'd come around the corner and start yelling at us, 'You bastards!' and then we'd yell back at him 'We're working hard!' He was just freakin' out! But they couldn't fire you; in the good old days, they couldn't fire you. They really had to have a person there full-time to watch us, but they just couldn't, so we'd go swimming, take off from work for four hours. If the foreman showed up, you'd go, 'Well, they're all in the bathroom!' Then the yelling match would happen again.

"Then they moved us into Barkerville, taking wallpaper off the inside of the walls to re-do those houses, but again, you had people like Alan and Mike who were really respected, they were the good workers. The rest of us were just laughing our heads off…That summer, Bert Rosin threatened to fire me because of my farts! It was in the days we were just starting to learn about soybeans. So I remember letting one loose, and Bert going, 'That's disgusting! You do that again, you're not working here—one more of those, you're finished!'

"There was a guy in Wells named Ole Kessler [sp?]. Ole was quite an amazing artist. I don't know where he came from, but he did incredible wood carvings, little wood statues. I think his wife's name was Judy, and they had a little boy. They were up there for the summer, and they were selling their stuff at Brian's [leather shop] too.

"So that summer, 1972, Trudeau comes to Barkerville! We all go to see Trudeau, meet Trudeau—so cool. Comes in on a little Cessna or something. I'm there with Ole's little boy, Mark, and we're holding one of his father's statues. Trudeau just forgets about waiting for the ladder to come to the plane; he just jumps out. We walk right up to him—he was surrounded by secret service guys and everything—and we've got this carving. I go, 'Here, Mark, give this to Mr. Trudeau!' Trudeau says, 'Thank you very much.'

"Two months later we got a letter! It was addressed to me, but there was a big argument as to who should get it, whether I should get it, Brian should get it, or Ole should get it! I mean, I couldn't care less myself at that time, but now it would have been really great to have that letter from Trudeau. You know, 'Dear Mr. Gillespie, Thank you very much for the statue…'"

JUDY CAMPBELL: "Work was seasonal and seemed to come in chunks. There was the spring/summer chunk, which usually started with Barkerville. An incredible number of people seemed to get seasonal work there in the 1970s. My first summer in Wells, 1974, all of my friends had started jobs at Barkerville, including my partner, John. I didn't really have any labourer skills (in fact, I don't think I really had any skills except academic). Finally, a job came up as an assistant to Clarence Wood, the curator. Basically, I tagged along in Clarence's ever-present cloud of pipe smoke, assisted him in the installation of displays, and poked around in the disorganized wooden filing cabinets that were the 'archives.' There were a couple of other young women who had

Pierre Trudeau comes to Barkerville! Stage driver is Herb Carter. BP3025 © Barkerville Historic Town Archives.

been hired to give guided tours, and I also had to assist on their days off, which meant I actually had to get up and speak in public—something I had never done before and greatly feared, but later came to enjoy...In time, I formed a fairly permanent attachment to Barkerville both winter and summer.

"After my first summer in Barkerville, I was asked by J.O.P. [John Premischook, the Park Supervisor] to stay on for the winter to develop educational programs. I got all fired up about this and developed the travelling trunk Edukit (which is still in use) and then, the next year, introduced the Wendle House program, which at that

Judy Campbell at Barkerville, mid-1970s, with the travelling EduKit. BP0845 © Barkerville Historic Town Archives.

time was a full-day interactive program for a class of thirty-five who 'lived' in Barkerville. About that time, I introduced the notion of the people giving tours wearing historic costumes. This was met with resistance from Victor Bopp, the then manager, who thought that women in long dresses would be mistaken for hippies. As a compromise, we introduced the first costume, an 1875 bustle dress, on Peggy Bryant, who worked with her husband, Harvey, in the Cariboo Sentinel Office. She was in her late forties and not likely to be mistaken [for a hippie]. It was such a success that we soon moved into a comprehensive costuming program.

"To start with we just had the Wendle House Program (which included the Cornish Wheel and the Carpentry Shop) and the School House Program. During the summer this morphed a bit to include guided tours of the town. We all usually gave tours at some point...

"We considered Barkerville 'ours' and definitely, by the end of the summer, resented sharing it with others. This led to antics like 'chew and show' and 'grizzly bears' hopping out of mine shafts during tours—pranks that still make *us* laugh, but must have left the visitors confused."

VISITORS TO THE HISTORIC TOWN OF BARKERVILLE THIS YEAR WILL BE TREATED TO SEVERAL NEW DISPLAYS

Clarence Wood, Barkerville Historic Park display technician, says an attempt is being made to put more emphasis on the Chinese section and on "live" displays. Work has been completed on two new cabins, one of them a miner's cabin in Barkerville's Chinatown section. The other is what is translated from the Chinese as a "death house." It is a reconstruction of an old men's home, where Chinese men went to live out their old age.

"There has also been extensive upgrading of existing exhibits," says Mr. Wood.

The two new live exhibits will feature individuals skilled in the use of tools of the early Barkerville period, who will demonstrate these by working with them. One will be in the cabinetmakers's shop and the other in the combination wheelwright and blacksmith shop.

Meanwhile, the women working at the Barkerville Museum have constructed a display in honor of International Women's Year. The museum lobby has

Jane Manthey (L) and Della Hubensky in costume at the Admin Building in Barkerville. Photo: Leanne Davies.

been divided into two sections, with one side feature blown up original photographs of women of early Barkerville and including a display case with some of their "womanly" artifacts. The other half is devoted to Lottie Bowron, whom the display organizers felt epitomized women in the early Cariboo."

El Dorado concession, Barkerville 1973. L to R: Karin Luddit, John Pavich, Donna Redlin, and Pam Stoddard. Photo: Karin Luddit.

NATHAN KEW: "The midnight shift [working in security at Barkerville] was the best because the Nicol Hotel was full of actors, and they were always partying until the wee hours of the morning. We had a punch clock [for recording security guards' rounds through Barkerville.] There was a clock in the kitchen of the Nicol, so we had to go in there to punch the clock. There was usually a party happening, so we'd stop and have a drink and roll a joint and maybe go upstairs and party for awhile. It was the last punch before you got back to the guard shack. I worked with John, a tall, slender, blond guy, and he and I would be partnered up on these midnight shifts. We'd take turns. On my rounds, there'd be an hour of partying at the Nicol, and I'd get back down in time to pass the clock off, then he'd get a round and do an hour of partying at the hotel.

"In the summer mornings, about six or seven o'clock, at the end of the shift, you'd go out and unlock all the exhibits. The baker would be baking; it was just beautiful in the mornings. All winter, though, you'd be there all by yourself...I remember this one night, it was snowing and there was some event in town. Scotty came out for one of his infamous surprise inspections. Well, I had made this big thing of marijuana brownies. John and I had eaten some of them and, of course, got the munchies, and ate—more brownies! So we are just toasted, and we're on this whole 'Securrrity' thing. We scrounged around and dressed John up with tall leather boots and with some spare belts, made him a Sam Browne belt. He's wearing sunglasses—at two o'clock in the morning. We are totally baked. Shortly after John leaves on his rounds, Scotty comes in. He's talking away to me and doesn't notice that I'm higher than a kite. Then, in walks John, dressed up like this Nazi thing, and Scotty's jaw just drops! John's got his sunglasses on and is just chatting away, blah, blah, blah.

"But that summer, there was a complaint to security that pork chops were going missing from the deep freezer in the Wake-Up Jake restaurant. Of course, we were all keeping an eye out, as we knew we had to catch the pork chop culprit. Scotty didn't tell us, but he planned a little sting. In those days, it was easy to drive up the back road, and you could almost drive right into town, and then you just walked across the creek. Scotty hiked in the back way from Wells in the evening, so he was coming into the back of town just as it got dark. He watched us go by on our rounds, and after we went by, he'd follow along for a few minutes. He tippy-toed into the back of the Jake and sat down in a dark corner and waited for the culprit to open the freezer—and there was John! John got fired for stealing pork chops. That was the end of him.

"Another summer, I worked security with Jim M., a nice guy, big heart. One night, he went on his rounds, and when he came back, he was just white and shaken. So we're all, 'Jim, what's up?' And he says, 'I'm not gonna tell you. I just want Ivan to take the next shift and tell me if you see anything.' So Ivan came back from his round, about an hour later, and he was very affected, too. And he said, 'Well, let's make a deal. Jim and I will stay here'—because they were going to get off work at midnight and John and I were starting our shift—'and only after everybody's done their rounds, we'll talk about it.' So then it was time for my round.

"I went up into the back of the theatre. And there was this piece of light, and when I turned around, it was floating in front of me. It sort of had the shape of a woman's handkerchief blowing in the wind. And you could see where it was being held. You know how, at night, everything's black and white? You're seeing with your black-and-white cones. This was a green light, very faint, just floating there. It started to move down the hallway, so I followed it. It came up to a dead end in the hallway, and it went between two cardboard boxes that were piled on each other. Now the hairs are standing up on the back of my head! I turned around, and there was a little sphere of light behind me, where I just came from, now ten feet away, floating there. It went into the backstage area, and I saw it go through the curtains onto the front stage. I followed it. And there was a woman floating up above the seats in this long dress, dancing. Her feet were about the level of the chairs, and she was just dancing slowly, twirling around…"

Chain of Lakes

Bowron Lakes, named after John Bowron, the Gold Commissioner in Barkerville in the 1870s, is a rectangular canoe circuit in the Cariboo Mountains that circumnavigates through lakes, rivers, and short portages (paths on which the canoes have to be carried on one's head or dragged before the Parks supplied wheels that could be attached to the canoes). It became a Class A Provincial Park in 1961 and by the end of the decade, offered a number of seasonal bush jobs to residents of Wells and area.

MIKE HALL first came to the Wells–Barkerville area in 1968—the year after the mine shut down, and before any hippies had moved to town—to vacation at Bowron Lakes Park with his parents and younger sister. He was seventeen years old. Their family was planning to paddle the whole circuit, but car trouble left them time to paddle only the west side of the lake chain. After finishing the canoe trip, they camped for a night below where the Bowron Lakes Nature House was later built. (There were no campgrounds yet.) Having enjoyed his experience at Bowron, Mike decided he wanted to work there. He walked over to Park Supervisor Davey Davidson's trailer. "He told me I was in luck, as he'd just fired someone,"

Aerial view, looking toward Isaac Lake over Indian Point Lake, Bowron Lakes Chain. Photo: Tom Adair.

Mike said. "So Dad gave me his boots and I started work." His parents left him there for the summer.

Mike recalled, in conversation with his wife Marguerite, that he did "whatever he was told to do: he shovelled, raked, and hammered, bucked and split timber, and helped to make trails and build the campsites and the Nature House (now the Registration Centre). At the end of the summer, he went back to high school, but returned in the summer of 1969. He had done yard work for his parents' neighbours in West Vancouver, and that was the sum total of his experience as a labourer and woodsman.

MARGUERITE HALL: As soon as his exams were over the following year, Mike headed back to Bowron. That year he worked on the chain. He learned how to use a chainsaw to fall trees and turn them into lumber and slabs needed for outhouse construction and trail work. Mike and the crew worked a ten-day shift; they would go one way, all around the chain, stopping to fix or construct campsites and fix or construct outhouses and fall and haul firewood. They made sure each campsite had firewood. They had four days off, then went around the chain again, this time backwards, since the boats were now at the 'other end' of the lakes.

"Mike sometimes hitchhiked home to Vancouver on his four days off. Loggers would take him into Quesnel, where he would get on the highway and hitch a ride, often making it home early on his first official day off. Sometimes he'd be sitting in the Jack at 11:00, in Quesnel by 12:30, stuck in front of the railway until 9:00 a.m., in Vancouver by 9:00 p.m. He usually took the bus back to Quesnel. On other days off he sometimes hiked the local mountains; he climbed Indianpoint Mountain a couple of times. He explored the caves near the upper Bowron River, and in the fall he watched the grizzlies fish from the relative safety of platforms along the river.

Aerial view of Indian Point Lake, Bowron Lakes Chain. Photo: Tom Adair.

"For the first summer and the second, at least, Mike said the crew, when in camp, lived in wood-framed canvas tents in what is now the old parking lot, or the overflow parking lot. That is where the headquarters and Davey's trailer were located and where Davey cooked meals for the crew when they were in camp.

"When out on the chain, the crew stayed in old, small cabins on Indianpoint Lake, Moxley Creek (Isaac Lake), McLeary Lake, Rum Lake, Pat's Point, and the River Cabin. These were either old trappers' cabins or old cabins that had been used by guides during the days when Frank Kibbee [later the first game warden at Bowron Lake] guided hunting trips. They fought a never-ending battle with mice: they set traps—dozens of them—then

Bowron Youth Crew Camp, 1976. Photo: Tom Adair.

had barely any sleep at night as the traps were triggered, one after the other, all night long; they put buckets over food, and they made sure the water bucket was covered or there would be floaters in the morning! Spring cleanup was gruesome, especially the spring after a fall when someone left a lot of food in the cabin and the mice population exploded, then there was nothing left to eat and…The only time mice problems abated somewhat was when a weasel would move into the neighbourhood for a while.

"The crew did it all. At first, all fuel for the boats had to be carried out to Bowron from town. Mike remembers many trips with a full ten-gallon gas can strapped to his 'Trapper Nelson' [a wood-frame canvas backpack], and a chainsaw in one hand and other supplies in the other, setting off down the portage trails. The trails themselves were rough compared to today's trails, with shin-deep mud in places that could not be avoided. They cut and delivered all the firewood. Mike remembers someone sinking a riverboat because he'd overloaded it with firewood.

"Mike learned all his skills on the job. They 'made' all the lumber for the outhouses. All they carried in to Bowron were the nails and spikes to put them together. At Pat's Point they made all the shakes for the outhouses on the chain, as there is cedar there.

"Mike remembers one tough trip. They had a small boat, which they were supposed to get up to McLeary Lake or the southern part of Isaac Lake. Mike's job was to tow the small boat with a larger river boat from Rum Lake, through Sandy Lake and the lower Cariboo River, up Lanezi, up the Cariboo River, and into McLeary Lake. He started off quite early in the morning by himself—eighteen or nineteen years old. Partway up the river, approaching McLeary Lake, the engine died on the larger boat. Mike had to turn around in the river, still towing the small boat, and make his way downstream without a motor. He remembers bouncing off the banks all the way down, despite having oars, and then rowing all the way back to Bowron Lake. There was no radio contact then, and he was on his own. He got back to headquarters well after midnight.

"Other memories include the crews who were brought in to construct corduroy on the trails. He remembers the fellow from Victoria who came in with his tape measure and mapped out where the roads and campsites would go in the hay meadow, and that became the campsite. Mike remembers planting many of the trees. That campsite has turned into a beautiful spot that not a lot of people know about now.

"The park itself was not widely known [in the 1970s], not like it is today, but it did have a steady stream of visitors, some who knew what they were doing, and some who did not. It was a long trip to get to the park, along an active logging road that was just a single lane in some spots, and a mostly gravel and much windier road from Quesnel. Mike doesn't remember too many rescues. The folks who came out there knew the risks and knew they had to look after themselves. He remembers the story of one camper who had inadvertently been mauled by a bear. He was using his pack as a pillow and the bear tried to snag it through the tent walls, but got the fellow's scalp instead.

"Mike had fun, but he worked hard at Bowron. He learned to drive there, taught by Davey Davidson in his '68 Oldsmobile. He took home about $197 a month. Mike fished a lot, and came to rely on fish for fresh meat while out on the chain. They ate mostly canned goods. Any fresh food they took out on their ten-day shifts was eaten early in the shift. Then it was butter from a can, canned corned beef, and canned veggies. One year, a young man from Quesnel was in the crew. (Mike is still incredulous about this, 'He was a boy from the Cariboo, for fuck's sake!') When it was his turn to cook breakfast—Red River Cereal, which Mike will not touch to this day—the young man managed to botch the meal by building the fire in the oven of the cookstove, not the firebox.

"He loved the beauty of the park. He still feels lucky to have been able to work in that incredible wilderness. He saw scenes and animals that most people would never dream of seeing. He saw every kind of animal he could in the park, and his favourite times of year were the spring and the fall when few tourists were about. He remembers with fondness helping Frank Cushman build his home on Indian Lake Road.

"In 1972, Mike and Dave Lockyer were asked to go to Barkerville and work for the winter. 'It was tough,' Mike recalls, 'because most of the people we knew then weren't working. We'd be partying all night, and then have to go to work the next day, and everybody else was hungover and they didn't have to be anywhere, it didn't make any difference to them.'"

TOM ADAIR: "My job title when I worked out on the lake chain, which was generally May (when the ice came off) to September or October, was 'Park Ranger.' But that was my second year.

"When I first started in 1972, I worked with Nathan Kew between Kibbee and Indian-point Lakes building corduroy trail. Nick Mole felled trees and cut them in half and then into four-foot lengths, which Nathan and the son of the owner of Canyon Airways and I would manhandle out of the bush. We'd then fit and nail them onto stringers, trees that were cut down and come-a-longed to the trail and placed three feet apart as support. We had a crew of four: three randy guys and Nick, who had no teeth and ate boiled potatoes with butter every night because that's what he could chew. We worked five days on and had the weekends off, and didn't mix much with the rest of the crew out at Bowron. I headed into Quesnel most weekends, but started to spend time with Nathan out at Bowron after he invited me to his family cabin on our days off. It was the beginning of our forty-year-long friendship.

"It was hard work. The four of us stayed in a small cabin on Kibbee that had not been stayed in for many years when we started. Mice, mosquitoes, and an outhouse. Rustic. But a great experience. I didn't realize how lucky I was to have the experience at the time, but it shaped me.

"I went back to university [in Victoria] in the fall but quit early in the spring. (In reality, I just stopped going.) I came up again to Bowron and got a job on the lake chain with the south-side crew at Unna and Babcock Creek area to McCleary Lake. There were three of us. Kevin was the boss; he was a hippie-biker type who knew how to run a chainsaw and taught me how over the summer. We would cut down dead snags in the forest as close to the campsite as possible and, after cutting them into lengths, haul the firewood close enough to the campsite so the tourists could find it. But we needed to cut wood along the edges of the lakes in the bush and then haul that wood to the boat, which we would fill to brimming, with very little freeboard (hull out of the water) and deliver it to the campsites. A cord of wood would disappear in minutes when we dropped

Tom Adair at Bowron Lake. Photo: Sue Safyan.

it off on the beach at a busy campsite, which could have fifty to sixty people in it. And everyone liked having a fire—the bigger, the better. At that time, most canoeists cooked over the wood fires. You can't do that now; you have to bring your own stove. We were lucky we didn't kill ourselves. Cutting dead trees down in standing timber is one of the most dangerous falling manoeuvres you can attempt. I learned how to be a faller as a result and measure risk carefully.

"We also dug outhouse holes, as close as we could to an existing, usually over-filled, outhouse, and slid the outhouse over on skids and covered in the mess afterwards. Usually, we would have to put a new seat in at the same time, as the porcupines loved that salt and would chew the hell out of the seats. We would also clean the campsites, maintain the trails, put up signage, rescue upturned canoeists, and give campers shit for leaving a campfire going. On more than one occasion when I was able to identify a camper that had left a fire still smoking, I would get in the powerboat and chase them down the lake and make them come back and put it out themselves. Amazing what a couple of 'Park Board' patches on the semi-military style shirts they issued us could do! We were a pretty rank group, working ten days on and four days off."

Trees for the Forest

The Cariboo's forest industry was thriving in the 1970s when logging of the Bowron clear-cut began, a 500-square kilometre eyesore, so enormous it is apparently visible from space. Forestry work could be steady and almost year-round (falling, driving truck) or seasonal. The loggers and Old Wells locals did most of the full-time work, and the newcomers picked up the seasonal jobs.

MIKE HEENAN recalls that a number of his years in Wells "were dotted with gigs for Forestry: tree planting, picking cones, slash burning, spacing, and firefighting:

"In the fall of 1977, John [Campbell] and I worked for Bruce Fraser and Brian McNaughton on a pre-commercial tree thinning project that Forestry concocted. Bruce and Brian worked for the provincial Ministry of Forests and were based out of Wells. Bruce and Brian took up residence about May of 1977. There had been a town-wide recruitment drive the previous spring by Forestry to get everyone on UIC planting trees. I think Bruce and Brian ingratiated themselves in Wells due to their fondness for beer and playing pool. They were two single guys, probably twenty-five or twenty-six, stuck in this small town in the middle of nowhere. They became friends with everyone that year in no small part because they were able to get lots of small projects going that employed the locals. The loggers liked them as well; I assume they didn't cramp their logging operations very much. With not a lick of experience, Brian and Bruce took John [Campbell] and I out into the bush with government-issued chainsaws and showed us how to fall a tree. It was apparently a new idea from Forestry that stands of trees, about ten years prior to harvest, could be thinned out and thus give them ten years of faster growth before they were harvested. This plan resulted in John and I falling fairly large trees, and it was a miracle that we managed to come out of it unscathed. I think we worked for about a month, mid-September to mid-October…"

TOM ADAIR: "The crummy, a passenger van, would pick us up in the mornings and drive us out to the landing, the cleared area in the forest where the trees were dragged, cut to length, their branches removed, stacked up into piles, and eventually loaded, now 'logs,' onto the trucks. These were active logging roads, and we didn't have radios [to be in communication with the logging trucks], of course, because we were just fallers, just sacrificial lambs to the forest company, a dime a dozen. Pay 'em lots of money; they kill themselves. So one morning, *ka-wham*! the van's hood flies up as we're driving along the logging road. We slow down, find a little bit of a pull-off to the side of the road. The crummy driver gets out, bangs the hood down, gets back in the truck, and just as we get going, these logging trucks come the other way. That was close.

"After cone-picking, we went out with chainsaws and cleaned up the ditches. We did that for a couple weeks. Some of those trees would be loaded with cones. I remember one especially. The forester guy had his four-by-four there and ended up hooking a cable onto it, because it was that rich, and they pulled it onto the road; it had just bags of cones.

"Of course, everyone's making money, everyone's drinking like crazy, and doing whatever. One night, I can't even remember where I ended up staying—I shouldn't have been where I was—and they needed me because I had the chainsaw. They ended up finding me and getting me out of bed. This van with eight people shows up to get me—you can forget about trying to hide!"

Like a Fish Needs a Bicycle

Some young hippie women spent a good part of their early years in Wells in traditional gender roles—baking bread in their wood stoves, sewing clothes for themselves and their families, knitting buffalo-wool caps and sweaters. And simulating the 1870s in Barkerville meant that, at work, men performed most of the traditional 'men's work,' (carpentry, blacksmithing, portraying authority figures such as Judge Begbie) while most women portrayed schoolteachers, hurdy-gurdy girls, and seamstresses—but there were exceptions. There were some opportunities for women to break out of old stereotypes with jobs in the forestry and mining industries. Work for the highways seemed to be gender-segregated; men drove the trucks and women flagged or, as described below, worked in the weigh stations.

Chinking a log cabin. On ladder, Barb Sargent; on ground either Marguerite Hall or Nancy Premischook. BP593 © Barkerville Historic Town Archives.

Women who'd learned how to do their own plumbing, electrical, and carpentry work could use those skills not only to maintain their independence ("a woman needs a man like a fish needs a bicycle," as the saying went) but to hire themselves out to local residents and businesses in Wells.

JUDY CAMPBELL: "After Barkerville closed down on Labour Day, the next chunk of work mainly consisted of fall forestry silviculture work, slash burning being the most common. Weldwood often hired a Wells-based crew, and I think in the early days West Fraser did as well. Rosie [Rose Danby] was the person I knew that had an in with Ross [Olsen], the crew boss from Weldwood. Ross liked to hire female crews because they were most productive. We would meet at a marshalling area in the early morning (seven-ish), typically somewhere like the Northwoods [Inn, a trucker's café on the highway in South Wells] to

Naturalist Marguerite Hall at Bowron Lake Nature house, demonstrating the physics of insect wings. Photo: Marguerite Hall.

be transported to the area where we would work. Ross or another forester would have figured out where we were going to burn by looking at the weather, wind, updrafts, etc. They would tell us the overall plan. If we were burning windrows, we would all start together on the upwind side of a clearcut, working in pairs, one on each side of a windrow, and move along parallel to each other, no one pair getting too far ahead of any other, in order not to smoke anyone out. Unless you were Tony, who was such a pyromaniac he would leap over piles, lighting everything in sight. One time, when working a linear pattern like this, the wind changed and a group of us was cut off from our route to safety. It was very easy to become disoriented and move towards the fire instead of away. We ended up having to crawl on our bellies to avoid smoke inhalation across a marsh to get to safe ground.

"If it was a broadcast burn, we would work in a circular pattern starting at the centre and working out. This produced a huge column of heat and smoke that created its own convection, sucking things into its vortex. One day we created such a firestorm we had to hold on to our hard hats to keep them on our heads while we made a run for it. At least with that type of burn it was easy to tell what direction to run.

"A drip torch was a tank that was filled with some sort of diesel or jet fuel, that 'dripped' blobs of flame (see photo, p. 184). There were versions you wore on your back and some that were hand-held. You aimed for the 'red dead' material (dried needles) in the brush piles, as they ignited easily. You walked/ climbed/ scurried over the piles of brush, some up to ten feet high, lighting up as you went. When conditions were dry, you needed to move quite fast to keep ahead of the blaze. I often wondered what would happen if you fell into a pile and couldn't get out!

"One time we were working some steep ground out on the Indian Lake Road, past Cushmans'. We were working with a helicopter pilot who was dropping what was essentially napalm from the air to get things going and then we were going in to clean up any missed areas. It was our female crew, the usual band of suspects—Rose, Sharon, me. The pilot had run out of fuel, so he was grounded and busy getting the next batch ready. For some reason, he felt it was important to stir the vat of fuel, and because he had the undivided attention of the female crew, he stirred it with his bare hand. 'Has he never heard of Agent Orange?' we wondered to ourselves. A few moments later, he produced a lovely Briar pipe, probably old and English, and flourished it while explaining to his captive audience the finer points of flying a helicopter so close to the mountainside. As he took out his lighter, he mistook our wide-eyed looks of horror as rapt attention, but soon forgot all about us as his hand and beautiful pipe exploded in flames.

"Other than hard hats there was no safety gear, not even steel-toed boots. And I think the first couple of years, we didn't even wear hard hats. At the end of the day, you were covered in soot, and your clothes had lots of scorched edges. We usually did two to four separate burns a day, so there was time in between to have lunch and a pee break.

"Cone picking was another variety of fall work, but didn't seem to happen as regularly as slash burning, which was a pretty regular fall event. We worked behind a 'feller buncher,' which is a huge pair of scissors that snips off pine trees and lays them down on their sides. We would come in and pick the cones off them before they were limbed and sent to the mill. The cones were sent to the nursery at Red Rock to be grown into little seedlings for tree planting.

"Tree planting was a fairly new concept in the '70s, and I didn't really get into it, though Marion and Mike DeWeese, Suzanne, [and others] did. Sharon did quite a bit of cooking for tree-planting camps."

SHARON BROWN: "The drip torch parade was to keep Uncle Ross (Ross Olsen of West Fraser, our slash-burning boss) on his toes. He never knew what we would come up with. We had the only mostly women slash-burning crew in the Cariboo, and we did the best job. Once, we won a trophy made by Gordie Gunson of West Fraser.

"That was my favourite job around Wells, and I did it for nine seasons. The things that stand out are the kindness of Ross (he was the head Mormon for northern BC and we never heard him swear, even when our lives were in danger), the amount of time it took to get to the bush, thereby delaying the work day, and us trying to get Ross to eat mountain mix or gorp [raisins and peanuts mixed with M&Ms]. His favourite expression was 'pot lickin'.'

"One day we were all near Indian Lake. Mike Heenan was on the crew. A truck was stuck in a big mud hole, and because Mike was the only guy, Ross instructed him to go get the truck out of the mud hole. Judy and Rose and I looked at each other, and it took a minute, but we all said at the same time, 'But Mike doesn't have a licence!' It didn't take Ross long to figure out that us women were all very capable, and he treated us very well.

"Another bush job I had was pine cone picking with Harold as our crew chief. I worked alongside his wife, Margaret, and thought I was working as fast as her, but at the end of the day I had a bag and she had a bag and a half. Harold would often get drunk during the day, so I would then commandeer the truck keys to drive us all home."

JUDY CAMPBELL: "Rose and John Boutwell and I were walking uptown one day. Rose was wearing coveralls. I kind of noticed she'd been gaining a little bit of weight, but it didn't really twig on me. But John says to Rose, 'So, Rose, you got a bun in the oven?' and Rose says, 'Yeah, but you can't tell anyone.'"

ROSE DANBY: "It was a secret from the whole town. I had to keep it quiet because I wanted to work slash burning that fall, and Ross wouldn't have hired me if he knew I was pregnant, right? So I was out there when I was three, four months pregnant, slash burning. Ross came back to town about two months after I'd had Sarah May. I was carrying this little baby, and he stops, rolls down the window, and he goes, 'That is not your baby.'

"I said, 'Actually, she is.'

"Now his jaw is on the floor. 'You were pregnant when you were working for me?!'

"'Ross,' I said, 'I couldn't tell you or you wouldn't have hired me!'"

BEV DANBY: "I worked [falling] with Brad Davies. I wasn't sure how good I was at that point, but after working with him, he said to me, 'You know, I've hired a lot of guys to work with me on slashing contracts, but you've worked out to be one of the better fallers.' He knew I wasn't stupid. If I got a tree that was a snag and gave me trouble, I would just stop. I wouldn't even mess with it. I'd say [whistles], Brad! He'd come over and take care of it. He was happy that I didn't take stupid risks. He had some guys who'd get stuck and be, 'Yeah, I'm tough!' Me, I knew when to say no, I'm not sure."

Until the late 1980s, the Highways Department was based in Wells and was a department of the provincial government. Highways employed half a dozen people year round to repair or pave the roads, both gravel and asphalt, between Bowron Lakes and Wells and between Wells and partway to Quesnel, to keep them ploughed and sprinkled with gravel or salt in the winter, to trim the bush in the ditches and right-of-ways along the side of the highway and, in the summer and fall, hired seasonal workers to direct traffic (i.e., flag), dig and fill in holes, and operate the truck scales.

SUZANNE BESSETTE: "One summer, Tom and Sally Wilson were working [for a private company that did paving], and they told me the company was looking for a scale girl and I should apply for the job. I went out and got the job. I was working for the company on the scales, and Peggy Manthey was working for Highways.

"It was an actual scale, nothing was electronic or digital. You had these big Highways trucks called belly dumps. I had to identify the truck before it came into the gravel pit. Each truck had a different weight, and I had to set the front axle weight on the scale before it came in. They were being paid by the load. I had to pay attention. They told me that if I wasn't fast enough, the drivers would get pissed off and dump their load on the scale and just shut the whole operation down. So I was wound up. I'd hear their jake brakes, *brrrrr*, and I'd fly out, and set the scale.

"But in between trucks, there was absolutely nothing to do. Peggy Manthey and I sat in this little shack. Sharon Brown [with whom Suzanne shared a house] made my lunch every day. This was the beginning of her food thing. She would go, 'Suzanne, in your lunch today I have some lovely Friulano cheese that I bought at the Italian delicatessen in Quesnel, and I'm going to put this with this, and try this'— and I would have this huge bag of food. That kept me awake throughout the day. Then I would just, oh, try to remember every man I'd slept with, count them and put them in order, just to keep from falling asleep!

"And then it got hot, so there were rumours going around that they weren't going to be able to pave, and we might have a day off. We were working straight through. So I decided that would be a good night to get really drunk. I went to Stromville. I don't know why Rob [Danby, her boyfriend] wasn't there, but I got really, really drunk. I was drinking Yalumba—there was a liquor store in town with this wonderful man who would tell us about all the different wines. So we were drinking Yalumba, which was kind of a sweet white wine, with apricot brandy. When I tried to walk back home, I was so drunk, I had to tell my feet, 'left, right, left, right!' This is how I remember it, but Rob might remember it differently. I think he stopped and picked me up and took me back to his place. I was

Suzanne Bessette (L) and Sharon Brown, c. 1975. Photo: Sharon Brown.

terrible; I was belligerent, and he was trying to help me get my clothes off—it was really bad! Then I settled down, and I thought, okay, whatever; I'll just sleep this off, and I have a day off tomorrow because we're not paving. But at five o'clock in the morning, there's a knock on the door, and Rob gets up. It's the Manthey girl, and she says they're looking for me—and they knew how to find me, right? As soon as I sat up, that Yalumba and the apricot brandy was just right here [taps throat]. But I went out to sit in the gravel pit all day—and there was no port-a-potty or anything like that. If you had to go to the bathroom, you had to run up the hill. I was so hungover and I had a pounding headache. I was at the scale, setting the thing, when I thought, oh my god, I'm going to get sick! I had to run up the hill, pulling on roots and things to get up there, and I laid on the ground and threw up.

"While I was up there, a truck came through. Now I'd missed a truck, and I was in trouble. The foreman came by to see what had happened. I said, 'I can't do it, I'm too sick.' He was so mad! He drove me back into town. Nobody was at our house, and I got into bed, which was just a platform with a mattress that had been built on the porch. I was lying there with my head throbbing, and I thought, *I gotta get up*. I got up and walked to the Good Eats. Bud was there. He laughed at me when I walked in the door, and I said 'Oh Bud, I'm so hungover!' He goes, 'Ehhhh, I'll fix you up! You know what's good for a hangover? Lotta pepper!' He gave me some soup with a lot of pepper in it. I sat there and had my soup. My head was pounding, and Bud was just killing himself laughing. That was one of the worst hangovers I've ever had in my whole life!"

SHARON BROWN: "When I was nineteen I got a job soil-sampling with a sub-contractor to Rio Tinto [a multinational mining company that did exploration work]. I worked with six guys out the Cariboo–Hudson Road, and we lived in a tiny camp out there with a Coleman stove in the cook shack. We took turns cooking. I was hired by the second-in-command (who I had been sleeping with), and the first day on the job I overheard them all saying that maybe Sharon should sleep with everyone! In those days there was little or no respect for women doing what was considered man's work.

"The head geologist did not believe women should be in the bush, so he was always mean to me. We all took turns in pairs, and worked with a different person every day. When I worked with that geologist, he went like hell to lose me, but I always managed to keep up. Sometimes I would look down the slope we were about to sample and wondered if I had ever skied anything that steep!"

BEV DANBY: "I worked in the Jack O' Clubs hotel. I did everything—cleaning out the sewer lines, fixing the plumbing, cleaning rooms. I served beer in the bar, I cooked in the restaurant for Virginia [who ran the café]. One morning, in fact, I started out waitressing in the café, but when Virginia didn't get back [from her trip to Quesnel to buy supplies], all of a sudden I was the cook for lunch!

"I was short of money one day, and I said to Ron [Barkwell, the proprietor], 'I haven't done any work on the faucets in a long time, they're probably all dripping. I should go up and check 'em and change what needs changing. How about you pay me forty bucks for the whole works?' 'Fine,' he says. Bloody took me two hours to check all the taps. I replaced all the washers at twenty bits each. But I had forty bucks to spend, and could last another good week."

Ace Consortium

The hippies also learned that a set of tools or a set of skills were theirs to loan, barter, or just plain give. They excavated each others' foundations, nailed on roofs, and fixed leaky plumbing—in return for a case of beer, drywalling, a little cash, or for free, simply because there was time enough and generous spirit enough to help out. With a little help from their friends—including some of the more accepting Old Wells people—it was quite possible to get by without a house and garage full of the newest trucks and tools. Whether it was hippie-communal philosophy or simply survival skills in a small, isolated, northern town with a harsh climate, people looked after one another in a way that was not practised, maybe not even practicable, in the big cities from which they'd come.

Ace Consortium was an informal and occasional group of locals (including Mike Hall, Mike Heenan, Tom Adair, and Dave Lockyer) who did carpentry and fix-it jobs in town sometimes for money and more often for traded favours. Ace sometimes simply "ran on cold bottled beer and various other substances." The pouring of the foundation for a large, brand new log house—thirteen yards of hand-poured concrete—was one of Ace's biggest contracts. The house owner had enough presence of mind not to pull out the "good drugs" (hashish) until later in the pour. In the first six hours, not a single wheelbarrow load of material was dumped wrong. After he pulled out the hash—"Would you like something to eat?" he asked his hard-working helpers—the next two wheelbarrows were "dumped before they left the mixer." But when they finally finished the foundation, the house owner took them all to Bud's Good Eats Café for massive steak dinners.

The Pogey Ski Team

After working for just eight weeks of the year, it was possible, in the early 1970s, to collect unemployment insurance, known as UIC or pogey ("No, No, No, Yes, No").

BEV DANBY: "We moved to Wells just because it was possible to buy a house there. We didn't even wonder if there'd be work. The first year we lived on unemployment insurance. That was it."

JUDY CAMPBELL: "Winter time was generally thought of as 'kick-back time' with the UI ski team in full swing. There really wasn't any work in Wells in the winter, so this wasn't necessarily voluntary. If you wanted to work, you needed to leave town."

MIKE HEENAN: "It was a new concept that when you did have money, you spread it around—everyone did then. When a UIC cheque came, it was at least one or two rounds for the house. In Mad John's case, it was pizza ordered from Quesnel via taxi. As I remember, his unemployment insurance claim had been held up for some reason or another, and when it was finally cleared, he got something like fourteen cheques all at once!"

Rose Danby likes to tell the story of how she had long coveted the recipe for a friend's chocolate peanut butter balls, but the friend jealously guarded the recipe as her secret. When this friend went to Mexico for several weeks while collecting pogey, Rose agreed to fill in her unemployment insurance cards and mail them in—if the friend gave up her recipe. With much reluctance, cursing, and swearing, she gave it to Rose, who made the treats and gave them away, along with the recipe, to all her friends in town that Christmas.

Winter Works

In November 1971, Canada Manpower introduced the Local Initiatives Program (LIP), which provided government-subsidized work for unemployed seasonal workers and those on welfare, specifically during the winter months. The Winter Works projects were meant to enhance their local communities; daycare centres were set up, heritage buildings were restored (such as the Sunset Theatre in Wells), performance arts companies were started, and bridges were built. In its first year, $100 million went toward such worthwhile projects in towns all over the country. LIP lasted until 1977. While indisputably laudable in its intent, the "make work" nature of some of the projects was perhaps responsible for the disdain felt by both those receiving Winter Works job-creation funding and those ostensibly benefiting from these "community betterment" projects.

As Zubin Gillespie recalls, in the mid-1970s in Wells, for example, "Winter Works built this amazing wharf at the Jack of Clubs Lake, at the end of the lake closest to town. The wharf cost $50,000 and the outhouses were, like, $6,000 each, which, in today's value, is about $30,000 for an outhouse. Sure enough, the wharf came off its moorings and floated straight to my house, and we tied it up. It was fantastic!"

MIKE HEENAN: "I took a two-week holiday to Hawaii and returned to Wells some time in the winter, either in November or December, and after filing for UIC, started working with John [Campbell] on the Winter Works program.

"Daylyn was the bookkeeper for the program, and our office was in the downstairs of the Community Hall where one of our duties was to keep the fire stoked so the hall was warm all winter. Bud Williams, John, and I installed a new furnace in the Sunset Theatre that winter, and I spent many days under the floor putting in the ductwork for the furnace. We shovelled out the fire hydrants and chopped ice off the eves of some of the houses on the Crescent for the first part of the grant and then cut a trail around Wendle Lake [a local swimming hole located on the Bowron Lake Road]. I remember many days driving out there with John and his dog, Jessie, when it was frigid. Because there was so much snow, we ended up cutting a lot of branches that were two or three feet higher than they needed to be for the trail. At one point, John and I decided to ski home from Wendle using a map and compass. It was a tough slog; we walked out the One-Mile Road, and Daylyn had to come and pick us up."

Not Just a Set of Wheels

All roads lead to Wells, but only one road goes through town—and road travel meant cars. Funky, inexpensive, and demanding old cars had to be kept running so their owners could get to work in Barkerville or go "to town" (Quesnel) to shop for food, building supplies, gumboots and, of course, car parts.

TOM ADAIR: "I remember that for weeks on end in the winter, the whole entertainment for the day was to go visit everybody and help whichever one car out of the fleet of junkers we all had that would start. The next day it would be a different car that was successfully started. All day was spent getting the car going so we could get up to the bar for the night. And then drive home, of course. Drinking and driving was the norm."

FRANK FITTON: "Alphonso de Credenza was my first car, a 1960 Chevy with terminal rust. I remember driving down Hastings Street in Vancouver with several friends in the back seat. They started fighting (in a friendly manner—this was the 1970s). The piece of plywood that I had put over the rust holes in the back floor got knocked aside and beer bottles started falling out, like a ship laying mines! Shortly after that, the car and I and several pairs of skis headed to Wells. My friend Yuri Pelech, who is no longer with us, named the car Alphonso, then he amended it to Alphonso de Credenza, Italian Sports Car. He felt that someone such as me should be driving only a

Fixing Alan McMaster's truck, view toward Twin Sisters from the front yard couch (behind Paula McGladry). Photo: Louise Futcher.

prestigious car! We ranted a lot in those days about many subjects! I don't know how long the car lasted after Rob Danby bought it from me (and it was a definite it—not he or she!), but my relationship with it ended when Alphonso blew a tire and launched me into Devil's Canyon in the middle of winter. It took two tow trucks two hours to pull it back on the road and cost me twenty bucks. In the week that it rested in Devil's Canyon, some Wells cowboy smashed the back window with a beer bottle."

SUZANNE BESSETTE: "Rob had this Chev that he called Alphonso. I'll never forget the first time he took me out the Bowron Lake Road, because he gave me a kerchief to put over my face. The car was all rusted out and he had just pieces of plywood in the back, and so when you'd go down the road all the dust would [waves hands in front of face] so we both had to wear bandanas."

ROB DANBY: "I took a photo on the Monday of a long weekend, I believe it was the Canada Day weekend, and it was the day before Pooley Street was paved in 1972. I was still living in Vancouver, and a group of us drove to Wells for the weekend in Rose's Pontiac.

"I also had a 1952 Pontiac (mine was blue), but for some reason I had Rose's car. I was probably doing work on it. Those that travelled with me were [my sister] Heather, her friend Monica, [my sister] Kathy, and Prudence and Mary Jane. On the way to Wells, the hood flew up at highway speed and smashed the windshield. I managed to get my head out the window and get things under control. Then we had to get up and jump onto it, to try and flatten out the hood. We had limited success but managed to get it good enough to tie it down with a whole bunch of rope. Next we had to deal with the now severely cracked windshield, which I managed to tape up with some red (of all colours) electrical tape that I happened to have. That kept the cracked and saggy windshield together for the rest of the trip. I think you can see the red tape in the photo if you look closely…

"On the return trip, Mary Jane was driving and speeding through Clinton and we got pulled over. The cop asked for the papers. He went back to the first car he'd pulled over, and Mary Jane, who didn't have a driver's licence, woke up Prudence, who was napping beside her. Right under the cop's nose, they switched places and Prudence popped up in the driver's seat just in time to get a speeding ticket for while she was sleeping! She was none too happy when she realized what had happened…

"In my first year living in Wells, 1973, I had my blue Pontiac. There were many old beaters, and people shared cars and licence plates—that was quite common—but Rose and I had one of the cleverest, an almost-as-good-as-legal plan. These were the days before ICBC, so you had two separate documents, vehicle registration and a 'pink slip' from your private insurance company. As we both had 1952 Pontiacs, we thought, why not put both of them in Rose's name and just get a policy for one car and split the cost? The only discrepancies were a couple of details like colour of vehicle and a few digits on the serial number. The insurance company gave out a hand-written pink slip when you paid and then sent another typed one in the mail, giving us the necessary two slips.

"One summer evening, I was in a hurry to get to Hong's General Store before it closed. I drove uptown and parked right on the corner between the store and the Good Eats, which was alive and well at the time and filled with people having their dinners. I parked by the store facing downhill on the wrong side of the road and jumped out of the car. Being

Gaylord and Rosie in the Caddie on Pooley Street. Photo: Rob Danby.

a safety-minded guy, I threw my parking brake in place as I ran towards the store to get in the door in time. My parking brake was a large block of wood. In my haste, I didn't place it quite snug against the wheel, and the car, although in gear, was sitting on a fairly steep grade. As I ran to the corner, I looked back and saw the car move. It had just enough momentum to hop over the block and start chugging in slow motion (because it was in gear) toward the front of this fancy camper van parked properly facing uphill. I ran to try

Shelley Schwartz and Dave Austin (in car), 1977. Photo: Judy Campbell.

and catch up to the car, flung open the door, dove in, and just as my foot hit the brake the car crashed into the camper. All of this was being watched by the patrons of the Good Eats, including the camper owner—as luck would have it, a vacationing RCMP officer. Needless to say, our local constable, Don Gillespie, was quickly on scene. He had a look at my car, walked around to the driver's side, reached in, pulled on the parking brake, and it came off in his hand. His only words were, 'See me in my office,' as he walked away with my licence in hand. The few minor details [of colour and serial number discrepancy] on the paperwork went unnoticed, and I walked away with a ticket for no parking brake.

"Peter van Deursen had a 1951 Chevy parked...in the Stromville parking lot. He made a deal to trade [it], and I agreed to tow it to Quesnel if he got the tow bar. It was too hard to get the cars lined up in the parking lot to hook up the tow bar, so we decided to tow Peter's car up onto the highway using just a cable and then have the two cars level for hooking up the tow bar, which would be much easier. It seemed like a good idea, but when the car with no motor (which was therefore much lighter and had no steering) came over the hump at the top of the driveway, it shot toward me at quite a speed! I thought, if I pull my car, the blue '52 Pontiac, across the road, the cable will just tighten up and the car will stop. When the motorless car got to the end of its rope, the front wheels (with the steering disconnected) worked just like a shopping cart and spun right around when the cable tightened up. The driverless car came flying at me twice as fast. Still not figuring out what was happening, I tried my cable-tightening trick again to avoid getting smacked by this angry car. Yes, it did it again, this time coming at me four times as fast. I tried my trick once more just to be sure it wouldn't work, and this time it was going so fast that the cable broke and the driverless car flew over the bank heading straight for the Stromville house. The gods intervened and the car missed the house by inches before coming to rest beside the house.

"Okay, it looked like we needed a tow truck. Esso Dave's tow truck just happens to drive by with, I'm pretty sure, Frank Everton at the wheel. He agrees to pull the car out, and just as he is crossways on the road, with the car halfway up the bank, along comes a loaded gravel truck one way and a loaded logging truck the other way with barely half a lane to get by. After lots of screeching and squealing of tires, everybody manages to get stopped, and when the dust clears, there's the cop! He caught one of the cars with the wrong licence plates and gave it a ticket, but my '52 Pontiac, with the slight inaccuracies in the paperwork, snuck through again!"

TOM ADAIR: "Zubin [who is well over six feet tall] had this Volkswagen bug, which he'd camperized so completely he could lie down full-length in it."

ZUBIN GILLESPIE: "I bought my first Volkswagen off Guido Manthey. It was a 1956 Volkswagen, and it was my first car. When I bought it off Guido, he had every purchase that he'd ever bought for the car entered into a book that came with it. The day that I bought it was the day it started going downhill. Every day, I'd be working on that Volkswagen outside of my house in sixty below!"

BEV DANBY: "The first vehicle I drove to Wells was my old '52 Fargo panel van. That was a pretty good vehicle. I bought that down at the coast, before I left. I spent the winter getting all kinds of work done on it; I had the engine rebuilt, I had the exhaust system redone, I had the brakes all redone. And that turned out to be the party van of Wells that first summer. We'd find people that were into having a drink—a wee sip of wine!—and off we'd go, driving out in the boonies. We'd fill 'er up with people and booze and away we'd go! One time, bouncing down the Mickeyville road, we hit the frame and shorted out [the electrics], so we had a bit of a walk back to town that day. We found someone with another vehicle, got her boosted, and away we went again. It was my nifty bush vehicle, with big skookum tires. It was my hippie van. I was just happening with that thing! I had it for a couple of years."

ROB DANBY: "Andy Stitnick had a car called Brutus—an old 1960s Valiant. It would never start; it didn't start with the key and there was something wrong with the solenoid, but you could short it out under the hood with a screwdriver to start it, or it would start if it was in drive. It had this goofy pushbutton automatic set-up. One day in the middle of winter we were stopped on the highway, and Andy sticks his head under the hood and accidentally puts it in drive. It goes, *spgh, spgh*, and starts up and starts driving away by itself. Andy's standing there shouting 'Brutus, come back here!' He starts running down the highway, yelling 'Brutus!' Finally he catches up with Brutus and jumps in, and says, 'Brutus! Don't you ever do that again!'"

NATHAN KEW: "I had a black Valiant. It was always covered in dust; it hadn't been washed in, like, eight months. And somebody traced a big five-pointed star, like a sheriff's star, on the dust of the driver's door and wrote 'Stromville' across the top and 'Sheriff' underneath! I never washed the car after that. I thought—I can't wash this!"

Andy Stitnick with his Valiant, Brutus, on the Beaver Pass Road, October 28, 1973. Photo: Karin Ludditt.

Volunteering

Working in Wells also included volunteer work in the community. While the Town Fathers looked after the governance, maintenance, and basic well-being of the town, even essential services, such as the fire department and those that were non-essential but important, like the library, survived only because of volunteers. This was also true of numerous clubs (Rod and Reel, Curling, Snowmobile) and organizations (church and school groups, Guides and Scouts, and others).

When the hippies arrived in Wells, they saw the fire department as a "closed shop" for the good old boys of the town, but in time, younger men and women (including sons and daughters of Old Wells) joined the department. Practices were held every Wednesday night at 7:00 p.m., when the fire siren was sounded and could be heard all over town and all the way out to Stromville.

ROB DANBY: "When I joined the fire brigade, Trev Davies was the fire chief. He actually had been a professional full-time firefighter in North Vancouver many years before and then, for whatever reason, moved to Wells. There was no training whatsoever, but everyone relied heavily on Trev because he knew everything, right? So if Trev wasn't there, then we were in trouble. It was a pretty loosey-goosey situation, and nobody really knew much, and there was no real plan. There weren't too many [fire] calls, so you could afford to be complacent for long stretches of time without having to acknowledge that you didn't have a clue what you were doing. But the big turning point was when Trev died.

"It was the middle of the night. We headed up to Trev's house, two trucks and a bunch of guys, but not having any training or plan. Everything that could go wrong, just about, went wrong. The house was up a steep hill, the hydrant didn't work, and we drove both trucks nose-in. It was dark and there weren't any lights. We had no way to get out and didn't have water. It was a stage-three fire too, which means when it's oxygen-starved and ready to blow up—but we didn't know anything about that then. First it starts small; it's burning and it's using the oxygen in the room, so it's no problem, then it burns a little more and gets hotter and hotter. Eventually the fire uses up all the oxygen and the flames go out, and that's when it's super dangerous because it's superheated gases. It's oxygen-starved, and so with the first puff of air it explodes. If you open the door, you get a big fireball, so you have to recognize that situation and ventilate it and get the hot gases out first to be ready to go in, otherwise you lose the whole house. Well, we didn't know anything about that.

"The deputy chief grabs on to the hose—which is the wrong thing to do; the guy in charge isn't supposed to be on the front line, he's supposed to be standing back, sizing it up, directing everybody; well, he grabs the hose and runs to the door. We think there's probably somebody in there—and it's Trev's house—and he kicks in the front door, and of course the oxygen just goes *boom*! Roger Tierney and I ran around to the other end of the house with a ladder to try to get up to the bedroom to see if we could find anybody. The flames blew out of the door at the back too, so we ran around to the side, put the ladder up, and I started to climb up the ladder; when I was about four rungs up, all of a sudden the whole roof just went *kahboooshh*! A big fireball went up, flames shot right up the whole side of the house, and the window exploded. I jumped off the ladder and ran back to the front. Everybody's standing there; there's this huge fireball and we've got no water, nothing's working—things have gone totally wrong. Then we look up and see that the power lines to the house go right over the top of the driveway, right over both trucks that are nose-in, in the dark, with no backup lights, and the house is on fire, and the line's sparking, the live line, getting ready to drop down on these two trucks.

"So, yeah, Trev was inside, and, I mean, at least he was probably long dead from the smoke, long before we got there, even if we'd had a proper plan, but that was when I started to get involved with the fire brigade. I'd gotten pulled into the secretary-treasurer job and then, after that scenario, I thought, whoa, if we're going to do this, we better figure it out. And just at that time, the Justice Institute had started the Fire Academy. I took some really good courses at the Justice Institute. I thought, let's get these guys up here and show us what the hell to do. I mean, we didn't have a freakin' clue. So that was when I was fire chief. They sent up some guys, and we had our first real, live training and figured out exactly how it all worked, had a basic plan.

"Which didn't always work. Remember the Snowball days? There were various tournaments in different places. There was a Snowball tournament in 150 Mile House, and those out-of-town tournaments were really popular, everybody wanted to go, they were total fun. Well, I remember thinking it would be a good idea to have some firefighters stay behind, just in case. So I agreed to stay in town, and everyone else said 'See ya!' and off they went to have a really great weekend.

"I had a fire phone in my house. The system with the fire phones was that they all rang when the number was called, and we each had a button to activate the big siren if there was a fire. And so when it rang that weekend, I answered it, and sure enough, somebody was reporting a fire. It was Lucky Swede's place. I set off the siren and started running up my stairs. I can see flames and smoke shooting up from the tailings [the south side of Wells]. The lady across the road from me, Gay Carter, and I had a plan; if she was around and the fire alarm went off and I had the kids, she'd pick them up. So I got the kids ready really fast, and fortunately Gay was standing there waiting outside her door, and took the kids.

227

"I ran to the fire hall and thought, *oh my god, who's left in town*? When I get there, the siren's already quit, and there's nobody there, the door's closed still, so that means I'm first there. I get in the truck and roar down the street. I see Fred May; he knew there was nobody around, and he used to be in the fire brigade, so he came running from his house as I'm rounding the corner with the fire truck, still half-asleep, rubbing my eyes. I picked up somebody else along the way, too. We got there, and I saw Lucky standing outside his house—*phew!* So I gave the hose to somebody and I said, 'Hook this up to the hydrant.' I had to run the pump, and then I got on the hose—it was like a one-man band!

"Another good fire brigade story was the one where there were two chimney fires in one night. The first truck, the Seagrave, broke down. It was a 1953 open cab, and it had this V12 motor, dual everything, and there was nothing like it on the planet. It had a dual electrical system as a safety backup because it was an emergency vehicle, so it had two spark plugs for every cylinder—twelve cylinders, twenty-four spark plugs—so you can imagine this nightmare of wires, two of everything, two of this, two of that, all plugged back, except to the distributor; the one weak link in the chain was that it had a single drive from the distributor to power both these units, and that's what broke. And on the way to the fire, literally in an intersection, it died. I was in the other truck; it was a six-wheel drive, a 1941 ex-airforce foam truck, with a top speed of about twenty miles per hour, but it would go anywhere, and it worked. It wasn't very fast, but it was really simple; you just stuck in the clutch, pulled on this lever, turned on the hose, step on the gas! Everybody could figure it out.

"But there were two chimney fires that night, so we responded to the first one and everything was okay. Then, somebody came running over, saying, 'There's another fire down in the tailings!' So I drove the truck up the road past the curling club when, all of a sudden, it starts overheating. It was forty below zero, and the other truck had crapped out already. We're like a block and a half from Judy's, which is where the fire was. I stayed with the truck to try and figure out what to do, and it was just like something out of the Keystone

Cops: the firemen jump off the truck, grab fire extinguishers, grab the ladder, and start running down the road. We went up to the roof, grabbed handfuls of snow, and threw snow down the chimney; it was the simplest thing to do, and it put out the fire."

TOM ADAIR: "Once there was a Wednesday night fire practice just before a long weekend. We took the truck out of the fire hall, and the beam under the flooring broke. So suddenly we couldn't get the truck back into the hall; we had to fix this, right now. We had a work bee, and it was all rebuilt over the weekend. All these people just dropped whatever they were doing and came together to do all this building stuff. That was what was so neat about being in the fire department."

ISLAND MOUNTAIN SCHOOL OF ARTS

WELLS NEWS

A Vancouver woman wants to establish a "Cariboo School of the Summer School of Arts" in the community of Wells, about 60 miles east of Quesnel.

Mrs. Mildred Crammeten says she wants to lease Cariboo Gold Quartz apartments in Wells and is applying for a federal winter works program grant to realize the dream. Her idea is that the federal "Local Initiatives Program" would pay for the restoration of the property, the apartment furnishings, labour, materials and a one-year lease, while community colleges would pay for the art materials, equipment and instructors. Income would come from students' fees and winter rental of the apartments.

Quesnel town council has endorsed the proposal to give added weight to Mrs. Crammeten's application for the federal money.

Reprint courtesy of: *Cariboo Observer*, Wednesday, December 15, 1971

In 1977, the Island Mountain School of Arts was started in Wells by members of the Central Interior Arts Council, who wanted to see a "retreat" for artists in the Cariboo. In 1976, there was a meeting in the Community Hall, and the people of Wells were receptive to the idea of a summer arts school (another idea being considered for Wells at this time was a maximum security prison). The archives don't mention what became of Mrs. Crammeten of Vancouver, but notes that Brenda Smith was elected School's President, Nancy Lagana its Corresponding Secretary, Ken Scopic its Coordinator, and Sally Service its Treasurer. Three classes were offered the first summer: Advanced Acting, Advanced Painting, and Beginning Photography. A story about the school's second year, which drew students from beyond Wells, throughout the Cariboo, and even around the province, appeared in the *Quesnel Cariboo Observer*:

> **WELLS NEWS**
> Island Mountain School of Arts, 1978 is over, but it will remain in the memories of all involved as an unqualified success.
>
> For eight days, students numbering 115, from five years to 75 years, were guided through various artistic disciplines by nine eminently qualified instructors.
>
> While children studied painting, crafts, pottery and movement, their parents developed their own skills as painters—novice or experienced, as actors or musicians, or learned the finer points of photographic composition. The sense of family that is so important to Island Mountain continued after school hours as students participated in an assortment of activities—picnics, trips to Bowron Lake Park and Barkerville, a coffee house, movies at the Sunset Theatre, workshops, or just getting together with new friends. Wells offers a unique setting for a school such as Island Mountain—a chance to get away from everyday life and relax, while at the same time, providing so much inspiration for creativity.
>
> Many aspects of the Wells community have been permanently recorded on canvas or in photos this past week by students who found choosing only one subject so difficult.

The Open House on Saturday saw friends of Island Mountain travel to Wells to join local residents in viewing the efforts of the weeks' study. Children's painting and crafts were on display, as were the photographs, drawing and painting of the adults, and the audience was treated to royal entertainment by the Renaissance Musicians and by the Actors.

These festivities brought Island Mountain to a close for 1978, but plans are already in the works for next summer plans that will see more and different courses and that will bring old friends back to Wells and introduce new ones to Island Mountain School of Arts.

Reprint courtesy of: *Quesnel Cariboo Observer*, Wednesday, August 23, 1978

The Tomato House, 1977. Photo: Judy Campbell.

A VERY, VERY, VERY FINE HOUSE

AFTER THE MINE SHUT DOWN, THE SMALL WOODEN HOUSES OF THE MINERS and their families were left empty to decay—roofs to buckle under the weight of winter snow, paint to fade, curl, and chip off the now grey wooden siding. Car parts, old stoves, dented freezers, mining equipment, and big propane tanks rusted in front yards. By 1975, correspondence from the Cariboo Regional District (CRD) to the Improvement District of Wells clearly indicated concern about the "vandalized, dilapidated and apparently abandoned buildings" in town—some of them occupied by the hippies. The CRD considered these buildings "firetraps present[ing] a hazard to the residents of the Community" and some were scheduled for demolition "under s. 873 of the Municipal Act." In one such letter, buildings were identified by lot and block number and the "type of cleanup required" was listed, e.g.: "Burn building and clear"; "Remove car bodies"; "Dept. of Highways to knock down building, burn and clear"; "Remove rubbish"; "Burn when not occupied," etc.[1]

In abandoned or cheaply purchased or rented shacks, the hippies found threadbare overstuffed chairs and sofas on floors of "painted" linoleum and warm, red fir, old calendars (Bud's Taxi, 1964) pinned to scarred walls of donnacona painted pink or mint green, cracked and peeling wooden furniture, perhaps a logger's checked shirt hanging from a nail behind the door. A Stromville cabin was "decorated" with a gun above the doorway,

Friends helping put a new foundation under Judy's house, September 1977.
Photo: Judy Campbell.

a very dusty sprayed-gold sheet-metal crown, a poster of Scott, the King of Stromville, standing on the cabin's rooftop, a couple of Wild Bill Hickok posters, snowshoes hanging on the wall and, in the kitchen, a clock which had been, on some historic drunken occasion, snipped in the wire and left perpetually at 5:10 (happy hour). The houses were heated primarily with wood stoves (airtights), although some of the larger homes had oil furnaces. (The oil trucks would come to Wells once or twice a year to fill up the tanks.) The airtights were more practical than decorative, and as relative affluence spread amongst the newcomers, beautiful wood cookstoves and heating stoves became a sign of success as well as a means of comfort. The miners' houses had small kitchens, tiny or no indoor bathrooms (they had outhouses), small windows, and were without built-in closets. Much of the home restoration, initially, wasn't done to lovingly preserve the 1930s-style architectural details, but to make the homes more liveable—i.e., less cold, more spacious. They were given new foundations, the wiring and plumbing were updated, insulation was added against the winter weather, the donnacona was replaced with Gyproc, kitchens were enlarged and given new appliances, windows were enlarged and double-paned to let in more natural light without letting in more cold.

But at first, the rustic shacks were often simply decorated with macramé and leather, silver-veined Indian scarves and printed Indian bedspreads brought up from the coast. Big glass jars of flour, beans, nuts, herbs, and dried fruits sat on open shelves beside pottery (heavy, brown, handmade), potted plants (and pot plants, yes), the *Tassajara Bread Book* and *Laurel's Kitchen*. The hippies kept their record collections in stacked wooden crates, and you could be reasonably certain to find an acoustic guitar leaning up against the wall beside the record player in most homes. Without running water or electricity, taking care of domestic basics (heat, laundry, meals, housework) while also often looking after small chil-

Judy's $300 house begins to undergo renovations, September 1977. Photo: Judy Campbell.

dren demanded long hours and exceptional multi-tasking skills. The newcomers, born and bred in middle-class city homes, learned how to survive "ten months of deep winter, how to bake bread, chop wood, unfreeze the outhouse, escape cabin fires, sew leather, and roast beaver," recalls Jude Goodwin, who, with her partner, musician Duncan Bray, moved to Wells in the early 1970s from the west side of Vancouver and started a family with their baby named Sky. In their funky houses, the young hippies experienced minus forty- to fifty-degree winter storms and snow falling a foot deep, night after night, which had to be shovelled each morning in order to get to the outhouse.

The Seasons of Wells

In the Cariboo Mountains, at forty-thousand feet above sea level, there is no month of the year that can boast guaranteed frost-free days. The winter storms will put down altogether twenty-five feet of snow in this high-elevation valley. Snow begins to fall in October, and by Halloween there is a solid foot or more of it already on the ground. The sun's path and the height of the hills and mountains that surround the town mean that sunlight doesn't directly hit many houses—especially in south Wells—for more than a couple of hours a day: a northern winter day in the shadows of the hills can be dark...and gloomy. Spring is "breakup" season—referring to the breakup of the ice on Jack of Clubs Lake, the occasional shattering of sanity after a long winter's cabin fever, and the break-up of couples, in the midst of that temporary insanity, as they endured alternating and seemingly unending snow and rain throughout April, May and June, when even in Quesnel, one could see the more traditional harbingers of spring (flowers, birds, warm weather). In spring, the mud on the roads was deep enough to suck a gumboot off a foot. Spring was also known as mud-and-dogshit-season, for when the snow melted, what had been left in the yard over winter was revealed—and no hippie yard was complete without a dog or two. In summer, the mosquitoes, no-see-ums, and blackflies were unrelenting and ferocious (when it wasn't raining or hailing). Fall (a.k.a. "Indian Summer") brought mornings of deep blue skies, heavy hoarfrost, and the aromatic pleasures of "spruce juice" on newly cut firewood. In the fall, the swamp between Wells and Barkerville turned tawny; fall, though brief, could be heartbreakingly beautiful.

Living in the Bush

Some hippies chose an isolated existence outside of the townsite, living on traplines, mining claims, and other squats out in the bush without electricity or running water and only wood heat. The back-to-the-land dream was shaped by visions of Thoreau-like solitary self-sufficiency (now called "living off the grid"). Miles from Wells itself, the most rugged or reclusive newcomers appropriated abandoned shacks (most of these on played-out mining claims) or built their own houses in remote places.

Louise Futcher: "Peter and I and another couple from southwest Ontario moved into a log cabin several miles out of town, past the [Jack of Clubs] Lake on an old gold mining creek. It had obviously been deserted for years. We made no effort to find out if it belonged to anyone and if we should be paying rent. (We did not even consider that this might be the socially appropriate thing to do.) There was another cabin a little closer to town on the same bush road, and another couple from our group moved into that cabin. Not long after we arrived in Wells, the Land Rover that I had driven from Ontario broke down on that road (a broken axle) and I abandoned it, along with the payments due to the bank. Years later, I saw it driving around town—someone had bought it from the bank and repaired it.

"Now, none of us 'settlers' had anticipated the ferocity of a Wells winter, the isolation, the silence, the poverty. We did not know how cold it could get, or how much snow there would be. Certainly we did not expect the isolation and the distance from the rest of the world. There was also the expectation that we could live off the land and grow our own food; we did not realize that the climate in Wells was inhospitable to such attempts. We had brought tomatoes from our farm in Ontario, picked green, packed in boxes, and wrapped in newspaper. They lasted for many months. And, although we shared similar idealism, we discovered to our surprise that our values sometimes differed, and this created conflict and stress. For example, Peter and I were vegetarians, and we shared our cabin with a hunter who insisted that shooting deer was an essential way to live off the land. It seemed immoral to me; we had a big fight about what it meant to live in harmony with the land.

"By mid-winter, I was living alone in my cabin. Peter left Wells, and the hunter and his girlfriend moved into the cabin closer to town (its former inhabitants left when winter started). To reach my cabin from town, I would hike out along the road, backpack full of supplies, and then snowshoe in from the road. Later, I heard of two tragedies associated with that locale. Apparently a man who lived in that cabin died of exposure while snowshoeing home along the trail. And some years after I left, my cabin was burned down, an act that people thought was probably arson.

"I had unemployment insurance and was able to support myself financially for a period of time. I can't remember how I managed when the money ran out. I must have lived off the kindness of others.

"I once had a chimney fire—flames roaring twenty feet high into the black night sky. There was only a wood cookstove, and it was inadequate to heat the house well. Massive icicles grew inside the house in the corners, about eighteen to twenty-four inches long. This, of course, indicates the quality of the roof, but also shows how well my stove heated the house!"

ERIC ACKERLY: "Ellen, Peter Best, and I were living in a cabin half a mile out of town toward Barkerville [in Stromville], the one up the hill with the tower on it. Well, this is how it got the tower: It was a warm spring, May, I think it was, when the stove pipe blew off and landed so that it caught the lip of the pipe just above the dry, old wooden shingled roof.

"I am lying in bed when I hear Peter yelling 'FIRE!' The first thing I see when I open my eyes is fire dancing up the roof boards of the cabin. Bare-ass and buck-naked, I jump up and start knocking boards off the roof. Meanwhile, Ellen climbs on the roof; Peter is throwing snow up to her to put on the fire. We got it out, but lost about a third of the roof, and Ellen sprained her ankle when she slid off the roof.

"This was the end of winter and we were broke, so Peter and I scraped up some boards and some old twenty-gallon drums from the mine dump. We took the bottom of the drums out and pounded them flat for the roof. Then the Cottonwood fire broke out. We were broke, and $1.10 per hour [for firefighting] went a lot further then, so we went to work—as did half of Wells—on the fire. Ellen was left in a half burnt-out cabin...then came the rain...snow...rain, you know Wells weather in May; anything goes and it did. The cabin was a disaster. Ellen wound up staying in the cabin on the lake until Peter and I got back and finished the roof.

"The reason for the tower was twofold: first, the view of the sun crossing the moose flats turning silver to gold, and second was so we could see the chimney and make sure we had no more roof fires."

ZUBIN GILLESPIE: "We were all renting three houses, a barn, and a garage for five dollars a month in Stromville. There was the tiny little house that [Brian's friend John] Angrignon lived in, then up the hill was the log house we all were living in. There'd been a fire in the log house, which had burned a hole in the roof, and so we built a tower where the hole had been. We used to do LSD and drive the world around up there in the tower!

"So we were all living in the log house, about fifteen of us with our girlfriends and boyfriends. [Building the tree house] cost me two dollars, and the two dollars was for the plastic for the windows. There were old buildings falling down everywhere, and you could pull all these old buildings apart and take out the nails, straighten out the nails. The tree house was in five trees, pie shaped, with triangular rooms, split-level—the kitchen was down, the living room was up, and the bedroom was down a foot. At nighttime, the whole house would move in the wind. It had beautiful Indian bedspreads and all that. Tons of candles. The kitchen was just a Coleman stove, some shelves, that kind of stuff. But it was a pretty great job, considering.

"There was a yellow house [in Stromville] where Duncan Bray, who was a brilliant guitarist, lived. His dream was to work on his music all winter and then go and play music

Zubin Gillespie in his tree house, with winter coming on, early 1970s. Photo: Al McMaster.

Lower Stromville cabin, summer 1979. Photo: Sue Safyan.

down in New Orleans with Leon Russell. Now this house was probably twenty-feet square, with not a stitch of insulation in it. There's a hill going up behind it. Well, with all the snow here, to get into the house you had to walk around the back. In the winter the snow got so deep, and it turned into ice. In order for Duncan to get into the house, he had to climb up this hill—Duncan wasn't the kind of guy who wanted to carve out steps in the ice. He would sit on top of this hill and then come flying down into the house. This is how we had to visit Duncan: climb to the top of the hill, sit down, stick your feet out, and come sliding into the kitchen. And there was Duncan with gloves on, cut off at the fingers so he could play his guitar. He'd have the airtight going, with a gallon pot of soybeans boiling on it. The door, of course, never closed properly, because there was all this builtup ice, so he just hung a blanket over the door.

"The next spring, Paula and I moved into the teepee together, out French Creek road. I lived in the teepee; Al McMaster and his girlfriend Jane were living down below on Spud Murphy's property. This was at the very beginning of the health revolution. I remember going out and collecting stinging nettles. I lived on stinging nettles and rice that second year! Quite healthy.

"Then I moved into Clarence Wood's house on the [Jack of Clubs] Lake. I bought it off Clarence for $1,500. Who knows who built it, but it was built in the 1920s. That log house was really an amazing place. In the wintertime, you'd get into bed and put all your clothes on, because otherwise you'd be frozen in the morning. We had a wood stove, but it was so low-tech at that time, you only had one option: the airtight, which made your house 150 degrees, and then in fifteen minutes it would be minus twenty again."

Larry Fourchalk: "When I moved up in 1974, I moved onto [a friend's] mining claim up the Downey Pass Road. It was two and a half miles from Wells. The offer was that I could build a cabin that was adjacent to his in exchange for helping him out (Rob was sixty-seven). Further, he would teach me about bush living, placer mining, and other stuff that a city boy needed to know in a new environment. And then, somewhere down the road, I'd move on and the cabin would be his.

"Although I didn't choose the location, it was a nice one; it was at the top of the pass with a nice view down the valley. It was an eight by twelve [foot] log house with a loft, free form, and Rob was very helpful in teaching me to use a chainsaw, loaning me his saw and truck to get the logs, physically helping in the construction, and generally mentoring me. The most unique feature of the cabin was that it utilized the windshield from a vehicle as my livingroom window, and the view was down the valley. I put in part of a winter there before taking off for a visit to Vancouver. There I met my future wife, Corinne, and wasn't to return to live in Wells until 1977 when I moved back with Corinne and our five-month-old son, Gabe.

"We moved onto a friend's mining claim out in Big Valley. My friend and I soon became mining partners and initially had a tent camp set up. The view of Two Sisters Mountain was spectacular; it was a gorgeous spot to build a home. There was a series of one-acre meadows that stretched down the valley next to the old mining/logging road, and our claim encompassed all of the meadows. We never intended to mine for gold there; we just wanted a claim to build our homes on. Our placer mine was elsewhere.

"I designed and built a hexagonal log house, eighteen feet in diameter. It was a pretty cool house. I also built the interior furnishings—counter, table, bed, and crib. My proudest

accomplishment was a fir door with a diamond-shaped stained-glass window in the centre and a yew-wood handle. It was a beauty! I had some help from friends, but I built the cabin mostly on my own in about four weeks. I then helped my partner build his rectangular log cabin, which stood about an acre away.

"We lived there for the best part of five years, though I only spent one entire winter out there. The summers were nice and we commuted to work in Barkerville and at my placer mine that was on the Bowron Lake Road. Aesthetically, it was a beautiful place to live. Autumn was spectacular. We left for all or part of most winters largely due to inadequate transportation to town, which was nine and a half miles away. We spent winters in town and one in California. After trying out various forms of winter transportation, such as legs, snowshoes, skis, horses, and a Land Rover, and these all proved

Rick Brownhill and Toke the dog at Big Valley, 1978. Photo: Larry Fourchalk.

to be inadequate, I bought a brand new snowmobile one winter. This enabled us to winter there for the first time.

"Winter presented many challenges such as transportation, hauling water from a creek up the road by sled (or melting snow on the stove), getting firewood (if I ran out), and missing social contact. Even the year that I finally had a snowmobile to haul water and supplies, I found that I went to town most days to socialize. Spring was always a problem as no form of transportation was adequate. Also, there was significant flooding in the valley and sometimes there was close to two feet of water in the cabin.

"My mining partner and his family left after a year and a half. My friend Rick moved out to join us in the summer of '78 and set up a tent camp in a meadow across the road. After Barry left, Rick moved into his cabin. Shortly after, Rick's girlfriend Rose moved out as well and set up a tent camp in another adjacent meadow. We moved into Wells for the winters and summered in Big Valley. Eventually, we just stayed in Wells in 1981, where we had work, more conveniences, an easier life, and a social scene. The cabin continued to be used as a getaway until we eventually left Wells in 1983. We left Wells so Gabe could go to school in a larger centre and Corinne could go to college. Rick and Rose eventually married and had a child, Seth (who was conceived in Big Valley, as I recall), and moved to town.

"As something to do and also as a creative outlet, Barry and I started writing newspapers that we delivered to each other's door. Barry published the *Moose Meadows Monitor*, I published the *Stewart Creek Sentinel*, Rick published the *Big Valley Blatt*, and Rose published *The Last Resort Report*. These newspapers had drawings and photographs. We took real-life events in our daily lives in the valley and exaggerated them to outrageous proportions, making them into humorous stories. For example, a cold outhouse

The *Big Valley Bugle and* the *Stewart Creek Sentinel, 1978, courtesy of Larry Fourchalk.*

toilet seat in the winter became a story of one of us being frozen to it and neighbours having to go to extreme measures such as hot water and a crowbar to pry the person off. Some stories were purely fictional. We poked as much fun at ourselves as anyone."

ROB DANBY: "It was kind of exciting moving out to Antler Creek; it was adventurous, and we were going on a different path. There was a crazy party scene in town, with lots of drinking, and suddenly Suzanne was pregnant; we're looking at having a baby and we didn't want to be around that scene..."

SUZANNE BESSETTE (DANBY): "We decided that we needed to get away from Wells and that we would like to live together. And it just happened that Tom and Sally were looking for someone to look after their cabin out at Antler Creek for the winter...When I found out I was pregnant, in September, our whole thing changed. I was in my Madonna stage, and we loved it out there!"

ROB: "We were in the middle of freakin' nowhere, and there was no power, nothing, nobody; they hadn't even hauled a single load of logs past Antler Creek Bridge in those days. Here we are in the middle of nowhere with no electricity, no running water, wood heat. And it was a real funky, cool log cabin, but it was your basic old log cabin. It had no foundation, so the bottom three logs were rotting into the ground. It had this kind of decrepit, falling-apart floor and so it was drafty, and there were mice everywhere. It had a big living room with an airtight and it had a big kitchen with a wood stove, and a separate bedroom.

"It was exciting, the whole back-to-the-land thing, there was something magical about life being so basic. And, of course, not having to go to work and not being stressed about money, you had the time to tend to the basics of life—and you needed it. It took you basically all day long just to survive; you had to chop all your wood, get your water, and that was everything, that's your life, and cook, and that's all you had time for. And I loved that, after coming from Vancouver.

"I fixed up the bedroom. I put a little oil heater in there and stuck the chimney out the window and hung blankets and mosquito netting to keep it somewhat civilized for

Aura [the baby]. We had this brand new baby in the middle of nowhere. I remember that we came home from the hospital, and we had the best of intentions, but we knew nothing. So we got all these cloth diapers."

SUZANNE: "Disposable diapers were around then, but we just thought that was wrong, you know? We wouldn't be doing that. We had this idea that we would just save up the cloth diapers and take them into Quesnel and wash them."

ROB: "Suddenly we had this mountain of messy diapers in this log cabin and no water and no laundry."

SUZANNE: "That was pretty disgusting, that wasn't working! So then one day, at Willis Harper [the hardware store in Quesnel] we noticed there was this plunger thing, it was supposed to be a hand-agitator. So we got a galvanized tub and the plunger and we decided we were going to do diapers at home. There was sort of a well, so we filled up some buckets. We put the tub on top of the wood stove and then we threw the buckets of water in and we got the fire going and heated it up, and then we threw the diapers in. And then we threw some soap in and we started agitating. Well…it wasn't too long before the hot, pissy water slopped onto the top of the cookstove, and we went [makes bad-smell face], 'Oh! That's not working!' We realized that now we had put eight buckets

Suzanne Bessette (Danby) with baby James. Photo: Rob Danby.

of water into this thing, and how were we going to get it out? Rob was convinced that he could pick it up and carry it out. He picked it up by the handles, and the handles just bent."

ROB: "So I was pretty discouraged on day one, and then Mike Hall showed up with a present. It was a package of Pampers! We went, 'Woo hooo! Alright! Let's get a truckload! This is way better; my bleeding hands are very happy!'"

View from back porch of lower Strom-ville cabin the author's first winter in Wells. Photo: Sue Safyan.

SUZANNE: "That was the end of our diaper washing and that was the story of how we started using Pampers. Aura was born in May. There were mice in the cabin; it was making me mental. I had her in a basket with mosquito net, and there'd be mouse turds on top of the mosquito net, so they were running over her at night, and I said, 'We have to get out of here.' Lars Fossberg had a cabin that was closer to the lake, and it had plywood floors, so we thought that was pretty good. We rented that from him, and we stayed there until the fall."

ROB: "We lived [at Fossberg's] until the end of October when my work finished. By that point, the weather was brutal; the dog's dishes froze onto the floor. Aura was crawling around on the floor, and everything was frozen up. We thought, *hmm*. Once you have a baby, you go, 'Now we understand why they invented running water! I think I understand why they invented electricity! And showers! Furniture—wow—that's a neat idea!' We started to kind of swing back the other way."

Winter Wonderland

LOUISE FUTCHER: "One winter, they said it was about minus sixty, and the logs in Terry and Bernice's log house were cracking like gunshots in the cold."

MIKE HEENAN: "When you realized that the winter weather in Wells could literally kill you, it was an achievement and badge of honour to have survived it. Everyone becomes much friendlier when it's cold out; cars are jumped, firewood is found, and plumbing is unfrozen. People really seemed to pull together when winter sets in. It was a survivalist kind of mentality. Status was conferred on anyone who spent the winter in Wells.

"It was always nice to look forward to the first frost, the first snowfall. After that, the realization that you'd be shovelling snow and dressing in long johns for the next six months became a tad tiresome. But it made for great stories when I went back to the coast and told my Vancouver friends what I'd been up to. It's funny how you can make living in a shack freezing your knackers off sound romantic! You are so far removed from the real world that it is simply the best place to be in the world.

"My first few winter lessons were as follows:

1. Always designate one chair at the bar for coats, toques, gloves, and scarves.
2. Sissy Vancouver winter boots and coats just did not cut it at minus forty degrees.
3. Don't cheap out on snow packs.
4. Buy extra [felt-pack] liners and change them often (when you're outside).
5. Learn to recognize the smell of burning liners on an airtight.
6. Nose hair freezes and snow starts to make crunching sounds at exactly minus zero degrees F.
7. Cayenne pepper will keep your feet warm/hot for about a minute until they overheat, start to sweat, the sweat freezes, and your feet freeze.
8. It's easy to split wood when it's minus forty degrees!
9. Make sure you really have to take a dump before you go to the outhouse when it's minus forty degrees.
10. Those guys were just pulling my leg when they said that when you pee outside when it's minus forty degrees that you had to break it off against a tree.
11. You don't feel the cold quite as much when you're drinking.
12. Despite the flame, coal-oil lights don't throw off any heat.
13. The itch from wool long johns is worth it when it's really cold.
14. The colder it gets, the more people want to drink.

Bev Danby about to take a slide with a square of snow off the roof in Wells, January 31, 1974. Photo: Karin Ludditt.

15. There is nothing like sitting in the Wells Hotel with the fireplace going when the thermometer's at minus forty degrees."

NATHAN KEW: "I was on the afternoon shift at Barkerville and was coming home at midnight, after Bill Jeffreys had come out to spell me off. By the time I got down to the flats, where the big campsite is, Jeffreys' tire tracks were gone—that's how hard it was snowing. The road and the ditch and everything was white. I kept having to get out of my car and walk down the shoulder of the highway, then turn around and come back to the car and follow my own footprints until I got back to town."

BEV DANBY: "We'd be shovelling snow off the roof and get a big chunk ready to go, then jump on it and, eeeeha!, ride 'er down! Off the second, third storey, whatever. There was so much snow down below it wouldn't hurt very hard when you landed. Unless you came off the Curling Rink roof when you were shovelling and you'd end up buried right up to your armpits; because the roof was curved, you couldn't get out."

SHARON BROWN: "One day we borrowed Randy Russell's 1963 Biscayne station wagon to go to Quesnel, and we had to push snow with the front bumper most of the way home."

MARGUERITE HALL: "We were living out at Stromville [without running water or plumbing]. It was my first winter in Wells. I went to the Jack O' Clubs Hotel in the middle of the day to have a bath and wash my hair. Dave Thatcher, who lived across the highway from us, said, 'I'll give you a ride home on the back of my snowmobile.' My hair was still wet. We went across the swamp [about a five-minute-long ride], and by the time I got home, my hair was frozen solid, and I had to be careful not to break it off underneath my hood."

MIKE HALL, (winking): "I preferred to wait in the bar until my hair dried."

TOM ADAIR: "In winter, you could just go into the bar and yell, 'Round for the house!' because there were only three other people in the bar."

Wildlife

Wells is situated in the vastness of the Cariboo Mountains at the confluence of several valleys and at the edge of a large swamp. Bears, moose, mice and, last but not least, horseflies and mosquitoes shared the natural environment with the hippies.

SUZANNE BESSETTE: "My parents came to visit us from Tennessee. We knew there was a bear around because the dogs were always barking at night. We had heard it was a grizzly; it had been sighted out at the Bowron Lake road, so we thought, well, we'll take my parents out for a drive, and maybe we'll see the grizzly. And there was the grizzly in the meadow, and it was quite amazing. It stood up. My mother said, 'Rob, do you think maybe that grizzly got away from the zoo?' And we went, 'Mom, this is the zoo!'"

BEV DANBY lived in one of the small cabins in Stromville that were, especially in summer, infested with mice. She was used to hearing them skitter across the floors at night and, although she was fastidious about putting food in rodent-proof containers, she could also hear them occasionally nibbling. But one night, she recalls, "I kept hearing the mice, and they were making a hell of a racket, running and jumping and banging into things. I got up and lit a lamp to see if I could find out what was making them so noisy and clumsy…Well, I hadn't put the bag of pot away; they had eaten most of it and were stoned out of their little minds."

JUDE GOODWIN: "The horseflies were huge. I remember putting my baby down by the side of a little lake and wading in for just a moment. She started crying, so I went back to her and her face was covered in blood from horsefly bites!"

Duncan Bray, Jude Goodwin, and baby Sky outside their home, fall 1973. Photo: Jude Goodwin.

MIKE HEENAN: "The bugs initially weren't an issue. Nobody really seemed to notice other than the occasional scream when a horsefly had drawn blood. But the longer you stayed there the more noticeable the bugs were and the more you realized that just keeping the little buggers at bay became a major part of your day."

ZUBIN GILLESPIE: "There was a guy named Danny living in one of the houses out at Stromville—a really spiritual, mystic kind of guy. While we were all being eaten alive by mosquitoes, I remember there wasn't one bug on Danny. Maybe he was using bug spray, but we thought it was because he was so mystical."

Living in Town

As the hippies settled in, they bought houses in Wells (available for as little as $300) and began to fix them up. Living in the bush was rough, but moving into town didn't guarantee that one's house would have water or power.

Home ownership, as the 1970s saw the rustic beginnings of the now multi-billion-dollar do-it-yourself movement, involved learning about plumbing, electricity, and insulation, cleaning chimneys, and digging foundations. Along the way, the newcomers endured indoor icicles and flame-throwing chimney fires. They also learned how to forage for food, grow it or raise it, and—this was an eye-opener— butcher it, and they formed a buying cooperative for bulk and organic foods, as the health food/organics movement began to spread across the continent.

JUDE GOODWIN: "I moved up with my newborn, Sky, and her dad, Duncan Bray, in the early summer of 1973. We rented a cabin. It was a tiny two-room log cabin with a big wood stove and an outhouse. There was a hinged window, which acted as a cooler in the spring and fall, but in the winter it was our freezer! We were what Duncan liked to call 'volunteer peasants.' We did not come with baby gear, for example. We had no stroller, high chair, etc. All I had was a sling and a bag of sleepers. Our clothes were all reused, our home was furnished with gifted items, handmade items, or second-hand stuff. I loved mending our things with big patches. I loved building things out of pieces of the world outside our cozy home. We had a big wood stove and an oil heater. All the walls were thick with black soot. I tried to clean it all away, covered a bunch of it with tapestries, and we installed our shiny new airtight heater. It was very cozy. None of our homes were very big.

Don Rutledge and Sky ("Sky liked to play with rolling papers..."). Photo: Jude Goodwin.

"We had an outhouse. In the winter our 'droppings' would freeze almost before they hit the pile, creating tall, pointed stacks. We would drop bags of lime onto these, which melted them down. We had oil lamps, and did all our evening stuff with them. I boiled my daughter's diapers (cloth, of course) on the wood stove. We had no laundry. There was a laundry in town, but it was a long walk. My baby had horrible diaper rash. Probably from inadequate rinsing. We had no running water, but Duncan would get the water from in town. Somewhere we came upon a sled, and I would pile my daughter in that sled and walk into town every day in the winter.

"Our first winter in Wells was beautiful—simple. We learned to chop wood, and bake bread on a big old wood stove. We did lots of crafts. I wrote a lot and drew and learned astrology. Duncan played with the Cow Mountain Boogie Band. Sky grew, bathed in an enamel basin, wore things that I crocheted (another new skill), played with handmade things. I remember I made her a board covered in things like doorknobs and hinges and

Baby Jenny [Futcher] in a home-made crib with peeled logs and macramé sides. Photo: Louise Futcher.

locks with keys. Similar to what you can find in the toy aisle at Walmart these days, but Sky's were made of rusty pieces of real equipment!

"Her crib was something I made out of ash twigs, easy enough to get her head stuck between but I didn't know any better! Safety issues were not common knowledge then as they are now. She ate a very healthy diet of mom's milk and wheat germ and yogurt; I had good books about food but not much else to go by.

"One night it was very cold—it got to sixty below that winter. Duncan or I had gotten up and stoked the new airtight and things were pretty cozy. I had nursed the baby, and we were just falling back to sleep when I noticed an orange pinpoint in the ceiling. It was getting bigger. Suddenly, I really looked and saw that the chimney of the airtight was red hot, and I realized the attic was on fire. We leapt out of bed, Duncan ran to grab what water we had and started throwing it at the ceiling. This did nothing, of course. I wrapped the baby in a bunch of blankets and tore down the snowy roadway to the nearest house, about a block away. I hammered on their door and yelled, 'Call the fire brigade! Call the fire brigade!' but these folks didn't have a phone. I ran to the next house and tried again, but there was no answer.

"Realizing everything I owned in the world was in that little cabin, including photos and all the baby's stuff, I ran back up. The fire hadn't made its way into the cabin at this point, so I put the baby down on the kitchen floor and started clearing everything out of the bedroom, specifically all her clothes. At one point some people came, and a man with a fire extinguisher used it up on the ceiling. By this time Duncan was outside on the roof shovelling snow. Someone yelled at me that they would take the baby to their house. They wrapped her back up and disappeared. I dragged our oval rug out onto the snow and started tossing everything I owned onto that rug.

"While I was doing this, a fire truck appeared. Volunteer crowd, I gather. They couldn't get the pump working on the water tank. I remember it took a long time for any water to start happening.

"And that's all I remember of that night. The little cabin was destroyed, but it didn't burn to the ground so they must have been able to get the fire out at some point. Anything left in the cabin was ruined.

"I have no idea where we stayed that night or how I got my baby back, but the next day we moved what we had left into a house in town and spent the rest of the winter there. It had a big wood furnace in the basement that terrified me. That spring, we moved into a house outside of Wells towards Barkerville. There was a kind of neighbourhood there. Our home had a circular driveway, I remember, and I thought it was pretty awesome.

"Lots of the locals liked to tell the story of the hippie chick who set her newborn down in the middle of a house fire in order to save her stuff! The townspeople must have been a big help getting us settled in after that fire, and I'm grateful in hindsight for their kindness."

Louise Futcher: "I rented a little house in south Wells for a small amount, perhaps $35 a month. I believe it belonged to a woman in Quesnel. I renovated it, ripping out all the old wall coverings and replacing these with barn wood and bright fabrics. I also ripped out the ceiling in the kitchen to find a beautiful, shiplapped arched ceiling. I had no running water

Louise Futcher and baby Jenny, 1973. Photo: Jude Goodwin.

Louise's house in winter. Photo: Louise Futcher.

and had to haul water in buckets from a well down the road (which, I realized years later, was probably contaminated by mine tailings). In the winter, I pulled the baby on a toboggan into town [that is, uptown Wells]. I had rigged up a box on the toboggan to hold groceries and supplies and laundry. We did our laundry at the hotel and had our baths there as well. I had no bathtub, and would rent the use of a bathroom with a tub once a week.

"I had become an astrologer and did charts for lots of people based on their birth time and location. I provided them with future forecasts and personality interpretations. On my kitchen wall I had pasted many hand-drawn astrology charts. This was a lot of fun, served a social function, and also provided me with some intellectual stimulation. Jude Goodwin was also into astrology and we used to talk about it often. I was also a tarot card reader.

"Living in the house next to me in 1973 (later Judy Campbell's house) were Gail, Frank, and their son Nathan. Behind me were Jacquie and Blaine. My sister moved to Wells that year. In 1973–74, more 'hippies' moved to Wells. I remember many days sitting around playing bridge. Shelley Schwartz and Paula were friends who came up from Vancouver. Shelley lived with Don Rutledge.

"In January 1974, my daughter Jennifer became very sick. She developed a high fever, and the glands in her throat were severely swollen and painful. There was no doctor in town. I took the Wells Stage into Quesnel, where Jennifer had surgery and was hospitalized for a few days, then we took the Stage home. (This also speaks to my lack of transportation and perhaps social isolation?). When I came home, I found my house completely frozen; the temperatures were extremely cold, no one had thought to start a fire in my house (and I had not thought to request this) and so I brought my sick baby back into this freezer of a house, and it took a day or more for the house to warm up completely. I still feel sad when I think of this. This also brings up the issue of communications; I don't know if anyone had phones.

"So, another aspect of life in Wells was the poor access to medical care...For example, within a month or two of arriving in Wells in 1970, I sliced my finger quite badly with an axe when making kindling. The finger needed stitches, but instead I simply bound it up. It healed okay, although I still have the scar. It would have been too difficult to go all the way into Quesnel. I'd have to hike several miles out of the bush, get the Stage the next day, and then it probably would have been too late for treatment. While renovating what later became the Tomato House in the summer 1973, I stepped on a nail, which completely penetrated my foot. I had to go into the hospital in Quesnel for tetanus shots and X-rays and treatment. The dentist was in Quesnel. I had no money for dental care, and so had a tooth removed rather than the expensive filling or root canal that he recommended. And that dentist was also very disrespectful to me as a hippie."

MIKE HEENAN: "When I went up there, I stayed in a little cabin next to Lucky's that had no power, no nothing. It had a nice big picture window, looking right onto the lake; you could see storms coming in off the lake. Just a little tiny airtight stove. When I went down to Vancouver one winter and came back in March, it had burned down…

"Then I lived in the corner house on Lowhee and whatever the back street is, in a tiny little blue house that Mad John had previously lived in. It was about ten feet by ten feet and had a very old and decrepit outhouse around the side, partly covered in willows. The entrance was at the front on the right-hand side and led directly into a shed. An immediate left took you through a door into the kitchen which was about eight by six and consisted of an airtight heater in the corner and a table and chair, which were in front of a window of about three by three feet. The other room was a bedroom with a single wooden cot along the side wall of the building. It must have been about four by eight (I doubt all of these measurements will equal what I thought the original size of the shack was). I remember cooking egg sandwiches with my cast iron frying pan. I used to sprinkle salt on the top cover of the airtight to keep the bread from sticking to the stove when I was making toast. I kept mayo, butter, and milk just outside the door in the shed…I am still waiting for the cancer diagnosis from drinking all of that cyanide-laced water I used to haul out of the creek.

"My dad had just passed away. It was Christmas 1975. I had nowhere to live, and I was up there with Wanda and just wanted to get gonzo, and Ken said, 'Look, here's the deal, here's what you've got to do. Mert and Bert [Everton] have a solid place, right next door [to the Jack]; it's $1,200; you should buy it. Think about it.' And I said, 'You're right,' so I went over to the Evertons and said, 'There you go, done.' And they went, 'Man, did we ever just take the rookie here!' The Evertons were laughing, telling everybody in the bar that night how they'd taken me to the cleaners for $1,200. I look back on that and go, *thank goodness* Ken Scopic was there; I mean he steered me in a very clear direction."

BEV DANBY: "[My sister] Rose and I had gone up to Wells and bought this house. Rose decided we'd go back to Vancouver and she was going to get a job so she could afford to come back up in the spring. I went back to working in the bank. We worked all winter. We both saved money, and in the spring we just took off up to Wells. Brought tools with us and jacks for jacking the place up. Hardly knew which end of a hammer to use. But we proceeded to fix as much as we could. We froze the first winter and had to learn about wood heat. We bought a wood heater and put that in. Kitchen sink with cold running water—and that was it. No indoor toilet. We went to the Jack—it wasn't very far away, just up the stairs. We had steep, steep, horrible treacherous stairs. How we ever survived going up and down the hill with all the trips that we made…

"So the first winter was pretty amazing. The water froze up pretty well steadily. We ended up running a plastic hose from the shut-off up to the kitchen sink, because then if it froze, I had to pry it off, take it upstairs in front of the stove, and once it melted, pour the ice out, and hook it back up. One time we went to Quesnel and we were worried about the place freezing while we were gone; we didn't know how well our fires would last. Left a little water trickling in the kitchen sink, and the drain froze. When we got back, there was water all over the floor. One winter we did the usual, turning the water off [so the pipes wouldn't freeze]. But the valve broke in my hands, so water's just shooting into the house! My brother Rob was there, and we started the bucket brigade, hauling this water outside. It was freezing almost instantly as we dumped it out of the bucket, because it was forty below. We phoned around to find where Bud Williams was because he had the [town water] shut-off key. Then he had to get the propane torch out to thaw the ground so that he could dig it up and turn the water off. Then he had to try to find a valve that he might have hanging around to replace the one that broke. And he got it all fixed; it was amazing, just a total blur of activity and panic.

"So we did learn about insulation. We learned about having lots of friends over for parties. They would stoke the fire all night so Rose and I could go to bed and wake up in a nice warm house, and there would be someone like Fraser on a chair by the fire in the morning."

ROB DANBY: "I moved into a little cabin on the back street behind the Highways yard down on the tailings. Duncan Bray and Jude Goodwin had lived there. I think Zubin lived there, and Robin Jacobsen lived there after me. Whoever was the previous tenant had had a fire in there. They didn't wreck the place, didn't burn it down, but it was charred and damaged. It had no electricity and just an oil heater and wood cookstove and an outhouse. The Crotteaus owned the place. Rent was $35 a month. Since the place was kind of a mess I said, 'Well, how about I clean it up and move in?' Crotteau then got this idea to really fix the place up and put in electricity;

The little cabin on the back street where Duncan and Jude and Robin and Rob lived. Photo: Jude Goodwin.

he hired Pete Pelletier, and then he jacked the rent up to $50. But then I had electricity, so I was really settled in for the winter.

"That was one of the worst winters; there was crazy snow. I had a really good time! Mike Heenan lived just down the street. We'd take turns going to each other's place for breakfast to start the day off—typical laid-back, relaxed, party scene. That January, my first winter there, living in that little cabin, there was one week in January when every single day, morning and night, it snowed a foot. I'd get up in the morning and there'd be a foot of new snow, and I'd have to shovel it to get out to the outhouse, and then by nighttime there'd be another foot, next morning another foot, and this went on for the whole week. I started getting claustrophobic. The snowbanks were really something.

"And then spring came, and I went back to working at Barkerville. That was the spring of '74 when Suzanne and Marion arrived in town. Suzanne and I met and fell in love very quickly, and then she got pregnant. We were both really into it. We ended up moving out to that place on Antler Creek that Tom and Sally Wilson owned, a log cabin at Antler Flats.

"When we moved back to town, I found this little trailer for sale, it was as teeny as could be. It was hooked up to Esso Dave's garage. We bought it for $2,500, and it had a furnace and electricity. So I approached my sisters, Bev and Rose, who were living in the house they'd bought for $700, the swamp house. At this point, the house was beyond its last legs, and it needed constant fixing. But the electricity and the water were there. So I said, 'Do you mind if we just park the trailer beside the house and hook up for the winter?' And they were like, 'Yeah, sure, whatever.' You know how it was in Wells; it was pretty relaxed. In fact, legally, their lot was hardly bigger than the house, and they only owned this one little patch. But we didn't worry about details like that!

"That was one of the cool things about Wells that I loved, that everything was just so basic, and you just did it yourself. Need electricity? There was power to the house, it was 110, and I just went and rigged it all up by myself and wired it in. Bingo, electricity. Until I touched the door handles—*Fzzzzt!* Whoa! Then I learned about grounding! It was like that for a period of time. I remember Gaylord coming to visit once, and he had to jump in and jump out! As long as you didn't touch the door, once you were inside it was okay. And then, when it was time to leave, you opened the door and you jumped out!

"So then I learned about grounding. I just got a little chunk of metal water pipe and a sledgehammer and pounded it into the basement, into the ground, and took the ground wire and wrapped it around the pipe, and it worked just fine. It was so basic and crude and simple, but it worked, and I learned; it was wonderful. And same with the water; hooked up to the town water through the house, so we got that all going, and I hooked into the sewer line—all just learn-as-you-go. Well, the sewer line was hooked to a septic tank, and it worked fine for a while. But the next thing you know, our whole basement starts filling up with sewage. I actually made my own septic tank that got us through the winter. I got a forty-five-gallon drum and dug a big hole in the ground. I cut a hole in one side and stuck the line in, and had the main line just a little bit higher. All the solids settled and the rest ran out the drain, and it worked just fine. Moving into the trailer beside the swamp house was my first real kind of settling in. 'Yeah, I think I fit in here, I think I belong!'

"After being there a year, we started realizing that there were probably actually property lines and we, in fact, were probably not on our sister's property and were kind of squatting. In an attempt to legitimize it, I bought the swamp house from Bev and Rose. They had to get rid of it, and I offered them $700—what they paid for it. They got their money back; they broke even. The building was really shot; the floor was gone. Originally I was trying to salvage the building, build a garage or shop or something, but it was all so old and brittle. Looking at the front of the house, the middle was sort of hanging under the chimney and the outside walls had totally sunk and the joists were splitting. I was afraid to walk in the house at the end, fearing for my safety. I saved the front door, which I used in the house on the Crescent, and I saved some windows, and some of it got recycled. So we decided to torch it.

"I got photos of this. We lit the house on fire, and then I got Esso Dave to level off the property, and I moved the trailer back in and put it on the lot that I now actually owned. But see, I was a hippie in those days, and I didn't know anything about the fire

Rose and Bev burn their swamp house. Photo: Rob Danby.

department, but I knew Trev Davies was the fire chief. So I approached him and said, 'We want to burn this house down because it's just a wreck, and we want to get rid of it. There's nothing around, and I just wanted to let you know about it,' and he goes, 'Oh yeah, no problem.' But he forgot, and forgot to tell anybody else, and so I think I've got it all covered and there's no worries. As soon as the flames shoot up, we hear the fire siren go off, and a few minutes later the truck arrives. Charging down the hill on the hose is Rick Brownhill. He was the first of us to get converted to the fire department, because he lived in that cabin on the lake that burned up when Walter died. I hadn't met Rick at that point, and he's running down the bank with a hose and I'm yelling 'No! Stop!' There's a lot of confusion, but we finally got it all sorted out, and then Trev showed up. I said, 'Don't you remember me telling you about this?' And he goes, 'Oh, yeah...'

"So we got rid of the swamp house and cleaned it all up. We actually owned the little trailer and had our own garage—we were taxpayers! For Wells, that's the middle class! And because we had a baby, it was nice to have a job too, so that's when I started my Highways career. So I was in. I had full-time work, and a place, and a family.

"I put one little addition on the trailer and then, in the winter of '77, we bought the house on the Crescent for $10,000. We were looking for a substantial house we could live in, year round. It didn't have big gaping holes in the floor; most of the comparable houses were a few thousand less, they were around the $7,000 mark, but they all had crappy basements that needed work, which was a big job. And this one had a concrete foundation and did not need basement work—it was done—so we decided to move in."

SUZANNE BESSETTE: "When we lived in the trailer in Wells, we got a wringer-washer machine. One day, Aura was in her crib, watching me. I was really good at the wringer, so I could feed it and catch it and feed it and catch it, and I leaned over, and it caught my hair and wound me up right to the wringer. I turned it off so it stopped, but I was afraid to release it because it had a big kick-back. So there I was with my head against the wringer and Aura looking at me. Eventually I put my other hand up to block the blow and got my hair out. After that, I wore my hair in a ponytail.

"I would hang diapers out, I had a line. I would go and stand on our deck—this was in winter, and it was so cold that I would hang a diaper, and then I'd put my hands in the warm diapers, then hang a diaper. They were just frozen boards, hanging there. We loved our little trailer, but there was social stigma attached to that. People were really appalled that we had been living out in the bush and had been doing the right thing, and now we're living in a trailer—we'd sold out! But we had a furnace; every morning I'd get up and turn the furnace on and Aura and I would sit by the main blower and just warm up!"

BONNIE MAY: "Fred and I met at a New Year's Eve party at the Community Hall. (Fred had been celebrating a little and came and sat on my lap. Let's say he didn't make a good first impression!) It was the next year, on August 15, 1971—Gold Rush Night—that we started going out. In the summer of 1971, I decided to stay in Wells and finish grade twelve in Quesnel. I was working for Art and Oline Smith at the Wells Hotel, chambermaiding in the morning, working in the dining room in the evening. Fred used to drive around waiting for me to get off work. I'd turn out the lights while I was washing the floors so he'd know I was almost done. The loggers that boarded at the Wells loved to tell Fred that I'd already left and then tease me when I came out.

"We rented the house on the Crescent across from Berlin's Garage from my dad [Clarence Wood]. In 1972, Fred and I got married and bought a house across from the playground from Claire and Jackie Garvin for $5,000. In 1978 we bought a house on the Crescent from my dad. That house cost us $12,000. Prices were going up!"

Fred May and Bonnie Wood get married, June 1972.

"Wells was a fantastic place to raise young children—the kids had so much freedom. Where else could you go snowmobiling and skiing from your back door? When I had my first child, there were two doctors that used to come up once a month to Wells—Dr. McIntyre and Dr. Maile. By the time I had my second, you had to drive to Quesnel for appointments."

JUDY CAMPBELL [After she and her husband had been in town for a few days, living in the shack they'd built on the back of their truck]: "Eugene Crotteau took us around to see all these houses. And they were just beyond, most of them. Even by my standards, which were pretty low, they were pretty bad. After about three or four days of camping out in our little truck, we moved it to the back street. Frank and Gail were going to move out to a place on Antler Flats, a log cabin, so we got to move in to their place. We paid $20 a month rent. It was fabulous. The next spring, after John and I split up, I worked up the nerve to go across the street to ask Bert Covey [the landlord] if I could buy the house. He said, 'Well, yes, okay. Do you think $300 would be too much?' I said, 'Hmm, I think I can handle it'...

"Now, until the mid-1970s, electricity was supplied to the townsite by the mine generator—even after the mine had shut down. Then Hydro took on responsibility for providing electricity. I remember the process of the poles going up along the highway. There were a lot of power outages in the first year or so, and instead of being fifteen minutes long (about the time it took for Jim McKelvie to go down and kick the diesel generator with his one good leg), they were hours and hours long.

"Everyone was completely used to the hum of the generators, even me, and I lived very close to them. I do remember one night (before they put the Hydro in) I woke up in the middle of the night and couldn't figure out what woke me. Then I realized it was the silence. The generators had kicked out, and the silence woke me up."

TOM ADAIR: "Andy Stitnick and I rented a place from Dave Thatcher's dad for the winter. It was $60 a month, and it had an oil furnace in the basement. But the whole roof leaked, on the inside, along one side. So there were long trays on each of the windows, and you had to dump the trays every two hours, day and night, or they would overflow and the floor would get soaked!"

SHARON BROWN: "I lived with John Boutwell for nine months when I was nineteen. It was a two-room shack—my mother was horrified! He had a Norton motorbike in his bathroom where the bathtub should have been, and an airtight wood stove in the front room that we had to keep a thirty-pound rock on, so that the top didn't blow off in the middle of the night and start a fire. I showered at the Jack…Plumbing or electricity issues? We had neither, so there were no issues! I did not have electricity until I moved into the wee house on Mildred Avenue in 1977."

Chainsaw Rhapsody

With only wood stoves to heat their homes, the hippies had to cut firewood—or buy or barter it from someone else—in order to stay warm. Even on summer nights, it could be cold enough to create hoarfrost, so firewood wasn't needed only for winter and it wasn't a luxury; it was a survival necessity. Getting firewood every fall was an annual ritual; but if you didn't get enough, you'd have to go out in the winter when the bitter cold would quickly freeze chainsaws and truck engines, not to mention fingers and toes.

ROB DANBY: "There were great adventures, but they were crazy dangerous. I went out scouting for firewood one time with Andy Stitnick in Brutus, his Valiant. We're driving up the main highway with a jug of wine in the car—it was the middle of winter, snowing like crazy—and there was deep snow. Andy pulls over to the side of the road and looks up.

'Arghh,' he says, 'that looks like a good one!' He gets out and cuts this tree down right on the side of the public road. It hits the ground, and he goes, 'Oh, it's not dead.' We didn't have a clue what we were doing...But I realized that it was going to be dangerous, so I ended up getting a faller-bucker's handbook, teaching myself the proper way. I had a big truck, a three-ton 1948 white flat-deck that was so popular for hauling wood.

"The winter that I lived at Antler Creek we ran short of firewood because we went through a ton of it; that was such a drafty old place. I went scouting later in the winter, and there was nobody out there, Monday to Friday. So I went out cutting wood out at Barbara Barrows' place, and there was nobody on this road. There was this beautiful dead tree a little way up the bank, and I thought, I have my truck and I'll just drop it on the road and throw it in my truck. I'm cutting the tree, and just as I'm starting to back off the saw—I can't hear anything because it's so noisy—I hear Barbara yelling at me, screaming at me, and I look up and there's two little cars on the Bowron Lake road, right where the tree's going to land. There's been nobody all winter on that road, and I finally decide to cut down a tree and drop it on the road, and suddenly there are two cars! It was like a slow-motion thing; the tree's going *kkkk-kkkk* [gesture of tree keeling over] and I'm going *ahhgghh*, and the drivers of the cars look up and just in the nick of time stop, stuff it in reverse, and back up. And the tree went *phomt*!

"One time, [someone] had arranged that we could get firewood from a logging landing. It all sounded good, so I thought, okay, fine. We headed out with my truck on Saturday morning, and when we get out there, [our connection is] drunk. He works for this company. All we had to do was just buck 'em up on the landing and throw them in my truck—it seemed like a pretty simple plan. Now, this is the company's logging equipment. He hops on the skidder—he's really drunk—and heads out to go skid in some dead wood for us to cut up, but then he gets the skidder stuck—he's got this expensive machine stuck. Well, it's supposedly all on the up-and-up, so he comes back and gets another skidder to go pull out the first one. Somehow word gets out that [the head logger] is on his way out, and there are all these hippies around the logging show, and they've got the skidders stuck!

I think we ended up getting the skidders unstuck, but it was a very unsuccessful wood mission. I got the hell out of there before [someone] showed up."

TOM ADAIR: "I had this deal with Judy to use her and Boutwell's one-ton truck. For every four loads of wood I cut, the fourth load of wood was theirs in return for the use of the truck. I would go out and cut the wood and haul it into town and sell the rest of it. I ended up usually getting four or five loads in two days. That was my having-fun money—I was working ten days on at Bowron and four days off. I was doing it on my own, out there chainsawing, cutting the stuff down, putting it on the truck; it was a great way to spend the time, but when you think about it, probably not the safest thing to do."

MIKE HEENAN: "I remember ordering a half cord of wood from Mike Goorew for $12.50 and getting rounds that were about three to four feet in diameter and without a single knot."

BEV DANBY: "We bought firewood for the first while we lived in Wells, and then I decided I was going to be a logger, too, and bought a chainsaw…Rose and Judy and I went out to get wood in my three-ton truck. I got out there with my chainsaw. This bloody gust of wind knocked the tree back into my saw, but I got the saw out okay. So I thought, I guess I've got to knock that tree onto that tree. I didn't even stop to think about how to do that, I just kind of went, *rrrmm, rrrmm, rrrmm*, and the trees went *ka-boom, ka-boom*! Knocked them both down. All of a sudden Judy and Rose are yelling, 'Geez! What a lumberjack!' I just laughed and thought, 'God, I love living in Wells!' It was great; I just loved that. And I got pretty good."

ELLEN GODWIN: "We were doing wood parties, where all able-bodied persons and vehicles went to a likely site. After the logging crew had left a landing was the best plan; there

Sharon Brown at the woodshed, spring 1975. Photo: Judy Campbell.

was lots of already downed wood, too small for the company's use. These events were a delight—it reminded me of otters playing beside a river on an ice slide, only we were bowling rounds of wood."

Animal Farm

Self-sufficiency was a counterculture value, and the hippies of Wells were as keen as any to grow their own food. But in Wells it can snow or hail or both in July and August, and because of the altitude, the growing season is short—about two months. In town, most backyards were only large enough to grow a moderate plot of hardy vegetables (if the heavy, rock-laden clay soil could be coaxed with enough mulch and digging to grow anything besides the hardiest weeds), put up a small greenhouse made from re-purposed wood-frame windows, and keep chickens or turkeys in a heated henhouse. A few brave and adventurous souls raised pigs out in Stromville.

Rose Danby with Fatso. Photo: Judy Campbell.

ROB DANBY: "Just before the first summer I lived in Wells, I was sharing a five-acre hobby farm with a couple in Surrey, just outside of Vancouver. We decided to get some chickens. We had quite a few at one point and sold eggs. When we left, I got my half, about twenty chickens.

"So I was going to Wells. I thought if I travelled all night in the dark, it would probably be best for the chickens, it wouldn't upset them too much. I had an old beater car, one of many in my fleet of old clunkers. I filled up the wheel-wells in the back with feedbags, made it kind of level, then I put a sheet of plywood in to cover the whole seat and the feedbags so it was flat, a plywood platform. And then, before I put the feedbags in, I stuffed a couple of poles in the corners and I wrapped chicken wire between the poles so there was chicken wire between the front seat and the back seat. I threw a bunch of hay in there, and then we just started firing the chickens in. Filled the car up with chickens and away we went! They were doing a bunch of roadwork on the Barkerville Highway in Devil's Canyon, and they had the road closed all night. You had to wait until seven in the morning for it to open up so you could get through to Wells. We got there before it opened, and we're in this big long line-up, sitting there. All of a sudden, [rooster crowing imitation]. People are like, what the hell? And there was a guy on a big bulldozer, I can't remember his name, but he was some typical guy up there, drank a lot, was up all night working, and he's chugging along in his cab, looking all cool, looking down at all the cars, and all of a sudden he sees a car full of chickens—[worried look] 'uh oh, maybe I better stop drinking!' But we made it just fine; the chickens even laid a few eggs on the way up. We put them into the basement of the swamp house; it was kind of a barn-type thing."

ROSE DANBY: "And then there was Bruce the Rooster. When I went into the chicken house to collect eggs, I came out with welts on my arm; I'd have to put my arm up over my face, because he'd go for my eyes."

TOM ADAIR: "Bruce would take a run at whoever came into the coop. I would time it so that, right when he would leap, I would just step back a little and soccer-ball him back into the corner. *Whump*! Really kick him. Then he would just sort of [sigh]—and I'd quickly grab the eggs."

MARGUERITE HALL: "We had a bad rooster, a mean rooster named Bruce. When Mike would go in with different shoes on than he usually wore, Bruce would attack him because he thought he must be somebody different. Bruce lived for a very long time, though I think he was stew after awhile.

Marguerite Hall shows Graham the chickens, fall 1979. Photo: Sue Safyan.

Pig butchering at Stromville, 1974. L to R: Dave Lockyer, John Scott Angrignon, and (back to camera) Mike Hall. A local boy watches in fascination. Photo: Judy Campbell.

"One day Mike decides he's going to let the chickens out and they're going to peck all around Stromville and just forage for their food. Later that night, we wanted to go to the Jack, so we had to get the chickens back into the coop. But we couldn't get the chickens or the rooster back in the coop. So we said, 'Oh, let's just go to the bar.' Mike says, 'They'll just go on in the coop by themselves.' When we came home, it was dark. Mike goes into the chicken coop—and there are no chickens. We start looking for feathers; maybe a coyote got them. Damn...no chickens. In the morning, we go down the back steps at Stromville, and there they are, all roosting on the steps.

"Then we decided, in about 1977, that we were going to raise pigs. Paul Guiguet, Mike Hall, Don Rutledge, John Campbell, and I. Our job was to go get the pigs. Five pigs. We found a farmer in Quesnel—Land Pigs—they were land-raised pigs, whatever that means. They were $20 each. The best part about it was they were really cute, these little piglets. Mike had the money ready to pay the farmer; it was a hundred dollars, but we couldn't tell the guy it was a hundred dollars. He was a real typical farmer. Mike had that old green truck and he'd just built the nice wooden sides on it. The farmer took a pencil out from behind his ear and start scribbling all over the wood, 'Let's see, five pigs, $20 each...' Finally, 'That's a hundred dollars,' he said. So away we go, we take the pigs home. The guys have built a corral in behind Stromville. Posts dug down two feet; Mike made sure the posts were in really good.

"These pigs ate the slops from the Good Eats Café, and they got bigger and bigger. I fed them; they got big buckets of slop. Titsmeyer [Mike and Marguerite's cat] would walk along the top of the fence, and all five pigs would follow—*snort-snort-snort-snort*—waiting for the cat to fall in. Then the pigs got too big for that pigpen, so they had to build another. From the air it would've looked like a figure eight.

"When it came time to butcher them, to figure out if they were ready to be butchered, they had to catch one. They had to do some scientific measurement of the girth in their legs, and then they'd know how many pounds it was. Did you know pigs can jump like race-horses? So there's Paul Guiguet and Mike in their mine coveralls and Don Rutledge. They figured out how to get one pig apart from the rest. They put a barred gate across the pen to separate him from the other pigs, but that pig jumped the gate like a horse, just sailed over the gate onto the other side. So then they butchered a chicken and gutted it and put the chicken guts on newspaper in the middle of the pen. And I come out and—I was baking bread that day, it was a fall day—look down and there's these guys, standing there noncha-lantly, and these chicken guts are in the middle of the pen, and there's a *very suspicious* pig. The guys are pretending that they're just looking at the scenery, trying to get the pig to go over to the chicken guts. They finally got it, and then it was time to start butchering. Mike had a book, I think, about how to butcher pigs. Shoot the pig, slit the throat. They had a big tripod, and they'd haul it up and hang it."

MIKE: "But there's a story behind that, too. I was using my pistol, and it shoots round mus-ket balls. Pigs' heads are really hard; those bullets just bounced off. So I shot one, and this thing started squealing like you wouldn't believe. They could hear it all the way in town. It squealed for a long time. It really freaked the other pigs out. They were, uh, really fun to catch after that."

MARGUERITE: "I remember Mike coming in [to the house during butchering] and saying, 'I'm the only one that will pull the guts out. And it's bloody cold out there; I'm the only one with warm hands.'

"It was the first snow, the first skiff of snow, so this would be middle of October. We had had five pigs and were down to two. Bev Danby lived in that cabin across the road. So, we're sitting in the bar, having beer, playing pool one day, after having our baths at

Mike Hall and Paul Montgomery behead the turkeys. Photo: Marguerite Hall.

the Jack, and Bev comes in and says, 'You guys really owe me! I was walking into town, and I saw the biggest deer tracks I'd ever seen! Wow, I thought, this is a big deer! And we don't usually have deer in Wells. But it was one of your pigs, just high-tailing it straight into town from Stromville.' A big pig, ready to be butchered. He'd put his nose under the bars of the gate and slid them along to get out. He was like, 'Oh my god, they're dropping like flies; I'm outta here!' Bev had to herd him back into the pen…

"In the end, we did them all in and butchered them. One night, Mike and Dave took a rack or two of ribs out to the carpenter shop [in Barkerville] and used the band saw to cut them into pork chops. It worked like a hot damn, but the cleanup took forever! But they didn't get to eat very much of the meat because somebody had unplugged the freezer."

MIKE: "There was about five hundred pounds of bacon in there; we'd smoked it, salted it, used special barrels…That was Don Rutledge's freezer. He'd had this all in his freezer and then he had a fight with, I forget, and somehow the power got cut off, and all the bacon spoiled."

MARGUERITE: "Then we had turkeys."

MIKE: "Well, we let them get a little big. We had one tom who dressed out at thirty-two pounds. When it came time to butcher, it was all we could do for two of us to hang onto this bugger. We had to hold him down and then cut his head off. First of all, we tried stuffing him into a feed bag, because we were getting beaten to death by his wings. He actually broke one of his wings, he flapped so hard."

MARGUERITE: "Mike's parents had to cut their turkey in half because it wouldn't fit in the oven."

MIKE: "Man, those turkeys were good, though. Tasted nothing like the ones you buy in the store."

MARGUERITE: "We had twenty-five butchered turkeys hanging from our old porch. And then we took them all off so we could go to the bar that night. Mike laid them all out in the basement. When I went down to the basement, they were all laid out like in a mortuary, not just higgledy-piggledy, but all the feet went in the same direction."

MIKE: "That was a lot of turkey. That was four to five hundred pounds of turkey."

Twenty-five turkeys all in a row. Photo: Marguerite Hall.

MARGUERITE: "The first year that we moved into our house in Wells, we had the little turkey chicks. We put them in that pen for the rabbits. Mike built a little wire fence around it and put the little turkeys in there and let them run around; it was pretty cute. You could get down and pretend you were in another world, because all the leaves were really big and there were these little turkeys running through it. I came home one day and there was a big gaping hole in the chicken mesh. John Campbell's dog had gotten in there, a great big fluffy husky, and killed all of the turkeys. So we called John over. He said that he knew the way to stop the dog from doing this, and he hung the turkey carcasses from around the dog's neck."

MIKE: "Those weren't little chicks that the dog killed, they were almost butcher weight. You take the turkey and hang it from the dog's neck, and when he touches it, you whack on him. I didn't agree with it, but that's what he did. And the dog wasn't killing them to eat them, just killing to kill. You couldn't do anything with them after that, either, because they weren't bled properly, so you just had to throw them out. It was really a waste…He was a nice dog, though."

JOHN ANGRIGNON: "Nobody had raised a farm animal (at least a non-human animal) in Wells for a long time (except for horses). The hotels and restaurants gave us people food, which we mixed in with grain every day…the pigs loved it. One long weekend, there was no people food to be had, so I just gave them grain. I walked away from the feeding trough, and when I got to the gate I felt a nudge on my foot. All the pigs were staring at me with that 'Where's our real food?' look in their eyes. My pal Big Andy used to take food to them during the day so they could have a picnic together. It was fun. I used to cook the restaurant food in the kitchen to kill off any bugs, and several guests got quite offended by the smell of that sometimes.

"Then butchering day came. I had worked in a butcher shop in high school, so had a clue how to do it, but when I shot the first pig I didn't hit him right and he sat there staring at me and squealing loudly and we all got totally stressed, so we had to have a lot of intoxicants to finish the job. Never want to go through that again."

Dogtown

Whether old-timer or newcomer to Wells, almost everyone had a dog. Hippies, in particular, seemed to have dogs, who were steady—sometimes sensible and sometimes idiosyncratic— companions against the isolation; they were sometimes trial-run children for young couples in their twenties. When not inside, dogs were seldom tied up or confined to a yard but were allowed to have the run of the town. Inevitably, this meant that sometimes the dogs would "pack up" and attack another dog, an unwary cat, or some chickens. Parents expressed fears for the safety of small children, but no one has shared stories of dogs attacking kids. Still, it was occasionally unnerving to walk through the deserted town streets alone and see a pack of large panting dogs trotting with purpose and speed in your direction.

Fred Ludditt, describing Barkerville in the 1930s—equally apt for Wells in the 1970s: "One of the curious things about most mining towns is the large number of dogs that roam the streets, seemingly untended and un-owned."

Rose Danby: "It used to be hell, going uptown with your dog. The male dogs would try to just fight to the death. Fixed? What you mean, fixed? Nobody ever tied their dogs up or had leashes in those days. It was just a free-for-all."

Bonnie May: "I was driving down the main street one night and was about to turn the corner by the Wells Hotel when we stopped to talk to my dad. We had our dog, Billie Joe, and Gaylord's dog, Flag, in the back of our truck. As we were talking, Brian Humber's dog, Murdoch, jumped in the back of our truck and a dog fight ensued…So there was Fred and Gaylord grabbing dogs and then shovels, trying to break up this dog fight! Fred finally picked up Billie Joe. Murdoch made one last attempt and lunged at Billie's tail, but got Fred's leg instead."

Judy Campbell: "John Premischook's dog got killed by a bunch of other dogs, and apparently Fargo [Judy's dog] was in this pack. John's dog had been tied up on his porch. It was terrible."

Eric Ackerly: "Dave Williams had the motel and gas station on the flats. King was the name of his dog, who wasn't really a dog, he was a pure-bred wolf. He is the reason there were so many wolf-dogs in Wells, at least until he was fixed, or broken, depending on your point of view…Wells, at the time, had about 350 people and about 1,200 dogs, a good number of them wolf crosses."

Lisa Marie Duncan [née Wood]: "My brother Gaylord used to like to party at the Jack O' Clubs bar. He had a dog named Flag, who was very loyal. My dad used to go to work at about six in the morning; he'd see Flag sitting out in front of the Jack, waiting for my brother to come out. I guess Gaylord would have had too much to drink those nights and forget Flag was there, and he'd go out the back door. Flag would have sat there till the cows came home waiting for Gaylord if he could have, so Dad would have to stop, pick up Flag, take him home, and give Gaylord hell. This happened too many times to count."

JUDE GOODWIN: "My dog was poisoned. She was the best dog ever. I've had three others since, but Margarine (she was a black lab/spaniel cross) was my first love. She came home one day foaming at the mouth and died in convulsions a short while later. We all let our dogs run free. I guess a local got tired of her chasing their chickens or something. I still mourn that dog."

ROB DANBY: "Mister Ivan was a very special little guy. Thinking about all the adventures I had with him gets me all choked up. As for the 'Mister,' that title got attached to him pretty early on.

"At the start of my first summer in Wells, Paul [Guiguet] and I planned a camping trip on his family's lot at Bowron Lake. At the time, there was no house on the property, just a tent platform overlooking the lake. It was a very idyllic wilderness setting, and we thought it a perfect place to ingest some LSD to kick off our camping week. The night before this early-morning trip to Bowron Lake was spent in the Jack consuming way too much alcohol—hey, it was our last chance for a week! The next morning, we started out early and loaded up the canoe with our supplies and headed out. Not wanting to waste any of this precious day, we got right at the acid before fully evaluating the effects of the previous night's alcohol consumption. As the morning started to 'come alive,' my condition began to deteriorate and soon went from bad to worse. So here we are in the middle of nowhere with me feeling like I'm going to die and Paul getting very high and wondering what to do with me. We needed some guidance—and that's where Ivan came to the rescue with his grounded, at-one-with-the-forest energy keeping me from completely losing it. I believe that's where he first developed his roll of the eyes and 'Oh, brother' look that he laid on me many times since then, and which I probably deserved most of the time! Anyhow, while he was still pretty young, he earned the 'Mister' designation that day with his calm, quiet dignity and air of authority.

"Once in awhile, in the early days, I liked to indulge in a little marijuana in its baked form. As I like to be up early, I chose to bake the cookies in the morning before going to work so that when I got home I could dig right in. I arrived home after work and had a small repair job to do on my car that I wanted to get done before I indulged. Mister Ivan had spent the day inside while I was at work, so I let him out before working on my car. I noticed he was a little wobbly while walking down the path and I thought, 'Poor guy. He's getting old and having a little trouble walking.' I finished up my repair job and went inside all excited about the

Marvellous Mr. Ivan goes cross-country skiing with Tom Adair (L), and Sue Safyan. Photo: Rob Danby.

treat awaiting me. When I walked into the kitchen, there on the floor were the overturned cookie plate and the remains of my baking. I was really pissed and started yelling and screaming at Ivan and sent him back outside while I cleaned up the mess. There had been a dozen cookies on the plate, and as I was picking up the crumbs, I started to realize how much he must have actually eaten. Two or three cookies would have been a lot for me, and he must have had three quarters of the batch.

"Once it started to sink in how much he had eaten, I felt really bad, as I hadn't been very nice to him. I went outside to try and make up to him but he was nowhere to be found. Then I started to get really worried that he was stoned out of his mind and wandering the streets of Wells. The search was on, and I scoured every street looking for him. I eventually found him uptown with his tongue hanging out on the steps of the Jack. 'Hey, that's where Dad always goes when he's thirsty!' But they wouldn't let him in and nobody seemed to understand his predicament. I tried my best to make up to him for my awful behaviour and took him home. I made sure he had lots of water and food nearby as he didn't move much for the next few days. He had quite an appetite for just lying there all day! And I ate the remaining broken pieces and joined Mister Ivan in his blissed state!"

LOUISE FUTCHER: "Our group brought several dogs with us from Ontario. We ran out of dog food and discovered to our chagrin (we were vegetarians) that they could not digest rice well."

SUZANNE BESSETTE: "Boogie was my little white dog. When I first came to town, I would leave Boogie at home while I went to work. One day, I went directly uptown, and somebody said to me, 'Oh man, Sharon Forman's really pissed off at you!' Sharon had got her groceries in Quesnel, and when she came back to Wells, she went into the post office to check her mail or something. Boogie had somehow got into her car and grabbed a roast and ran down the street with it!"

ROSE DANBY: "Tannis was my Irish setter that I got in Vancouver as a puppy. We'd go out to Wendle Lake where there was a great echo. She would always think it was another dog, and she'd get totally freaked. She'd start just skulking around the edge of the lake, looking. Then she'd send out a warning *boof*! And a warning *boof*! would come back. She'd go *boof-boof* and then *boof-boof* came back! She'd carry on for hours, and nobody could shut her up...

"Now, Tyee was the most magnificent dog I've ever seen. I can remember the first day I laid eyes on him. He came to town with a guy named Steve Cook, who lasted around here for only about six months before he landed in jail and left the dog behind. Tyee was quite capable of taking care of himself; he just went visiting all the time and would eat at whoever's house he felt like eating at. Or he'd go out and disappear for days on end. He'd go hunting, then he'd come back to town when his belly was full. Periodically, different people would make claims on him and buy a leash and a collar, and say, 'You're my dog, you're coming home with me.' He'd humour them for a day or two and then cut loose and say, '*hasta la vista*, I'm outta here.'

"So [someone] had a trapline way out at Bowron. He claimed the dog, took him out there, chained him up, starved him, and beat him regularly to 'submit' him to his will. Well, I came home to Stromville one day, and there was this emaciated, four-legged furry thing lying in the driveway, pretty close to death. I walked right up and had to look him right in the eye before I went, 'Oh my god—Tyee? Is that you?' All he could do was just lift his head, look at me, and then, *clunk*, back down. So I went up to the cabin and got a bowl of water and a bowl of dog food, and I sat with him through the entire night. I fed him one little crunchy at a time and made him drink water, and one little crunchy. I could see that he was in such bad shape that if he ate or drank too much, it would kill him. I nursed him through the night and then the next morning I carried him up to the cabin and put him on the bed and just nursed him back to health. After that, he just said, 'I'm your man!' I swore to him—I said, 'I will never tie you up; I will never put you on a leash. You're free to come and go as you please.' He lived with me because it was his choice.

"Then he allowed me to put him in a harness and haul wood up the hill. It was quite remarkable, because I'd told him I would never leash him or tie him up. My firewood always got dumped down at the road, and it was a long ways uphill. One day, I just sat down and talked to him. 'Here's the deal: you're a husky, you can pull. I have a sled and I have a harness. Would you mind helping me bring the wood up to the cabin?' I just hooked him up and he did it. Never once complained.

"Then, when Rick and I got together and we got a job at a ranch, it became a big dilemma because if we brought him there, Tyee would've chased cows and been shot. I'd promised I would never tie him up, and I absolutely wasn't going to do it.

"Tyee hated men with a passion after that episode at Bowron. But Tyee and I were up seeing Edie [Decker] in Prince George one day, and these two guys showed up that were friends of hers. One guy sits down on the couch. Tyee walks straight up to him, sits down, and puts his head in his lap. I went, 'Holy fuck! Do you want a dog?' He looks at me like I'm insane, and he says, "You don't mean this dog, do you?' I said, 'Yeah, this dog just told me he wants to go with you. There's only one stipulation; you never tie him up and you never put him on a leash. And the guy said, 'That's no problem because I live on the trapline, and he can just run free all the time.'

"I kept in touch with him; the news would come from these guys to Edie to me. Tyee was just in heaven living out there on the trapline with these guys...One day he just never came back. Met his demise as he wanted to—free."

The Food Co-op

The "co-operative movement" in Canada, as the term applies to wholesalers of goods (wheat pools, dairy products, livestock) dates back to the nineteenth century. But in the 1970s, hippies formed food-buying co-operatives, specifically "natural food" co-ops, as part of their rejection of the unhealthy convenience foods—the corporate commercial foods—of their childhoods in the 1950s and early '60s (white bread, hot dogs, processed cheese, and tinned vegetables, fruits, and spaghetti). The co-ops bought natural or health foods (brown rice, whole wheat flour, dried beans, nuts, fruits, and herbs for teas and traditional medicines) in bulk from health food stores and, where possible, direct from growers, making the prices of these specialty items far more affordable than non-bulk retail purchases. The co-ops were also templates for countercultural business models—volunteer-run and non-hierarchic in structure, communal enterprises undertaken, ideally, with like-minded souls.

In Quesnel, the commercial centre nearest Wells, where there were supermarkets (Safeway, Overwaitea), hardware stories (Willis Harper), pubs (the Billy Barker, the Cariboo), restaurants (Savalas), and at least one health food store (Karin's Delicatessen & Health Food Store, still operating on Reid Street), a food co-op was formed in the mid-1970s that served the hippies who lived in Quesnel and the surrounding countryside, often in communes (The Hill, Bobb Inn, Dragon Mountain). The CRS Workers Co-operative in East Vancouver (later the East End Food Co-op, or EEFC) started Fed Up, a food-buying club, in the early '70s. According to an online history of the EEFC, its roots are founded

in "a larger social-environmental justice movement," which produced an "environment conducive to co-operative efforts...In the rural communities of BC, a truck would arrive at a community hall or church basement where collectives would unload the truck and divvy up the orders."[2]

SHARON BROWN recalls that the co-op in Quesnel was located on "Carson Street across from the old Hudson's Bay building. It was a big storefront next to Owen's department store. I remember tall ceilings; it must have been an old building."

LARRY FOURCHALK: "The first opportunity I had to meet a whole bunch of hippies all at once in Wells was

The travelling vegetable man came to town once a week. L to R: Joseph, Blaine, veg man, Alan, and Jane in front of Forman's store, c. 1973. Photo: Jude Goodwin.

when there was a meeting about forming a food co-op. The meeting was at Don and Shelley's house, as I recall."

JUDE GOODWIN: "We all got together and joined a food co-op (a big thing back then) and would drive into Quesnel now and then to get the shipment. The co-op was called Fed Up and was based in Vancouver. The deal was that all the small towns or groups that joined were obligated to send two people for two weeks' work once a year or something like that. In Duncan's words, as the members left the 'counterculture' and took up regular jobs, it became more and more problematic, and eventually the structure failed. Fed Up continued on as a street-level food co-op after that in Vancouver."

LOUISE FUTCHER: "We ordered lots of food in bulk. I remember wheels of cheese and other bulk purchases shared among the group. That worked well."

ROSE DANBY: "With the food co-op, I felt so wealthy every time we went to pick up a load. You'd have huge buckets of raisins and nuts. We had the honey in big buckets and we had to fill all the pails. It was just like liquid gold I was pouring out, stocking up for winter."

The Good Eats Café

Sometimes, however, the palate-pleasing ability of bulk health foods prepared at home seemed limited; ample opportunities for socializing and binging on steaks and sweets could be found at the Good Eats Café.

The Good Eats (the building itself still stands, though the restaurant is no longer) was located on Pooley Street, the main street in Wells. The triangular building had once been the site of the Wells Taxi Stand, a business run by Bud Williams, who with his wife, Ida, opened up the Good Eats in the 1960s. The café was famous for its sticky buns, (large doughy swirls filled with oodles of butter, cinnamon, and sugar), and was a popular hangout for both Old and New Wells until Bud and Ida closed the restaurant and retired in 1979.

THE GOOD EATS CAFE

The Good Eats Cafe - we spelled out the name,
The building we knew could not give it fame,
It had weathered the years - a triangular frame.

We entered its portal with many a doubt,
But our fears had vanished before we came out!
If the house was three-cornered, the meals were SQUARE,
With relish we tackled delectable fare!

If ever you're travelling the Barkerville-way,
Stop in at Wells, at the Good Eats Cafe.
This we can say (for we've tried it, we're sure)
You'll never regret passing in through its door.

Ed Hewlett

NATHAN KEW: "When I was young, the Good Eats was *the* place to go. My grandmother [Bea Kew] used to take us. And in those days Bud cut his own steaks. He had the little end for the tourists and the big end for the locals. You'd get your T-bone, and it'd be on one of those big oval platters, and three corners of the steak would be hanging off the platter."

TOM ADAIR: "On the last day of the year, because the Good Eats was only open in the summers, everyone got steak, and Bud would bring out liquor, and he'd pour you whiskey or tequila. He never had a liquor licence, he never had insurance; he was like, 'The amount of money I've saved by not getting insurance, and nothing ever happened…'

"The time I spent in the Good Eats! I was trying to figure it out: I was contracting in the summer, and I lived in town, so I wouldn't make a lunch, I wouldn't make a breakfast, I would just go to the Good Eats. Breakfast, lunch, and dinner, and then I started to figure out how much I was spending there. It was a good deal, but it was probably $20 a day, and so, work it out by the month. It was a lot. But it was good because the bar was right next door. You could just eat and drink!"

SUZANNE BESSETTE: "Bud and Ida were amazing characters. They taught me so much. I had never seen people work that hard. They made all their own buns and pies, and everything was from scratch. I remember when I first started working there [as a waitress], I thought, 'Oh wow, this'll be so great; they said I could have a free meal.' So on my first shift, I'm sitting there having a free meal with everything—I'm a slow eater—and all of a sudden I got this really weird feeling that somebody was looking at me. There was Ida staring at me through the coffee cups from the kitchen. I realized I didn't have time; I could only have soup and a bun and get back to it!

"She'd tell me to do something, and I'd go, 'Well, I was just, you know…' And she'd go, 'Hey, just say okay. I don't care what your excuses are, just say okay.' That was a huge, huge lesson. At night, when they'd finish, we'd do the cleanup. I had to do all the steam tables, the gravy thing, the potato thing and I'd be covered in sweat. But Bud always said, 'I look after my girls [his waitresses],' and he did. He was really proud that his girls didn't have to clean the toilet. We did the kitchen cleanup, but Bud cleaned the toilet. At the end of the shift, they'd go, 'Suzanne, crack out that bottle of rye and pour us a drink!' Bud was so funny. He'd tell stories about people and things that had happened in the restaurant and in the old days. He told me a story about a guy who blew himself up on the bridge down at the bottom of the Jack hill.

"One day I was waiting on a British couple, and they complained about the food. Well, you know that the food there was amazing. I went back to the kitchen and I told Bud. And he goes, 'Which table is this?' I pointed to the table, and he goes, 'Bloody limeys! I know their kind. I was with them in the war. Yeah, I'll go out and deal with them.' They almost got into a fist fight!"

JUDY CAMPBELL: "The sticky buns at the Good Eats Café were known far and wide as the best on the planet. I actually met someone in Hawaii who, when he found out I was from Wells, confirmed that the Good Eats made the world's best sticky buns. They were huge, doughy, and dripping with brown sugar syrup."

ERIC ACKERLY: "Bud Williams had the Good Eats Café and made the world's best sticky buns, bar none."

JUDE GOODWIN: "There was that little odd-shaped café with the sticky buns. We loved those sticky buns!"

BEV DANBY: "I could probably tell lots of stories of working breakfast with Bud at the Good Eats. I learned a lot about the sticky buns just watching him make them fresh every morning. He would also tell me the 'secret' is using real butter and lots of it."

This is how she remembers the recipe: In a small pot on medium-high, scald one-and-a-quarter cups of milk, then stir in two tablespoons butter, two teaspoons sugar, and one teaspoon salt. Set aside to cool. In small bowl, dissolve one package of yeast and one teaspoon of sugar in one-quarter cup lukewarm water. Set aside for ten minutes.

In large mixing bowl, combine cooled milk, yeast mixture, one tablespoon lemon juice, and one egg that's been lightly beaten. Add two cups of all-purpose flour and beat well for five minutes. Gradually add enough remaining flour (up to four cups in total) to make a soft dough. Knead on a lightly floured surface until smooth and elastic. Place in a greased bowl, turning to grease top. Cover and let rise in warm place for an hour.

After an hour, preheat your oven to 350 degrees (F). Punch the dough down and roll it into a nine by eighteen-inch rectangle. Spread with two to four tablespoons butter and sprinkle one-third cup brown sugar and one teaspoon cinnamon over top. Roll it up from the long side, pinching the long side to seal.

Spread a nine by thirteen-inch cake pan with half a cup butter. Evenly sprinkle half a cup brown sugar and one teaspoon cinnamon over top. Cut the long roll into one-and-a-half inch slices and place them in the pan. Bake for thirty-five minutes. Remove from oven and invert immediately onto tray. This makes twelve world-famous sticky buns.

All roads also lead to Stromville. Photo: Tom Adair.

AFTERWORD
OR WHY
ALL ROADS LEAD TO
WELLS

"I GET SO HOMESICK FOR HOME," LISA MARIE DUNCAN TOLD ME. "WELLS seems to get into your soul and stay." For many of the people who lived in Wells, it will always be "home." This is true whether they lived there in the 1940s as miners, the 1970s as hippies, or the 1990s as artists, whether they spent their whole childhoods there or visited once during a summer more than a lifetime ago. Bev Danby told me: "I grew up moving all over the place with my family, and then I got to Wells; it just felt like home. It still does." Suzanne Bessette added, "It's my hometown, my Canadian hometown." When Wellsites (a.k.a Wellsians) get together, they talk about Wells' "magic" and just what it is that makes the place so special. Why do they long for it in ways they might not long for the hometowns where they were born and raised? Why do the people they knew there feel like family? Was there a secret ingredient in the sticky buns?

   As in other small towns, the residents are familiar to each other—they're not anonymous strangers, potentially and vaguely threatening, as city-dwellers often seem to be. In Vancouver, for example, you might cross the street if a toothless, drunk, and grizzled man approached you; in Wells, you'd say, "Hey, [fill in favourite geezer name], I'm on my way to the post office. Buy you a beer in the Jack in five minutes?" In Wells, people don't lock their doors and they even sometimes leave their car keys in the ignition. There is a sense of trust. The family down the street may not like you much, but if you have a chimney fire or your water line's frozen, they'll help you if they can, as the hippies who came in the 1970s found out. And you may not like their politics or their small, yappy dog, but if they need to borrow a tiger torch or a cup of sugar, you will warmly oblige. There is a sense of personal and communal safety—especially for children and women—in a place where you've at least seen the faces of all of your fellow townsfolk. "For me, after growing up in Vancouver, it was a little piece of heaven to be able to go for a walk out to One-Mile or down to the lake or to Mickeyville and be totally alone," remembers Bonnie May. But a sense of safety is more or less true of all very small places.

Wells is isolated, geographically, from its closest neighbour, Quesnel, which is more than fifty miles away, and its solitude plays a role in the town's unique personality. Although Wellsites have to drive to Quesnel to get even basic supplies and services, there is a sense of proud independence from the outside world, of doing things their own way. (It's worth noting, too, that Wells remained unincorporated until the late 1990s.) When late-night talk turns apocalyptic, which happens sometimes at a table crowded with half-empty bottles, Wellsites half-jokingly shrug and say, "When the rest of the world collapses, we'll barricade the highway at Devil's Canyon!"—a steep, narrow, and therefore easily defensible, canyon outside the town. Just as there is something known as "island time," in which things move slower than on the Mainland, there is also "Wells time," a tempo unique to the place, its seasons and weather.

The beauty of the environs is part of Wells' magic. "I remember climbing Twin Sisters, going there after the bar closed, getting in somebody's vehicle and driving in it as far as we could and then hiking to the top to watch the sun rise," Rose Danby says. "You'd wake up and you'd be at the top of the world." Bonnie May remembers "the beautiful, sunny, snowy days in the winter, the stars at night—so clear, so many—and the northern lights," and Mike Heenan cannot forget "the wood smoke ('spruce juice') that, to this day, is for me the smell of walking home from the bar at night in the freezing cold. In the summer, it was the smell of sun-parched pine needles." But it is more than the scents and scenery that makes Wells special.

Part of it is a peculiar phenomenon behind the Wells saying that forms the title of this book: All roads lead to Wells. That is, if you have lived in Wells, no matter where you go, when you tell people where you're from, they will invariably say, "My uncle worked for the mine there in the 1950s!" or "I tree planted near there—man, we had some wild nights in the bar when we came to town!" or "My sister lived there two summers ago and worked in Barkerville" or "I was one of the last babies born in the hospital in Wells," or "My very first teaching job was in the school there," or "I bet you know my cousins there," or the person you've just met at a party, in a supermarket, at work, in a university course, while volunteering, or in some other situation, will turn out to have been at a Christmas party in Wells with you in 1982. You begin to wonder just how many people lived in what is now a town of less than two hundred people. "When I worked on the front desk of the Barker-ville Museum," Judy Campbell told me, "I constantly got, at least every day, a couple of people who'd walk in and say, 'Oh yeah, I was here for three months in the '30s.' There was a huge turnover in the mines, and I started to realize that Wells had a population of 4,500 people, but it was not the same 4,500 people on any given day!" Wells seems to lie at the centre, at the hub, of a network of invisible but meaningful connections. When feeling given to grandiose statements, some Wellsites will even say it is the centre of the universe; it is positioned, perhaps, over a major ley line, like the "magical" town of Findhorn in the UK.

Linked to this is the recurring circumstance that, when they travel, people from Wells seem to meet up with each other spontaneously in the far corners of the globe: "Dave Lock-yer went down to Puerto Vallarta in the late 1970s. He did some exploring on his first day there," Tom Adair told me. "Dave walked across this little bridge in the back end of the city, and who should he meet on the bridge, coming the other way, but [Wells resident] Paul

Guiguet?" Mike Heenan recalls: "Somewhere during the winter of 1976, John and I hatched a plan to drive from Wells to Las Vegas in the spring. And we met Tom Adair on his way north, driving along the Pacific Coast Highway in California." And so on. This doesn't seem to happen to residents of other small towns.

Further, many small towns and villages are notorious for the insularity of their clans and families. It can take years—it can take generations!—for newcomers to become locals. This is not the case in Wells: spend a winter or, better, two, living there and you're in.

JUDY CAMPBELL: "Wells has this very high ability to just accept people as they are…I found an interesting thing where I finally gained a high level of acceptance in Old Wells, not through being there for any length of time, but because I was the major person who made the [restoration of the] Community Hall project happen, which was dear to the heart of Old Wells. And I was the person who finally said, 'We're going to do this. I know how to make this happen.' So, since then, Dave and Mid say hello to me."

Even if you left as a small child, but your parents were involved in the town and were well-liked, you will be welcomed back.

MARGUERITE HALL: "My sons, Sean and Graham, were in grades two and six when we left Wells. When they were growing up, they knew they were from Wells, but it was academic knowledge. The first year that the casino in Wells opened [in the late-1990s] both boys worked up there. At a dance early in the summer, someone asked Graham who he was. He said he was Mike and Marguerite's son. They exclaimed and hugged him in delight and took him around to meet others, saying, 'This is Graham, Mike and Marguerite's son!' He told me that it was like coming home and being accepted in a place he never, ever thought he'd consider 'home.'"

For the people who came to Wells in the "hippie era," it was, as Zubin Gillespie put it, their "summer of '42"; their time in Wells was during their halcyon and salad days, and nostalgia naturally sweetens some memories.

ZUBIN GILLESPIE: "The whole thing was a party in a sense. We were working up in Barker-ville, but we were free, it was the very first time all of us were living with our boyfriends and girlfriends, and it was just so magical: we were healthy; we were naïve; we were opti-mistic. The people in town—some of them were totally whacked out themselves, so we fit in there quite well; everybody was a character. And at that time the climate was very extreme. The first summer we spent going up to the old garbage dump, digging for bottles, swim-ming, skinny-dipping…

"We were just so open when we moved up there out of the city. Every day that first summer [1970] was so fantastic; we had our health, we had our exuberance. There was an optimism at that time, it was a naïve optimism, about what the world was going to be, com-pared to what it is now, where everything's based on fear and the coming apocalypse. At that time, you just got a job, like that. Everything was very easy; food was cheap, rent was cheap, gas was cheap. The whole sexual revolution—there was no such thing as AIDS back then, no worries about becoming pregnant unless you wanted to become pregnant. It was one of the most optimistic times in human history."

MICHAEL WEISS: "I've been daydreaming a lot about Wells of late. With the first hint of fall in the air, I've been thinking of what it would be like to spend a winter in Wells, whether it would be great to live a quiet, snowbound existence for weeks at a time, or if I'd just go batty. It's weird that I usually start thinking about Wells as I'm drifting off to sleep. The set-ting is so firmly implanted in my mind—I guess you can do that with a small town—that it's easy to think of the place, the sounds in the Jack bar, the smell of wood-burning stoves, the cold air. I really don't quite know why it still has this hold on me—maybe because it repre-sents an escape from all the urban ills and work deadlines that clutter my world daily—but it does…I still think of my time in Wells as the most exhilarating of my life."

ELLEN GODWIN: "I think about Wells; it is the default run-away-from-home place for me. I rent a room at the Wells Hotel off-season, take over the maintenance chores or just the kitchen…"

MARYANN VAN DEURSEN: "Those were some of the best times of my life! I was sixteen to eighteen in those years…I remember the Tiddlywinks competition and the huge spaghetti dinners in Barkerville. I have great memories of Rosie, my heroine at the time, as she could do anything and everything, and her sister, Bev, who could also do anything…So many good memories—climbing the mountains, eating cinnamon buns, meeting the craziest and most entertaining people I had ever met."

SUZANNE BESSETTE: "I always felt, when I was there, like I was on top of the world; I felt really happy. I loved the way it smelled! I loved all of it, good and bad. So many important things happened to me there. It's where I grew up."

FRANK FITTON: "My time in Wells was personally very intense. I was a late bloomer in a lot of ways, always partying too much. The times in Wells happened in my twenties; I have gone through many changes since then, but I shall never forget those times."

There is nothing constant except change. In 1997, Wells residents voted to incorporate the town; the Cariboo Regional District, formed in the wake of the mine closure in 1967, would no longer govern Wells. This decision was not reached without some discord, however; ninety-two people voted for incorporation, but sixty-three voted against. Nevertheless, an official municipal government was elected: mayor Joseph Jourdain and six councillors (Judy Campbell, Barbara Cirotto, Dave Hendrixson, Carol McGregor, Robin Sharpe, and Virginia Wilkins). A series of mayors and councilors have continued to govern Wells, improve its basic utility services, develop an Official Community Plan and zoning bylaws, and supply funding for the town's fire department, ambulance service, elementary school, historic buildings, outdoor recreational trails and facilities, and cultural organizations and events. Many of the town's organizational amenities, however, remain strongly if not primarily volunteer-run.

By the mid-1990s, the grand old Community Hall, built in 1938, suffered from structural degradation and decay to the point where it was no longer considered safe to hold dances. Through strenuous and persistent work on the part of a number of volunteers, led by Judy Campbell, funds were raised, donations from around the world solicited, and grants obtained to restore the building. Throughout the 1990s and 2000s, a number of artists began to move to Wells, and the town claimed the highest number of art galleries per capita in the province. Island Mountain Arts ("School of the" was dropped from the name in the 1990s) has been running classes continuously since its inception in the 1970s, offering courses in a wide range of subjects for both children and adults. In 2003, the ArtsWells Festival was started on the initiative of artistic director Julie Fowler and others, and since that time, dozens of musicians and hundreds of audience members attend the Festival each year. It is now known as "BC's largest and best new indie arts festival."

Fire has continued to claim some of Wells' most beloved buildings; the Stromville cabin burned down in the late 1980s, the Lode Theatre building (then housing the Northwoods Inn restaurant) went up in flames, and on Valentine's Day 1994, the Jack O' Clubs Hotel went up in a spectacular nighttime fire; photographs show what appear to be faces in the flames and smoke that billowed above the Jack. Fortunately, no lives have been lost.

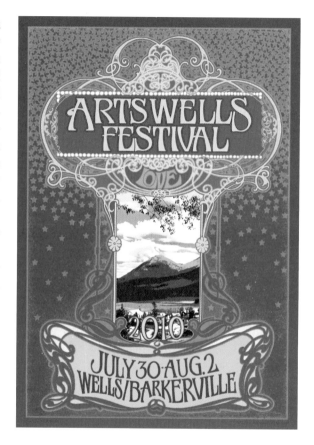

ArtsWells 2010 poster. Courtesy of Bob Masse.

Of all the people who were interviewed for this book and who lived in Wells in the 1970s, only a few remain there; the rest have scattered throughout North America and farther afield, and many are, to most of us, "whereabouts unknown." A core group, made up of both Old and New Wellsites, has remained in touch, remained friends. The Wells hippies have become truck drivers and poets, engineers, CEOs and teachers, designers, journalists and chefs, carpenters and counsellors, managers and massage therapists; they import exotic goods from the Far East; they work at odd jobs to make ends meet; they have retired and become grandparents. Some have died (including, from the 1970s group, John Campbell, Myron Kozak, Gaylord Wood, Brian Humber, Wayne Diggins, and David Lockyer) and are much missed at reunions.

Wells was and still is greater than the sum of its extraordinary and quite ordinary parts—its people (past and present), its isolation, size, climate, and scenery. And most Wellsites, an idiosyncratic, independent, smart and foolish, generous and territorial, wild and straight-laced tribe, cherish their memories of Wells.

"The best Wells stories," said Tom Adair, "we've probably forgotten because they were so amazing."

Stromville party, October 1975. L to R: Paula McGladry, (unidentified with back to camera), Vin Campbell, Linda Campbell, Deb Kell. Photo: Tom Adair.

The road home. Photo: Sue Safyan.

ENDNOTES

Preface

1. http://www.pbs.org/wgbh/nova/physics/fractal-detail.html.

Introduction

1. Jeffrey Jacob, *New Pioneers: The Back-to-the-Land Movement and the Search for a Sustainable Future*, Pennsylvania State University Press, 1997, pp. 20–21, 22.

2. Peter Warshall, "Prolog," *Whole Earth Catalog*, Issue 1340, Winter 1998, in which first edition reprinted in full. At wholearth.com/issue/1340/article/199/anniversaries.to.com.prolog. Jeffrey Jacob, *New Pioneers: The Back-to-the-Land Movement and the Search for a Sustainable Future*, Pennsylvania State University Press, 1997, pp. 20–21, 22.

3. Justine Brown, *All Possible Worlds: Utopian Experiments in British Columbia* Transmontanus/New Star Books, 1995, pp. 61-62.

4. "City politicians averse to hippies," CBC Archives. Broadcast date: March 18, 1968. http://archives.cbc.ca/society/youth/clips/3202/.

5. Quotations attributed to the speaker are derived from interviews conducted by the author between 2002 and 2011.

6. Rex Wyler, *Greenpeace: How a Group of Journalists, Ecologists and Visionaries Changed the World*, p.45.

7. Tina Loo, "Flower Children in Lotusland," *The Beaver*, February–March 1998; pp. 36–41.

8. The hippie years in Vancouver are explored at length in Lawrence Aronson, *City of Love and Revolution*, New Star, 2010.

9. Loo, 37.

Gold Town

1. Sandra Mather. Unpublished manuscript in the Wells Archives, p. 1

2. Fred W. Ludditt, *Campfire Sketches of the Cariboo*, [n.p.] 1974, p.18-19.

3. Mather, p. 5.

4. Mather, p.21.

5. Ibid.

6. Ibid.

7. *Mining the Motherlode*, http://wells.entirety.ca/, Accessed June 26, 2009.

8. Mather, p. 21.

9. Wells Heritage Townsite in *Measured Drawings: An Architectural of British Columbia*, http://bcheritage.ca/drawings/sites/site1/wells.html.

10. Fred W. Ludditt, *Barkerville Days*, Vancouver, BC, Mitchell Press, 1969, p. 20.

11. Harvey Bryant, *Harvey's Story: Memories of Cinema, Wells, and Quesnel*, Big Country Printers, 1978, p. 31-32

12. Robin Skelton, *They Call It the Cariboo*, Victoria, BC, Sono Nis, 1980, p. 213.

13. Bryant, p. 42

The Geezers

1. Gunanoot was a First Nations outlaw who evaded the police for thirteen years. See David R. Williams, *Simon Peter Gunanoot, Trapline Outlaw*, Victoria, BC: Sono Nis, 1982.

2. Lucky also told this story to Robin Skelton, and it is found in *They Call It the Cariboo*, Victoria, BC, Sono Nis, 216.

Are You Ready for the Country?

1. Bryant, p. 32-33

2. In 1971 an estimated fifty to eighty thousand "high school and university students, drop-outs, draft dodgers, freaks, heads, and hippies" hitchhiked across Canada. "By July 1971," writes Crystal Luxmore in 'Vice, Vagabonds, and VD' (*The Walrus* magazine, walrusmaga-zine.com/articles/2008.07-ephemera-vice-vagabonds-and-vd/), "there were so many teen-agers on the road that Secretary of State Gerard Pelletier announced an emergency measure to turn thirteen Canadian armouries into youth hostels for the 50,000 or more travelers on the road. In 1971…the transient youth phenomenon had reached epic proportions and

launched a National Hostel Program. Part of the Trudeau Government's effort to engage young radicals, more than $500,000 was doled out to youth groups and municipalities to open 116 makeshift hostels from Newfoundland to the Yukon. The program lasted until 1976."

A Very, Very, Very Fine House
1. Wells Archives. Record Group 34. Wells Improvement District. Collection Dates, Series #1–#3 1967–95. Letter from H.S. Tatchell, Land Commissioner to Mr. Harvey Bryant, Secretary, Improvement District of Wells, June 19, 1975.
2. http://www.learningcentre.coop/resource/east-end-food-co-operative.

REFERENCES

Aronson, Lawrence. *City of Love and Revolution*. New Star, 2010.

Brown, Justine. *All Possible Worlds: Utopian Experiments in British Columbia*. New Star Books, 1995.

Bryant, Harvey. *Harvey's Story: Memories of Cinema, Wells and Quesnel by Harvey Bryant*. Big Country Printers,1998.

Drinkwater, Diana Lynn. *Our Town...Our Times...Our History: A Collection of Photographs and Memories, Wells, BC* [n.p.]: 1991.

Jacob, Jeffrey. *New Pioneers: The Back-to-the-Land Movement and the Search for a Sustainable Future*. Pennsylvania State University Press, 1997.

Loo, Tina. "Flower Children in Lotusland," *The Beaver,* February–March 1998.

Ludditt, Fred W. *Barkerville Days*. Vancouver, BC, Mitchell Press, 1969.

Ludditt, Fred. *Campfire Sketches of the Cariboo*. Self-published, 1974.

Ludditt, Fred. *Gold in the Cariboo*, 2nd ed. Courtenay, BC, E.W. Bickle, 1978.

Reich, Charles A. *The Greening of America*. Random House, 1970.

Skelton, Robin. *They Call It the Cariboo*. Victoria, BC, Sono Nis, 1980.

Speare, Jean E. *Bowron: Chain of Lakes: Place Names and People*. Quesnel, BC: High-Plateau Publishing, 1983.

Vonnegut, Mark. *The Eden Express*. Seven Stories Press, 2002.

Wells Historical Society. *Wells: The 1930s: Photographs from the Wells Museum Collection 1930–1945*. [n.p.]: 1991.

Wyler, Rex. *Greenpeace: How a Group of Ecologists, Journalists, and Visionaries Changed the World*. Raincoast Books, 2004.

PERMISSIONS

Bryant, Harvey. *Harvey's Story: Memories of Cinema, Wells and Quesnel*. Quesnel, Big Country Printers, 1998. (Permission granted by Edmee Rosin and Peggy Bryant.)

Ludditt, Fred W. *Campfire Sketches of the Cariboo*. [Penticton, BC, Fred W. Ludditt], 1974. (Permission granted by Karin Ludditt.), *Barkerville Days*. Vancouver, BC, Mitchell Press, 1969. *Gold in the Cariboo*, 2nd ed. Courtenay, BC, E.W. Bickle, 1978.

Luxmore, Crystal. "Vice, Vagabonds, and VD," July 2008 online exclusive, *Walrus* magazine (walrusmagazine.com/articles/2008.07-ephemera-vice-vagabonds-and-vd/).

Quesnel Cariboo Observer, December 15, 1971, October 3, 1974, May 12, 1976, February 15, 1978, March 29, 1978, September 13, 1978, August 23, 1978. Courtesy *Quesnel Cariboo Observer*. All rights reserved.

Vonnegut, Mark. *Eden Express* New York, Seven Stories Press, 2002.

Heritage BC Conference, June 1979. Photo: Judy Campbell.

ACKNOWLEDGMENTS

MY FIRST THANK YOU IS FOR TOM ADAIR, WHO TOOK ME THERE.

My deepest gratitude to the people who made this book and for whom this book was made: Eric Ackerly, Tom Adair, John Scott Angrignon, Suzanne Bessette, Duncan Bray, Sharon Brown, Rick Brownhill, Bob Campbell, Judy Campbell, Bev Danby, Rob Danby, Rose Danby, Brad Davies (for his brilliant writing), Leanne Davies, Frank Doherty, Lisa Marie Duncan, Frank Fitton, Larry Fourchalk, Louise Futcher, Zubin Gillespie, Ellen Godwin, Jude Goodwin, Marguerite Hall, Mike Hall, Sally Hamm, Mike Heenan, Ann Moxley Humber, Deb Kell, Nate Kew, Anne Laing, Dave Lockyer, Karin Ludditt (and on behalf of Fred Ludditt), Richard Mackie (for his expert guidance, inspiration, and support), Alan McMaster, Bonnie May, Frank Parker, Sandy Pelletier, Edmee Rosin (on behalf of Harvey Bryant), Sam Thatcher, Tracey Townsend, Maryann van Deursen, Peter van Deursen, Michael Weiss (for mentoring, advice, and encouragement), and Mike Wigle. And everyone else who shared stories with me over the years.

I am also grateful to my first reader, friend, and encourager extraordinaire, Jen Nachlas; to Mandy Kilsby and Bill Quackenbush at Barkerville Historic Park (and Wells Archives) for providing archival materials; and to Tracey Roberts, publisher of the *Quesnel Cariboo Observer* for granting permission to reprint articles from the 1970s.

Thank you to Vici Johnstone and Patricia Wolfe at Caitlin Press for fine editing and design expertise and for their support and assistance. It's been wonderful working with you! Grateful hardly begins to express the thrill and honour of having Bob Masse's beautiful work on the cover of this book. Thanks to Julie Fowler for permission to adapt the Arts Wells poster.

INDEX

PHOTO NATHAN KEW

Susan Safyan moved to Wells from Los Angeles in 1980 and lived there until 1985. She returns to visit her friends in Wells every year and has dedicated herself to collecting and preserving their stories. Safyan works as an editor for Arsenal Pulp Press in Vancouver, BC, but still owns a useable pair of felt-packs and can kindle a fire in an airtight.